ZIM
The Autobiography
of Eugene Zimmerman

ZIM
The Autobiography of Eugene Zimmerman

Edited and annotated
with introductory commentary by

WALTER M. BRASCH

SELINSGROVE: SUSQUEHANNA UNIVERSITY
PRESS
LONDON AND TORONTO: ASSOCIATED
UNIVERSITY PRESSES

Associated University Presses
440 Forsgate Drive
Cranbury, NJ 08512

Associated University Presses
25 Sicilian Avenue
London WC1A 2QH, England

Associated University Presses
P.O. Box 488, Port Credit
Mississauga, Ontario
Canada L5G 4M2

The paper used in this publication meets the requirements
of the American National Standard for Permanence of Paper
for Printed Library Materials Z39.48-1984.

Library of Congress Cataloging-in-Publication Data

Zimmerman, Eugene, 1862–1935.
Zim : the autobiography of Eugene Zimmerman.

Bibliography: p.
Includes index.
1. Zimmerman, Eugene, 1862–1935.   2. Cartoonists—
United States—Biography.   I. Brasch, Walter M.,
1945–   . II. Title.
NC1429.Z48A2   1988   741.5′092′4[B]   85-63420
ISBN 0-941664-23-6 (alk. paper)

Printed in the United States of America

. . . to Sondy Kendall, who has given her time and energy to preserving the memory and art of Eugene Zimmerman, and who has spent uncounted hours helping locate information for this book.

and, as always,
. . . to Milton Brasch
and
Helen Haskin Brasch

Contents

Preface

E UGENE ZIMMERMAN (1862–1935), FOR-
ever known by the block scrawl signature, ZIM,
was the developer of the Grotesque school of caricature and one of the nation's most respected,
most original cartoonists of the latter two decades
of the nineteenth century.

At the age of two, he was sent to live with
relatives when his mother died; five years later,
with the coming Franco-Prussian War, he was sent
to America where he worked for his room and
board on farms, in a winery, and as a sign painter
for the next decade. In 1883, at the age of twenty,
Zimmerman was hired by *Puck,* the nation's most
influential humor magazine. Two years later, he
moved to *Judge,* which eventually surpassed *Puck* in
circulation and influence. By the time he was
thirty, Eugene Zimmerman, who had lived most
of his boyhood in poverty, was one of the nation's
best-known and wealthiest artists.

Not only was he a principal artist for *Judge,* the
leading American humor magazine, but he also did
formal portrait work as well as caricatures, wrote
newspaper and magazine articles, drew a newspaper comic strip ("Louie and Lena"), illustrated
numerous books, including those of Ring Lardner,
James Whitcomb Riley, and humorist Bill Nye,
designed posters and banners (a hold-over from his
teenage years), and created a cartoonist correspondence course.

The Judge Co. issued several reprints of his
works, knowing that the public would eagerly

Eugene Zimmerman, 1925

9

force publication of even more reprints. In the mid-1920s, ZIM became the founder and first president of the American Association of Cartoonists and Caricaturists.

Until his death in 1935, ZIM sold his cartoons to major national magazines—and also gave away innumerable sketches, portraits, and caricatures to friends, acquaintances, and charitable organizations.

★   ★   ★

Editing *any* manuscript presents numerous problems, for the editor must retain the essential style and substance of the writer, yet work with that writer to have the manuscript presented in a manner suitable for the intended audience.

In addition to basic line editing, checking for spelling, grammar, and style problems, editors look for "holes" in a manuscript, for inaccuracies, for redundancies; they look for ways to make the manuscript "flow" better, often moving sections around to help tighten the final product. A writer and editor working together can usually improve a manuscript.

But what happens when the writer is dead, and there is no opportunity for a give-and-take discussion? Some scholars believe that no editor should do more than the most essential changing of such a manuscript; some even believe that original spelling errors must be left in—"for historical accuracy." However, a manuscript is still just that—a manuscript. Except for certain manuscripts of the world's most outstanding writers and scholars, it usually makes no difference if the manuscript is a hundred years old, or just a few weeks. The task of a good editor should be to take that manuscript and work with it, to edit it as the writer may have wished, as if the writer were still living, as if the manuscript were not cut into stone. Although many editors will facetiously claim that it is far easier to work with dead writers than live ones, the reality is that with live writers editors can exchange information, discuss and argue through problems—and, when necessary, even suggest rewrites. With the manuscripts of writers who no longer are living, it becomes a major task to try to reason what the writers would say to certain suggestions, and how best to preserve the quality of the writer's ideas and style. My task in editing ZIM's auto-

biography was to edit it as if ZIM were still living, to look at the manuscript as a "living vehicle" for understanding a complex person. Thus, for *ZIM* I melded the three sketchy manuscripts, various diary entries, letters, and newspaper and magazine columns and sketches. For what now became a master working autobiography, I then created chapters; eliminated redundancies and superficial, sometimes meaningless chatter; analyzed, researched, and tried to eliminate all internal factual conflict; verified all major facts and as many minor facts as possible; researched the era to add explanatory information in many places; moved words, sentences, paragraphs, and even full sections to improve the flow; corrected all spelling and basic grammar errors; and occasionally changed word usage, but left in many phrases that showed the "spirit of the language." Always, I was concerned with retaining the spirit and life of ZIM, told as if ZIM himself had approved the final autobiography for publication.

ZIM's three different autobiographical manuscripts, written at different times, all three overlapping, occasionally conflicting, presented a number of routine problems, many of which were overcome by tight editing. For example, he jumped around, throwing information down seemingly at random; sometimes his grammar followed rules of French and German rather than English; he often used what in a different age we now recognize as clichés; and he misspelled many polysyllabic words, as might be expected of someone whose native language was not English. Within each version were also redundancies, some of them only phrases and sentences, some of them complete recollections.

But there were also more complex problems, magnified by the presence of the three separate autobiographical manuscripts—and numerous memos, letters, and diary entries that sometimes contradicted passages within one or more of the manuscripts. One of the three versions of ZIM's autobiography is a fictionalized one in which the central character is named Felix; another autobiography is written in the first person; the third is a series of disjointed and fragmented tales, some of which ZIM used for his various newspaper and magazine columns; others were just quick remembrances put into writing for the sake of recollection.

I also realized that ZIM himself covered up some of his tracks. As a writer, I know that writers usually prefer to tell their own stories, in their own ways, from their own perspectives. ZIM wanted to tell us his own story in his own words, but he would tell us just what it was that he wanted us to hear about him—no more, no less. About certain aspects of his life there was a plethora of information with more than adequate documentation. In other instances, he skipped years with barely a mention. What was important to him, he wrote about; what wasn't, and perhaps what was a little painful, he avoided.

Even the most credible autobiographies by the most seemingly objective writers are only subjective statements of what the writers perceive as truth, and are merely the reflection of what those writers choose to tell others. ZIM's autobiography is no exception. What ZIM chose not to put into the manuscripts is just as significant as what he did put in. The early part of his life he documented well, but he left substantial holes in the years that followed his emergence into fame. Perhaps after getting started on his autobiography, he became bored or wondered if anyone would be interested; perhaps he just didn't have time to finish the autobiography in a more complete form. It is still significant, however, that of ZIM's various accountings of his life, the most complete information is of his early life before leaving the Elmira-Horseheads area and going to New York City to work for *Puck*. Until he was in his early twenties, ZIM had lived a miserly life, one filled not only with poverty but also with hard work and problems associated with being foreign-born. Perhaps those years etched their history deeper into his soul than all the fame he would ever achieve.

ZIM says little about his years as a full-time staffer on *Judge* or of his numerous free-lance articles and cartoons published in many of the nation's leading magazines. At a time when mental problems were not discussed, were hidden from the public and friends, ZIM freely discussed the nervous collapse he suffered a couple of years after moving to *Judge*. Yet, he—perhaps from a sense of propriety—gave little insight into the personalities of many of his outstanding contemporaries. He wrote about Horseheads and its people, but glossed over his many contributions to the town, including designing, financing, and helping to build a bandshell and outfitting a town band, solely because he enjoyed music and thought Horseheads should have a band.

With the exception of passing references to his wife, and including a small chunk of his manuscript to Bill Marshall's wife—whose compulsion to yell at him helped him to decide to leave farm life at any early age—ZIM didn't refer to women in his various manuscripts. Extensive research, however, shows that he loved his daughter and adopted son, and tolerated his wife. Perhaps he didn't wish to inject his family into his professional life, to subject them to the same kind of public scrutiny that he had been subjected to since the mid-1880s. Perhaps an old-fashioned, yet much needed, chivalry combined with a Germanic chauvinism to exclude women not only from his manuscript, but from much of his cartooning art as well; very seldom did ZIM caricature women in his cartoons, unless they were Black, Irish, or Jewish—and even then, the number of ethnic men caricatured was far greater than the number of ethnic women. Although ZIM had done several outstanding portraits of Horseheads residents, only once did his subject include a woman. In his correspondence course, ZIM gave one possible explanation:

> Some of the things that women do are certainly laughable, but the man who deigns to criticize women's weaknesses is either unhappily linked himself or not up to the point of appreciating their good qualities. If you must make fun of women, confine it to those out of your immediate neighborhood. The wrath of the women singled out by your pencil may mean your undoing. Be respectful in such drawings or avoid the subject entirely.

Even if all three of ZIM's autobiographical manuscripts had been essentially the same, it would still have been difficult for a media historian to edit and annotate them. Although there was significant overlap, there were substantial differences—different wordings, different recollections, different remembrances about the same event. In one version, for example, he wrote harshly of a woman who was his "foster mother"; in a later version, he modified his attacks, almost as if saying, "Well, I guess she may not have been the greatest person to care for a young child, but I should now try to be compassionate."

Although most of his recollections were accu-

ZIM's house, Horseheads, New York, exterior

ZIM's house, Horseheads, New York, interior

when they appear within the text or as introductory comments to a chapter, they are set off by brackets; as explanatory footnotes, they are self-evident. The comments explain not only some of the things that ZIM referred to but also try to help the reader learn more about ZIM's life.

The selection of art for this book also presented numerous challenges. With the assistance of the Horseheads Historical Society and especially Sondy Kendall, curator of the ZIM House, I explored his art. During a sixty-year career, ZIM had drawn more than forty thousand sketches, black-and-white cartoons, caricatures, lithographs, and paintings. It was a challenge just to find the location of the surviving magazines. In addition, because of the fine work of the students of the Cooperstown Conservation of Historic and Artistic Graduate Works Program and of a small handful of volunteers from the Horseheads Historical Society, more than two thousand original drawings, many of them restored to near-mint condition, were available. To fully understand the range and scope of his art, it was necessary to look through every issue of *Puck* from 1883 through 1885, and *Judge* from 1885 through 1930, as well as numerous other major magazines for which ZIM had contributed. I searched through his published art, and also more than two thousand original drawings and paintings preserved by the ZIM House project of the Horseheads Historical Society. A large number of these originals had appeared in the mass media, and the quality of most of these drawings had been restored by volunteers from Cooperstown who also established a classification to aid the Historical Society.

Sondy Kendall, Rosemary Renn Brasch, and I spent several weeks selecting more than a hundred representative samples, each of us trying to get our personal "favorites" into the book; to our frustration, we soon realized that there were too many favorites to get them all in. And so we'd discuss, argue, even beg and cajole the others to include a "favorite," or to exclude one that we didn't think so favorably of.

Complicating the selection process was the painful question, What do we do about his ethnic art? Some in Horseheads thought that *no* ethnic art should be included within the book, believing that the inclusion of such art was itself racist, and demeaning not only to Blacks and Jews, but also to

rate, ZIM occasionally forgot, confused, or modified facts. Sometimes a diary entry, a memo, a letter to or from ZIM, or a reference by someone else about ZIM contradicts information within one of the autobiographical manuscripts. It became an intriguing challenge just to analyze these three versions, determine which parts were accurate, analyze relative placement of the various parts, and then create one autobiography from three, always keeping in mind the question, "Was this what ZIM would have wanted?"

Throughout the book appear editor's comments;

the people of Horseheads, most of whom are not racist and who are sensitive to the feelings of others. Some of the art is, indeed, painful, especially since the editor of this book is a member of one of the groups that ZIM caricatured so grotesquely. However, not to include a representative sample of ZIM's ethnic humor would be to whitewash a part of his—and America's—past. Even ZIM would probably have wanted a representative sample of his work included in his autobiography, hoping that people would understand that he had changed as the nation had changed. How can we even understand what this kind of art was if we can't see what it is we are so sensitive about?

Even a thorough analysis of ZIM's art would not be enough to answer some of the critical questions. If it is true that you cannot thoroughly understand writers and their works just by reading what they wrote, then it must also be equally true that there is far more to art than what appears on the page. I gained a basic understanding of ZIM by trying to understand his art, but I still knew little about the

man, his values and beliefs; what lay on the surface provided only some insight. To help me delve further into ZIM's life, to help me try to understand his place in cartoon history, and try to find out why ZIM and *Judge* were so little remembered, Sondy Kendall opened up another part of his world for me. I looked at the things ZIM saw, talked to some of the people he had once talked with, read magazines that he had read. And I dug into his memoirs, letters he had written and received, his newspaper columns, his publicity clippings, the local "humor histories" he wrote, and the three versions of his autobiographies he had written in the hope that he would not be forgotten. From all this data a deeper glimpse into his soul emerged.

It is my hope that the editing of this manuscript was done both as ZIM wished and as an editor must do to bring coherence and understanding. More importantly, it is my hope that ZIM—with all his greatness, but with a few flaws, as is the case with all of us—will again live, that his words will help us better understand ourselves—and our lives.

Acknowledgments

My DEEPEST APPRECIATION IS EX-
tended to Sondy Kendall who provided assistance
that can never be measured. As curator of the ZIM
House museum and as liaison with the Horseheads
Historical Society, Sondy was always available to
answer questions and to help in so many ways that
even to begin to list them would require a full
chapter.

Others from the Horseheads Historical Society
who helped were Leah Cramer, Mike Edwards,
Nadine Ferraioli, Esther McCann, and Helen Mc-
Cormick.

Rosemary Renn Brasch made numerous trips
with me to Horseheads and provided significant
help in many aspects of research and manuscript
preparation. Her ideas and suggestions were always carefully considered, contributing to a better
manuscript.

Jan Strasser Kather's thesis about ZIM provided a
good base from which to conduct further research.

Cartoonists Jud Hurd, Rick Marschall, Brian
Walker, and Art Wood all gave solid insight into the
nature of cartooning, and ZIM's place in cartoon
history.

Among those who provided competent and
much appreciated direction for the book were Dr.
David Wiley, director of Susquehanna University
Press; Thomas Yoseloff, designer and publisher;
Beth Gianfagna, managing editor; and Willa
Speiser, copy editor, all of Associated University
Presses. Dr. Charles Press reviewed the manuscript
and provided many solid suggestions. Tim Mac-
Neal provided photographic reproductions.

I never met Laura Zimmerman, daughter of Eugene and Mabel Zimmerman; Laura died in 1980,
almost a year before I had begun preliminary research. But it was Laura who preserved her parents' house, in which she had lived until her death,
and had willed to the Horseheads Historical Society the house, her father's original art, notes,
press clippings, letters, and many of his possessions (including furniture), and also provided a
trust fund to care for the house. The further preservation of materials and the restoration of the house
by the Horseheads Historical Society made my
research significantly easier.

Finally, to the people of Horseheads who took
the time to talk with me about ZIM and the town
they both loved, I extend my appreciation—and
admiration for allowing me to see a life that ZIM
had seen more than a half-century earlier.

A *zim* Chronology

May 25, 1862—Eugene Zimmerman is born in Basel, Switzerland. (Father: Joseph Zimmerman; mother: Amelie Klotz Zimmerman; brother: Adolph Zimmerman, 1860–1887; sister: Amelie Zimmerman, 1864–1930)

1864—Zimmerman is sent to Thann, Alsace, to live with an aunt and uncle; he attends a French school. His father secures bakery job in nearby city; Zimmerman's brother and sister remain in Basel with another aunt and uncle.

1867—Zimmerman's father and brother leave Western Europe and arrive in America, settling in Paterson, N.J.

1869—Faced by threat of what would become the Franco-Prussian War, Zimmerman's aunt and uncle send him to America to live with relatives.

1870–1871—Franco-Prussian War.

1869–1874—Zimmerman, in America, spends a few months with relatives, then moves to Paterson, N.J., to be with his father and older brother. He works several hours a day in the bakery, but also attends private German school, then switches to Old Van Houten public school.

1874—Bill Marshall hires Zimmerman as a chore boy, paying him three meals a day and giving him a room in the attic. Zimmerman

attends school irregularly the next couple years.

1876—At the age of fourteen, Zimmerman runs away from Marshall's house after being spanked by Marshall's wife and becomes a chore boy for Mr. Spangenmacher, farmer and wine merchant. Zimmerman often works from 6 A.M. to midnight, sleeping in the barn with a field hand and the horses.

1877—The winery burns and is rebuilt. William Brassington, a passing sign painter, admires Zimmerman's lettering of the winery name on the new windows and offers him an apprenticeship.

March 14, 1877—First issue of *Puck*.

1878—Brassington and Zimmerman move to Elmira, N.Y., after securing work at the Chemung County fair. Brassington establishes a sign-painting business in Elmira, at the corner of E. Water and Railroad streets.

1880—Sign painter J. T. Pope, of Horseheads, hires Zimmerman as head of his pictorial staff, at a salary of nine dollars a week.

1881—Zimmerman becomes a member of Acme Hose Company No. 2, Horseheads; serves as secretary until 1883; remains a member of the company until his death.

1881—Several artists from *Puck* leave to form a competing humor/political magazine, *The Judge*.

1882—Pope's business fails; Zimmerman is hired by sign painter Joe Densmore. During previous five or six years, Zimmerman had developed a desire to become a comic artist and work on the staff of a magazine. While in New York on a visit, he is persuaded to leave his portfolio with relatives, who show it to Joseph Kepler, publisher of *Puck*. Kepler is impressed. Densmore, an impoverished but kind and generous man, encourages Zimmerman and gives him the money to go to New York to accept Kepler's invitation for a meeting.

May 28, 1883—Zimmerman visits Keppler in New York and is hired for three years; salary to be five dollars a week the first year (almost poverty wages), ten dollars a week the second year, fifteen dollars a week the third year. By the end of first year, however, he is earning more than ten dollars a week from *Puck,* and extra money from businessmen who commission him to do advertising art. While at *Puck,* he begins drawing political cartoons and developing his style for grotesque distortion.

1885—Eugene Zimmerman drops the *merman* from his professional signature, becoming known as ZIM.

December 1885—ZIM and some other cartoonists, including Bernhard Gillam, leave *Puck* to join staff of the revitalized *Judge*. Billy Arkell becomes the publisher and establishes the standard that would lead *Judge* to become one of the nation's most important weekly magazines. I. M. Gregory, editor of the *New York Daily Graphic* and former city editor of the *Elmira Gazette,* becomes editor-in-chief of *Judge;* Gillam becomes art director. ZIM's contract specifies he is to be given stock options and be paid eighty dollars a week, with freedom to select ideas for his cartoons, a chance to draw the centerfold spread, and the option to do commercial work.

September 19, 1886—ZIM marries Mabel Alice Beard (1866–1958) of Horseheads; they move to Brooklyn.

1888?—ZIM suffers a nervous collapse, probably from exhaustion; he and Mabel go to Florida for a few months to recover. While in Florida, he continues to send art to *Judge.*

When ZIM and Mabel return from Florida, they establish a permanent residence in Horseheads; ZIM spends every other week in New York.

1888—ZIM and Mabel become parents of a daughter, Laura (1888–1980).

1889—ZIM and Mabel adopt Adolph Zimmerman, Jr. (1883–1908), orphaned son of ZIM's older brother.

1890—ZIM and his father-in-law, Alvah Peter Beard, complete major work on a new house at 601 Pine Street, Horseheads. The house features a two-story living room designed to be an art studio.

1891—ZIM is elected alderman of Horseheads.

1893—ZIM retires as alderman of Horseheads, after deciding that "fixing streets" and solving everyone's problems was causing him to lose too much of his own time.

January 19, 1896—Bernhard Gillam, ZIM's closest professional friend, dies of typhoid at the age of thirty-nine. Grant Hamilton becomes art director. Gillam's death forces ZIM and Hamilton to increase their work for *Judge;* ZIM reluctantly agrees to spend more time in New York and less time in Horseheads.

1896—ZIM meets Thomas A. Edison and becomes the first cartoonist to draw sketches while being filmed.

1897?—ZIM organizes town band in Horseheads; band disbands in 1900, reforms in 1909, and finally disbands in 1916.

1901—*Judge* is sold to Standard Oil of New Jersey. Austin Fletcher becomes president, taking over from Billy Arkell, who may have been forced out in bankruptcy proceedings.

1904 or 1905—John A. Sleicher, editor of *Leslie's Weekly,* becomes president of the merged Leslie-Judge Co.

1905—ZIM writes *This 'n' That About Caricature,* a "how-to" book for novice cartoonists. Two thousand copies of the book are sold at $1.50 each.

1906—ZIM receives patent for an automatic fire extinguisher; however, the automatic fire extinguisher, a very short-lived invention, causes more problems than it solves.

1908—Adolph Zimmerman, Jr., dies of tuberculosis.

1908—Fire destroys much of the *Judge* office; most of ZIM's original art is lost.

1909—Standard Oil of New Jersey reorganizes *Judge* to avoid financial collapse of the magazine. The page size becomes smaller and political issues are usually avoided.

1910—ZIM and his father-in-law design and build a bandstand for Teal Park, Horseheads.

1910—The Correspondence Institute of America in Scranton, Pennsylvania, buys the rights to ZIM's cartooning book, renames it *Cartoons and Caricature; Or, Making the World Laugh,* and prints fifteen thousand copies, although authorized to print only five thousand copies.

1911—The Correspondence Institute of America is brought into federal court, its officers charged with multiple counts of mail fraud. ZIM, caught in the middle, sends a form letter of explanation to as many people as he can, pointing out that he had revised the book and authorized the institute to sell it but was completely unaware of the Institute's business practices.

1911—ZIM writes the first of his "Foolish Histories," *ZIM's Foolish History of Horseheads.* Other versions are published in 1927 and 1929; his *Foolish History of Elmira* is published in 1911. The books become regional best-sellers.

1912—ZIM officially retires from *Judge* after contributing very little since the previous reorganization.

1913—ZIM begins his own correspondence school for cartooning, eventually writing twenty volumes. Students were urged to sign up for each of the twenty lessons; ZIM critiqued each student's work, encouraging each to develop to his or her fullest potential.

1916—ZIM begins writing "Homespun Phoolosophy" column for *Cartoons Magazine,* Chicago. Column continues through 1918.

1918—*Puck* dies, leaving only *Judge* and *Life* as the nation's major humor/comic magazines.

1921—Standard Oil of New Jersey withdraws its financial support, throwing *Judge* into bankruptcy. *Leslie's Weekly* is merged with *Judge.* The magazine gets a new editorial life when several outstanding writers—including William Allen White (editorials), Heywood Broun (sports), Ruth Hale (movies), George Jean Nathan (theatre), Ring Lardner, S. J. Perelman, and others—sign long-term contracts. Circulation increases to 250,000.

January 17, 1926—Grant Hamilton, dies almost penniless in Los Angeles, several years after leaving *Judge.*

1926—ZIM becomes the founder and first president of the American Association of Cartoonists and Caricaturists.

December 12, 1930—Billy Arkell, never having regained the power—or happiness—he had as *Judge's* publisher, dies in Los Angeles.

1932—*Judge,* after fifty years as a weekly, becomes a monthly. It is sold again and absorbs the subscription list and all the "humorous tradition and features" of its major rival, *Life;* Time, Inc., however, retains rights to the name of that magazine. *Judge* begins another slow decline and dies just before World War II.

March 21, 1935—ZIM becomes ill and is treated for indigestion.

March 26, 1935 (about 7:45 A.M.)—At the age of seventy-three, Eugene Zimmerman dies of a heart attack at his home in Horseheads.

ZIM
The Autobiography
of Eugene Zimmerman

Editor's Introduction

WHILE RESEARCHING MATERIAL FOR what would become the definitive social history of American Black English,[1] I became intrigued by *Judge* and *Puck* magazines, the two leading American humor and satire magazines during the 1880s and 1890s—an era marked by the proliferation of magazines. Within the weekly editions of *Judge* (which favored the Republicans) and *Puck* (which favored the Democrats) were essays, articles, jokes, pithy sayings, and outrageous mock speeches. All these combined with myriad cartoons, many of them in lithographic color, to bring a complex world of human nature and politics into perspective that almost any reader could not only laugh at, but also understand. In some ways, the absurdity of the humor, some of which would now be considered racist, drove home the political messages more forcefully than the most powerfully written newspaper editorial could have done.

By looking through *Judge, Puck,* and other magazines of the era, I became familiar with the names of Joseph Keppler, Bernhard Gillam, Frederick Burr Opper, E. W. Kemble, A. B. Frost, Sol Eytinge, Grant Hamilton, T. S. Sullivan, James A. Wales, Thomas Worth, Richard Felton Outcault, and Eugene Zimmerman, some of the leading cartoonists in America. Their humor was biting, their drawings equal to those of the finest draftsmen-artists. The cartoonists drew the foibles of man-

kind, exaggerated them; their depictions twisted and distorted their subjects—and tore into the political and social soul of America.

For *Black English and the Mass Media,* I could only devote a few pages to the place of *Puck* and *Judge* in America's social history. I was intrigued by them; I wanted to know more about them, these great cartoonists of the late nineteenth century, to learn about their lives, their values. Their cartoons are still witty, probing, entertaining, giving significant insight into the social conditions and politics of an era. But, also on my mind was why many of them chose to draw cartoons that by today's standards can only be seen as racist. Were they themselves racist? Or were they truly kind people caught up in an era of racism? Did they reflect society's values about America's minorities? Did they even consider that much of their art was derogatory, no matter how funny, no matter how real the situations appeared?

More important, haunting me throughout the research, was the question of what happened to these men in America's history. *Judge* and *Puck* in the 1880s and 1890s were as well known as *Time* and *Newsweek* are today; the cartoonists were as well known then as Bill Mauldin was in the 1940s and 1950s, as well known as Gary Trudeau, Herblock, and Pat Oliphant are today. What had history done to them that they and their magazines are now virtually neglected in the catacombs of journalism, forgotten in the history of our Republic?

Even a cursory look at the available information suggested that there was very little, if any, research on the great humor magazines and the great humor writers and cartoonists. In America's quest for the present and the immediately relevant, did we forget our past? Did we become so sensitive to some of the work that was being done in the latter 1800s that we deliberately chose to ignore it? To erase it from our collective consciousness, ignoring even that which would help us understand our past? What happened? *Why?* Why did these great writers fade into the vapors of history? Why does society forget? It nagged at me, burned within me, as I later tried to learn what happened a century ago, why people have allowed themselves to forget their past, and what the process was that allowed the famous to become the unknown.

A decade ago, I could not follow up on these questions, for there were other projects to initiate, other books to write. A few years later, I resumed my search, this time focusing upon Eugene Zimmerman, forever known by the block scrawl signature, ZIM. ZIM was the developer of the Grotesque school of caricature, and one of the most respected cartoonists of the latter two decades of the nineteenth century. He not only drew cartoons for magazines, he designed posters and banners (a holdover from his teenage years), did formal portrait work as well as portrait caricatures, wrote newspaper and magazine articles, drew a newspaper comic strip ("Louie and Lena"), and illustrated numerous books, including those of Ring Lardner, James Whitcomb Riley, and humorist Bill Nye. The Judge Co. had issued several reprints of his works, knowing that the public would eagerly demand publication of additional reprints. In the mid-1920s, ZIM became the founder and first president of the American Association of Cartoonists and Caricaturists. Because of his place in cartooning history, my research had to begin with an understanding of ZIM and of his world.

My initial research revealed that ZIM was even more famous in his time than I had originally believed. In 1904, journalist-historian Orison Swett Marden profiled ZIM in his popular book, *Little Visits With Great Americans. Munsey's Maga-*

zine, one of the most popular magazines at the turn of the century, profiled ZIM as "[standing] alone in the point of originality of conception and treatment. He is what artists denominate as an 'acrobat,' but a careful scrutiny of his work will reveal the truth behind his grotesque exaggerations." The article also noted that ZIM "views nature through a magnifying lens . . . and we cannot but feel that it is a merry lens, untempered with malice or spleen, and one that compels us to laugh with him."

In *This is the Life* (1926), the autobiography of Walt McDougall, a major American humor writer and journalist, ZIM was identified as "The greatest comic artist of the [1880s], after L. Hopkins of *The Graphic*." McDougall noted that ZIM's cartoons "are characterized by an insight into the political questions of the hour which is assisted rather than hindered by the sheer humor of his work." McDougall also noted that ZIM was

> . . . A splendid handler of pen and ink, utterly unspoiled by an immense success, who . . . made pictures that were funny in themselves, regardless of the subject matter. Few artists seemed then to recognize the distinction, perhaps because few were really humorous.

The *New York Herald* reported:

> He is a bundle of nerves. He memorizes his jokes sometimes, but as a rule he composes somewhat like this:—There is a whirl of arms and legs as ZIM darts into his studio. Another whirl as he fishes out crayons and squares himself before his board. Then, silence for ten minutes, perhaps half an hour.
>
> "Confound it, I can't think!" he exclaims as he paces the room nervously. Presently he sits down and begins to draw.
>
> R-r-rip! Away goes the bristol board. Another bit is tacked on swiftly. There is a rumbling and shrieking of little wheels as ZIM throws aside his chair. He swings a packing box to its place. Again silence for some minutes. Then *zip! zip! zip!* like the noise of a school boy sharpening his pencil. It is ZIM's pencil flying over the cardboard.
>
> Not another sound is heard for a half hour or so. Then comes the slam of the studio door. ZIM is gone home. On his desk lie two or three comics. Perhaps ZIM will come back the next day, or perhaps his next batch of jokes will arrive by mail with a note, dated in the northern wilderness of this state, in which ZIM explains that he is fishing now and mustn't be bothered with jokes for a week or two.

The *Chicago Tribune* noted that "Eugene Zimmerman is without exception the funniest cartoonist now living." William J. Arkell, former publisher of *Judge,* in his autobiography, *Old Friends and Some Acquaintances* (1926), wrote that ZIM "was the funniest artist this country has yet seen." Rube Goldberg,[2] writing in the *Saturday Evening Post,* described ZIM as one of the artists whose work inspired him to enter the world of pen-and-ink drawings. Tad Dorgan, another of the greatest American cartoonists, paid an unusual tribute to ZIM. In a cartoon entitled, "Trying to Tell an Aspiring Artist Just How Rotten His Stuff Is," an art director is checking the work of an egotistical job applicant. The applicant says, "Yes, yes, I know. You're going to say that there's something about them that reminds you of Bush and Davenport. Yes, my serious stuff does. And they say my comics are just like ZIM's." Nearby, members of the art staff are chuckling, one of them remarking, "If his comics are like ZIM's, then near beer is a ringer for Pilsner."

The *Elmira* (N.Y.) *Tidings,* which kept track of ZIM, noted that he was "the greatest caricaturist on earth. He is the only artist who can immortalize his work in the face, the hands, the legs and the whole body. Other artists are clever, but none can approach ZIM in originality." The *Elmira Telegram* humorously noted that "ZIM is the lion of Horseheads and when a stranger blows in and asks to see the sights, all hands chorus, 'Come and look at ZIM.'"

Among contemporary cartoonists, ZIM is still held in high esteem. Cartoonist Art Wood notes that "ZIM was a 'cartoonist's cartoonist.' His infectuous humor and penetrating character delineations set him apart as one of the key graphic artists of the late nineteenth and early twentieth centuries. He was a first-rate technician, and tops the list of America's funniest cartoonists. Today's political cartoonists are aware of style and the importance of drawing skills as stressed by ZIM." Richard Marschall, nationally syndicated cartoonist and editor of *Nemo, a Magazine of Classic Comics,* points out that ZIM was at the "forefront of an era" that was "set free from the wooden classic format [of cartooning]." Brian Walker, cartoonist and president of the Museum of Cartoon Art, calls ZIM "one of the greatest cartoonists in the classic examples of illustration and cartoon art. Many cartoonists bor-

row heavily from the standards that ZIM helped establish."

Jud Hurd, nationally syndicated cartoonist and editor of *Cartoonist Profiles,* agrees, noting, "There's no question about it; the quality of work is there. ZIM is undoubtedly one of the greatest cartoonists in pen-and-ink [style]. And, most important, his work in lithographic colors is only a shade below that of Kepler, perhaps the greatest cartoonist in lithographic reproduction."

That ZIM was a well-known cartoonist is easily recorded. But it is also noted that ZIM was not a compulsive worker. A popular folk impression was that he had a streak of laziness; this was an impression that both editors and his friends recorded, and one that he cultivated. In one of his most famous self-caricatures, ZIM depicted himself lying on a hammock, work needing to be done, while he absorbed the comforts and beauty around him. It would not be realistic, however, to believe the editors, his friends, or ZIM himself. He worked long and hard in the early mornings and late evenings, when there were few distractions, keeping the rest of the day for relaxation, reveling in a public perception of his "easy-going, non-caring" nature. Few actually saw him at work, but the sheer volume of what he produced suggests that no one could produce such an abundance of art and stories and be lazy.

He was generous with his time, and even more generous with his talent, drawing hundreds of posters for civic organizations and virtually thousands of caricatures for the people of Horseheads and Elmira. For more than three decades, no Chemung County fire convention or fair passed without a major ZIM contribution—almost always given without charge. ZIM loved children, taking time not only to exchange stories with them, but also to draw innumerable sketches, all of which he gave away. Even the books of his correspondence course in cartooning he gave away if the aspiring artist was poor.[3]

For the *Elmira Sunday Gazette* he drew weekly cartoons; for the *Chemung Valley Reporter* he wrote a weekly humor column, "Ea-Zy Pickings, the Rustling Reporter." Had he chosen to use the same time to draw more cartoons for the major newspapers and magazines, he would undoubtedly have been one of the wealthiest artists in America. But ZIM, as long as he was making people laugh and getting paid for it—no matter how little or how much—was content.

A century after *Judge* and *Puck* were born, much of ZIM's humor, as well as that of the other artists and writers, is still outrageously funny; much of it tears into social issues. Although *Puck* and *Judge* were established as vehicles for political satire—and the magazines' strengths came from full-color front and back cover and centerfold political cartoons—ZIM preferred, both professionally and personally, to stay away from many controversial issues. While at *Puck,* he contributed numerous ideas that Keppler and others then used for their own illustrations; at *Judge,* he assisted Gillam and Hamilton. Compared to Keppler, Gillam, and Hamilton, however, ZIM drew relatively few political cartoons; after 1910, when *Judge* lost its political soul, ZIM drew almost no political cartoons—not for *Judge,* not for any magazine. During World War I, although essentially a pacifist, ZIM did produce numerous sketches, watercolors, and pen-and-ink drawings on behalf of the war effort. His work was later commended by President Coolidge and by Franklin D. Roosevelt, who was assistant secretary of the navy at the time.

Although his political cartoons were usually as clever and biting as the best, ZIM preferred to look at the lighter side of life. An entire cartoon series, frequently reprinted, showed an inept fire company; the humor was well received by volunteer firefighters throughout the country—after all, ZIM was not only a famous and respected cartoonist, he was also a dedicated member of the Acme Hose Company of Horseheads. He may have poked fun at the human condition, but he thoroughly enjoyed life and just wanted to share his love and amusement with others, earning national fame in the process.

In his 1926 autobiography, Walt McDougall pointed out a reality of fame. According to him, "As years went on, 'ZIM' altered his style, growing funnier if less artistic, but through an inexplicable lack of recognition by the latter-day publishers he has retired into comparative obscurity" (p. 65).

Comparative obscurity? Even *during* his lifetime? Were the publishers who so readily accepted his material in the 1880s and 1890s now rejecting him? Why? Was it subject matter? Wasn't he "relevant"

anymore? Didn't he adapt to a changing society? Did ZIM tire of the writing life and force himself into obscurity? His "glory days" had been more than three decades earlier, in a different time, a different society. But even in death, he was remembered. *The New York Times* gave his obituary a two-column headline; other journals gave his death major notice. Had he died in the late 1800s, would he have received Page 1 coverage? Would *any* of the great cartoonists have received page 1 coverage?

For more than two decades, beginning in 1883, ZIM spent considerable time in New York City; because he drew for New York City-based magazines, he received significant recognition from the New York media at a time when New York City newspapers and magazines dominated the public's knowledge of people and issues. But ZIM preferred a quieter life than New York City could offer; he didn't seek out the metropolitan media for interviews and "gossip tidbits." By accepting the life of rural Horseheads, he almost cut himself off from the media, which *knew* that if it didn't happen in New York, it didn't happen at all.

His lack of long-lasting fame was also attributed by some to professional laziness. The critics claim that by maintaining the formula he developed in the 1880s, ZIM was professionally lazy, that his fame could not endure because he didn't experiment with new forms. But ZIM had popularized a *new* form, one that was characterized by broad, flowing brush strokes reminiscent of the lithographic grease pencil, by vivid colors, by the grotesque distortion, and by a visual humor that could bring laughter even before the audience read the captions. If ZIM had chosen to draw only in that style, his fame should have been assured; yet he is attacked for the kind of art he did, by critics who consider comic art the lowest form of art and would find any comic art inferior even to a mediocre wash-drawing landscape. Perhaps, as some claim, because he chose to deal only with "transitory" issues, ZIM could never have achieved enduring fame; such critics forget that the human condition never changes.

Also contributing to ZIM's lack of universal recognition today is the fact that he was never identified with any one character or any one issue. Only once, about 1915, did he draw a continuing comic strip; however, "Louie and Lena," distributed by

McClure's Syndicate, never became popular and did nothing to enhance ZIM's reputation. Even if he had been able to produce a daily comic strip for the million-circulation New York *World* or *Journal,* it is still doubtful that many people today would know who ZIM was; after all, how many people today know who Richard Felton Outcault, Winsor McKay, Rudolph Dirks, Bud Fisher, and George Herriman were? A few might know that Outcault's "Yellow Kid" gave "yellow journalism" its name; a few might even know Outcault's "Buster Brown." A very few may remember "Little Nemo" (McKay), "The Katzenjammer Kids" (Dirks), "Mutt 'n' Jeff" (Fisher), and "Krazy Kat" (Herriman). The reality is that the average person does not even notice, let alone retain, a credit line or byline; in contemporary society, the average person can recite the names of more hunk-actors and fluffy-haired actresses than the names or works of some of the best writers in Hollywood. The title of a book *might* be remembered, but the name of the author forgotten; the investigative feature might be remembered for a few days but the reporter's name forgotten or never known. The problem is magnified if the artists or writers are no longer living; if their work is no longer in front of the public, then to the vast majority of the public it is history and thus no longer relevant.

Five decades after he died, ZIM is virtually unknown except within the fraternity of cartoonists, and in Horseheads. It was in Horseheads that Eugene Zimmerman lived most his life after moving there in his teens; it was there that he became active in civic affairs; it was there that he died in 1935, in a house he and his father-in-law had built. Knowing this, I reasoned that if there were clues to the life of Eugene Zimmerman, Horseheads would have those clues. It would be the people of Horseheads who could provide insight; some who still survived would have known him; they could provide at least a direction.

Such was not the case, however. Even in his hometown, ZIM was only a name to many. They knew he had been a famous cartoonist; they could point to some of his cartoons, signs, and caricatures that were hanging in town. But he was of an older generation, and the people just couldn't remember much about him. A few whom I stopped on the street didn't even know who he

was. For many years, the Horseheads Historical Society had tried to keep his name alive; many of his drawings hung in the museum, in a special ZIM Room. But even this wasn't enough. In 1980, upon the death of his daughter, Laura, the Society began a massive volunteer project to restore his house and open it as a memorial to the man now identified as founder of the Grotesque school of caricature, a timid and gentle man who was one of the country's outstanding cartoonists.

Without doubt, ZIM—born in Switzerland, and raised in poverty in America—was a keen observer of the human condition and thoroughly understood American humor. Some critics, however, believe that ZIM's work is nothing more than "the worst in comic strip art." One critic argues that ZIM's art consists of "stale comic jokes, reminiscent of the worst of vaudeville." He argues:

> It is the kind of comic art where the last panel shows someone's feet up in the air with the big word "plop!" It is at its most typical, characteristic of "correspondence school art." The artist simplifies by offering clichés—"here is the way you draw a shoe, here is the way you draw a man's ear." The clichés extend beyond the characters as well. Not only are the Jew and Black drawn as stereotypes, but so are the English gentleman, etc. They all look like figures out of an unimaginative central casting.[4]

It is true that much of ZIM's comic humor is the "short take," the kind of humor that we now associate with the minstrelsy and, later, vaudeville. It is also true that by today's standards, the jokes are stale. But we cannot judge the comic humor of a century ago by today's standards; we need to ask the question, "Were the jokes stale when ZIM first illustrated them?" If they had been, then ZIM can properly be relegated to a minor place in America's comic art. But they were not. ZIM illustrated the jokes of a nation—and by doing so helped preserve them, perhaps to the point that they do indeed seem stale a century later. ZIM also created his own jokes to base the illustrations upon. The humor reflected what society at that time accepted. Undoubtedly, millions of Americans took ZIM's cartoons, showed them to their friends, repeated the jokes so that even within a generation they were so widespread that few remembered where they originated. By the second generation, the jokes were stale.

Each writer, each artist, learns to specialize in a form and a style. ZIM chose the pen-and-ink one-panel and comic strip formats—at some cost to his professional standing. Just as some consider satire secondary to tragicomedic stories, some believe that "belly-laugh" humor is secondary to serious satire. And ZIM was a belly-laugh humorist. In the political journals, the full-color covers and center-folds went to the political satirists and the inside pages went to the "comic" humorists. ZIM drew far fewer full-color illustrations than did some of his contemporaries, but his satire, when he did choose to create it, was as sharp as the best.

ZIM could not be influenced by money, for had he chosen to work full-time for *Scribner's, Harper's, Collier's,* or *Lippincott's* magazines instead of free-lancing for them, he would have been even wealthier. In the world of the capitalist, ZIM could have easily commanded fees of a thousand dollars or more for a major full-color portrait; yet he chose to give away much of his art to friends, civic clubs, and to fans, reasoning that he "made enough" from the art that he did sell—and sell at a premium—to the editors of some of the nation's most prestigious magazines. He would sell them his art and stories, most of them drawn or written in Horseheads, but he would not ever again—not after his nervous collapse while working for *Judge*—ever sell them his soul full-time.

ZIM actually needed to give away his art, to accede to even distant acquaintances for "just a little sketch," for it was through his art that he initially gained the love he missed so much in his preteen and teenage years. He generously gave of his time, his talent, of *himself,* possibly hoping that the people would respect him, love him, want him, *need* him. It was through his art, something he could give, that he could receive this recognition and this love.

ZIM had been born in Switzerland, sent to live with an aunt and uncle in French Alsace at the age of two, shortly after the death of his mother in childbirth, then sent to America at the age of seven to join his father and brother who had emigrated; he found himself living with other relatives in New York, however. Neither his father nor his brother accepted him, to give him the love he so desperately needed. Yet ZIM believed that it would be only

a short time until his father and brother could establish themselves; he accepted what little they did for him, hoping that by proving himself a good worker, he would be loved. He wrote to his sister in Switzerland, but he never saw her again. In America, still in the first decade of his life, he was shuffled from relatives to strangers, forced to work at odd jobs in order to survive, dependent upon the kindness of people who took pity upon what appeared to be a street urchin. He was Swiss by birth, a "foreigner" in the minds of Americans, yet dependent upon America for his survival. He determined, as he noted in his autobiography, to be a "100 percent American," for he believed that if he accepted American culture and conventions, America would accept him. He reached out, trying to identify all that was American, to *become* American. As an immigrant boy with minimal command of English, he learned what it was like to be a minority, shunned by others. As an adult, he would *be* the American he needed to be, even to the point of drawing what he thought America wanted him to draw.

ZIM needed Horseheads and the small town rural life it offered hours from metropolitan New York City. He needed to be able to walk down to Hanover Square, buy an ice cream, talk with his friends. He needed the beauty of Teal Park and the Chemung River. He needed to be not just a "famous" artist, but "one of the boys," someone whose generosity and civic responsibilities far outweighed his national reputation, for few of his friends and acquaintances truly knew how famous he really was. He accepted small-town America with all its benefits and prejudices, asking only that it accept him. And it is possible that he subconsciously mimicked American prejudices, drawing stereotypes and distortions of ethnic minorities not because he was a bigot but because he had learned that the American melting pot still did not really accept Blacks, Native Americans, Jews, and many other minorities. And, most importantly, he truly believed that he was not offending anyone, for he saw humor as universal, not confined to just one race, class, or ethnic group. Metropolitan New York had shown him all forms of prejudice and bigotry; ten thousand American towns and villages had shown him intolerance, often based upon a lack of knowledge. Prejudices against Jews he carried with him from

Alsace and saw reinforced by the prejudice of Keppler, who first hired him to work on a magazine. Prejudice against Blacks and Native Americans he learned in America. If a significant portion of his cartoons reflect what we in a different era call "racist," then we must also remember the kindness of a man who always had time for people, no matter what their race or religion. It was a kindness that many who claim to be tolerant and unbiased could use as their own models of behavior.

By reflecting American humor, ZIM also reflected American racism. Some of ZIM's cartoons and short sketches, more than one-third of his published work, is blatantly racist when judged by contemporary standards. For almost two centuries America's minorities were universally excluded from a national literature; by the late nineteenth century the media "found" Blacks as well as other minorities, many of whom had recently passed through America's immigration process. Appearing frequently were cartoons depicting big, dumb, drunken Irish cops or crooked politicians, conniving Jewish merchants with big noses and greedy hands, and Blacks who rolled dice, stole watermelons and chickens, got into fights, and told their feet to "do yo' thang." ZIM's cartoons were no more racist than other material that appeared in most American magazines of the era; they were no more blatant in their racism than what the majority-owned media accepted—and what readers tolerated. Some of the captions and much of the nonverbal caricaturization accurately reflected a West African language base.[5] Even the offended minorities found much to laugh at in the depiction of their race or ethnicity.

Why some of America's most talented writers and artists chose to enhance previously created stereotypes cannot be completely known. Perhaps ZIM, like many other humorists and satirists, recognized that sometimes the truth was too deep, perhaps too painful, to be satirized in traditional forms. Stinging indictments could be desensitized, yet still retain their importance, by being delivered in bastardized versions of American Black English, Yiddish English, or Irish brogue by Black, Jewish, and Irish stereotypes, rather than in Standard English by American-born whites. Audiences might be touched by the edge of a universal truth while also being entertained. Certainly, it would be only human to want to believe that no matter how badly off you were, there was always someone else worse off—less educated, more impoverished, with more family and business problems. The more discerning readers would probably have seen reflections of white society under the gross distortions, but many, undoubtedly, only saw their own prejudices reinforced by the cartoons, mock speeches, pithy sayings, and jokes.

Perhaps the reason for the proliferation of what we today call racist depictions is only as complex as an argument of circularity. As writers and artists realized that editors were publishing more and more racially and ethnically oriented work, they contributed more, recognizing that what had already appeared in print established the foundation for what would later be acceptable. As editors saw more and more such stories and art—whether in other magazines or among their own submissions—they assumed that the writers and artists were reflecting community-shared values and published the material in order not to be left behind.

ZIM was not the only *Judge* artist or writer to depict Blacks. E. W. Kemble, one of the country's leading cartoonists, drew several series, their titles as racist as the stereotypes they depicted—"A Coon Alphabet," "Blackberries," and "Pickaninnies." Among the other major "Black series" were J. A. Waldron's "Old Chocolate's Target Practice" and A. T. Worden's "Uncle Gabe's Sage Saws," each a series of eight or ten pithy sayings written in American Black English. Most of the sayings reflected human truths, and a number even attacked, through satire, racism. At the end of the nineteenth century, Richard Felton Outcault, who later became the nation's leading daily comic artist, drew "Shakespeare in Possumville," a series of twenty full-color illustrations that reflected what whites thought Blacks would do if the Blacks were Shakespearean actors. Major artists also contributed Black stereotypes to other magazines. For *Harper's Weekly,* beginning about 1872 and continuing through much of the 1880s, Sol Eytinge drew the "Blackville" series; for Currier and Ives, Thomas Worth drew "Darktown," a set of one hundred lithographed plates, each portraying a scene of Blacks in what whites thought was their society. Johann Ehrnhardt, whom many consider to be second only to Joseph Keppler as a lithographic artist, kept Black stereotypes in *Puck,* the cartoons recognized as a "circulation builder" among white audiences. In hundreds of other magazines, hundreds of other artists—famous, soon-to-be famous, and never-to-be famous—all depicted white images of Blacks, and for a two-decade period in the 1880s and 1890s, helped build mass circulations.

In the latter two decades of his life, ZIM was aware of the racism of the cartoons from the 1880s and 1890s. Certainly, it was not his intention to hurt people but rather to make them laugh. Undoubtedly, he felt some pain for having drawn the cartoons, knowing that it was his "bread-and-butter" for so many years. In his autobiography, he notes that in the 1930s "only the most stupid publishers" would print many of the cartoons. Times had changed, and so had ZIM.

In a new age, one that saw the Harlem Renaissance of the 1920s and 1930s and the civil rights struggle of the 1960s, the grotesque distortion was too caustic; by holding minorities up to ridicule, ZIM had held *all* Americans up to ridicule—the minorities for the comic humor, the others for having allowed it. In an effort to cleanse a nation's history, perhaps America deliberately tried to bury its past—and that included *all* art by *all* writers who used the stereotypes, even if much of their work was nonracist.

Whatever the reasons, many writers and artists *did* give realistic portrayals of America's minorities. Grant Hamilton, who became art director of *Judge* upon the death of Bernard Gillam in 1896, did not draw cartoons that included racial or ethnic stereotypes. But he, like many editors, was torn between the realities of readership preferences and the realities of his own values.

Why is ZIM forgotten now? Perhaps because of society's need to rid itself of the memory of early racism, forgetting that racism still exists, if in different forms. Perhaps society, or at least professional critics, determined that his art was "stale," not worthy of enduring. Perhaps the American people, in an era of "me-ism," of acquiring jobs and status, have determined that history is boring, that it is not as necessary to understand their past as

it is their "relevant" present. Why did ZIM choose the paths he did? Perhaps his overwhelming desire to be a part of a closely knit American society led him to seek acceptance and love rather than enduring fame. Perhaps he feared leaving the form that he knew best.

No amount of research can answer why people do not study their past, do not use it to understand their present and future. Perhaps the answer is as simple as knowing that a generation or two raised to believe that there are more important things than one's ancestors is the crux. But media historians must one day answer the question, What price has fame if it lasts so few years? Perhaps the restoration of ZIM's house by the volunteers of the Horseheads Historical Society will force people to see that the threads of human existence cut across all generations; that people, no matter when they lived, share basic values, hopes, beliefs, and aspirations; that they are faced with the same problems, the same glories. And, perhaps, when we see the role that Eugene Zimmerman played in American life, we can begin to understand the role that each of us plays.

NOTES

1. See Walter M. Brasch, *Black English and the Mass Media,* Amherst: University of Massachusetts Press, 1981; paperback rev. ed., Lanham, Md.: University Press of America, 1984.

2. Each year, the National Association of Cartoonists awards a Reuben statuette, named for Rube Goldberg, to the outstanding American newspaper cartoonist of the year.

3. Brian Walker calls ZIM's correspondence course "one of the best teaching tools for several decades." Cartoonist Grant Wood notes that "ZIM's correspondence course was one of the earliest and best, and because of this, he was able to pass on his tips and techniques to artists of yesterday and today."

4. Personal correspondence with Dr. Charles Press, professor of political science at Michigan State University; author of *The Political Cartoon.*

5. Many of the grammar rules found in ZIM's captions using American Black English reflect similar rules in Wes-Kos, the West African Pidgin English.

Autobiography
of Eugene Zimmerman

Introduction to My Life

MY ONLY EXCUSE FOR WRITING THIS book is a statement by Henryk Sienciewicz that it is every man's duty to leave behind him memoirs of his experiences for the benefit of posterity. Since I have produced about 40,000 sketches, counting those I have destroyed as unworthy of publication, and have associated with men and events which loomed large in a half-century's history of caricature, it occurred to me that readers might be interested in a personally conducted tour of my cartoon foundry.

"Why do you hide your light under a bushel in this small town?" I am often asked by visitors from the outside world. The incentive of big money coaxes many a youth into the hurly-burly of the metropolis. Some who have found out the truth, as I did, have returned to the simple life and crawled back under the bushel, out of the feverish turmoil where millionaires and paupers are made. A blossoming crabapple tree has more charm for me than phony palms under which one may sit in an expensive hotel and ruin his stomach with rich viands. Simple living keeps me fit for work or play.

Frugal meals. Temperate habits. Long walks and short rides. Hunting and fishing for relaxation. The omission of tobacco in every form.

All my life I have shunned tobacco. I don't know how many coughs there are in a carload; I have never joined in an anti-spit crusade, and I wouldn't walk a mile for any smoke unless it came from a campfire in the woods. Nevertheless, a local cigar maker named Ed Cannon christened a nickel perfecto with my name, about fifteen years ago, and later the United Cigar Stores offered him $1,000 for his rights to that cigar. I advised Ed to sell, as he had other brands to manufacture, but Ed would not listen to it; hence the ZIM cigar is still his property and its creator is still poor.

However, I have never been a prohibitionist, 'tis true, and the *Elmira Telegram* once gave me a sly dig in a news item announcing that the Acme Hose Company of Horseheads had presented me with a cut-glass water set; it concluded: "The only wonder is what Gene will do with a water set." The *Judge* staff used to reserve a secluded corner in the tap room of the Prince George Hotel, on Twenty-eighth Street, opposite the Brunswick Building, in which *Judge* was published; every noon, six to ten good fellows met there to talk shop over a social glass and a tasty luncheon. Whenever a contributing artist hit the city, we invited him to sit at the board and partake of our hospitality. And my friend, Emil Flohri, the artist, used to say: "If Prince George's wife brewed that ale, she was a crackerjack brewer."

To be tucked away in a small town in the Chemung Valley seems to fit my needs and nature exactly, for I can go out at will and breathe the free and balmy air without punching the time clock; besides, the hills, the woods and the streams are very soothing to the nervous system. Here, one is not annoyed by trolleys, elevateds, nor subways. Skyscrapers do not hinder the sun shining in every window, and the bills for maintenance and overhead expenses are considerably less than those that confront one in the great Metropolis.

I have no particular routine except that I retire with the chickens and arise at 5:30 quite regularly. Seven o'clock finds me at my desk and 8 o'clock at breakfast. After that, my day is divided between work and play. With the mail of my correspondence school attended to, I am ready to join a hunting, fishing or hiking outfit, and so on. It is easy to understand how one can fall in with a life such as this with its agreeable environment.

After having been amalgamated with the spirit of Horseheads, I had decided to stop working for landlords; whereupon I designed and built a home of my own. I purchased a double lot 100 by 160 feet, paying for it from week to week as I earned the money. My father-in-law was a carpenter and I became his helper. I toiled all day at sawing and nailing lumber, besides doing my art work at night. I believe I put in an average of sixteen hours a day in that double capacity.

As soon as the framework was finished and I had shingled the roof, my wife and I moved in. The interior was completed when finances permitted. Five years elapsed before I could call the job finished, and I have been living in that house for forty years.

When natives learned that I was seeking relics with which to deck the walls of my studio I became the recipient of such ancient trinkets as warming pans, book jacks, spinning wheels, spear

heads and old tin lanterns, until my attic bulged for lack of housing space, and I was obliged to hang out a signal of distress. On one occasion, a Negro porter at the *Judge* office delivered to me this information: "Mr. Zim, dey's a wooden bicycle downstairs fo' you; it came by Express." It was a disjointed four foot spinning wheel minus two of its legs.

Every man who builds a home for himself has a hobby. Mine was one tall room, with a balcony which I intended to use as a studio but which proved to be too public for that purpose, so I surrendered it for a quieter workshop. Children never annoyed me in my work. I often labored at my desk with Laura on my knee and Adolph playing around. Adolph Zimmerman was an orphaned nephew whom I adopted at the age of six. Occasionally the youngsters' prattle suggested ideas for comics.

I have lived an ideal life among the characters of my nimble pencil. I have seen the passing of farmers' chin whiskers and the coming of the automobile. On dull summer days, when the town characters gather at the old blacksmith shop to discuss the uppermost topics of the hour, I join in the discussions, and in this way I collect much of the material that later appears in ZIM cartoons.

I have watched my town grow from kerosene to gas, from gas to electric lights. I have seen the old base burner of the corner grocery replaced by a modern furnace. I have viewed the downfall of the stately prune, its price dropping from twenty-five cents net to three pounds for a quarter, and have seen our champagne thirst turn in the direction of wood alcohol. I have beheld periodic changes in transportation, the old stage coach succeeded by the horse car and then the electric trolley; as this narrative is being penned, the trolley is beginning to wobble out of commission and the luxurious bus is taking the lead.

I have no desire for travel except to roam the hills afoot or to fish from a flat-bottomed boat. To me, this is the life, this is luxury. I have never seen Niagara Falls, but I have sat upon ant-hills and studied the movement of insects. I have observed the trapping methods of the wood spider and have watched a weasel transfer her young to a new home in the springtime. I have seen the kingfisher dart into a stream and nab a fingerling. I like to notice these things and draw them in their wild surroundings. I also like to gather medicinal herbs and roots, berries and nuts.

My motto is "Never let business interfere with pleasure," for which I have been called lazy; but listen: A man who gets up at 5:30 and shaves before breakfast is not lazy. Never, as far back as I can recall, have I eaten breakfast in night robes. When I sit down to the morning meal, I am fully clothed for work or play—and possess a hired man's appetite. When I say *play* I don't mean bridge or golf. With an eight-pound gun, a pound of ammunition, lunch and heavy boots, try to follow a couple of fox hounds over ten or fifteen miles of rough country, and you will agree that the word lazy does not apply to the hunter.

My favorite vice is a fondness for preparing my own meals, whether at home or in camp. A cook book interests me more than a novel. If I dine at a hotel and find upon the menu an interesting dish that is new to me, I tip the waiter to get me its recipe. The enthusiasm of some sportsmen ends when the catch is landed or the game is bagged; with me it has just begun. I love to dress my fish or game, and do the cooking; after that I can eat it with relish.

As far as Prohibition is concerned, I'm abiding by the law and finishing up my days on clear spring water, delivered through the medium of an iron pipe at the regular meter rates.★ Nevertheless, my mind goes back to those pleasant days—which alas! are no more!—when I picked up many a good idea over a cool glass of Bock or India Pale Ale, when bars were open and thirst was eternal, and when I was annoyed by local panhandlers.

To give an idea of what half a century of cartooning means: In the course of one year I made more than 1,000 drawings for *Judge* alone. The list includes front and back covers and double-page spreads, also *Judge's* library covers, all in colors, some drawn on stone, in addition to black-and-white drawings. During a period of freelancing I worked for seventeen different publishers, from twelve to sixteen hours a day.

It is torture for artistic brains to toil on a time schedule like an alarm clock—every day I would

have to produce a fresh batch of ideas—especially when such labor is performed behind walls of steel and masonry under a boss's eye. The nature of our profession, aside from hack work, is pleasant and alluring, but so-called efficiency takes most of the joy out of it.

I remember what great pleasure I received from A. B. Frost's humorous book, *Stuff and Nonsense*, published by Harper Brothers. It was a perfect masterpiece of comic art. Comparing the art of Frost's period with the more modern productions, we find a certain deterioration. Big money and quantity production have brought this about. Artists are not to blame for turning out inferior drawings when larger incomes stand in the way of time and careful work. It seems that as long as the idea is acceptable, the public cares little how roughly the drawings are tendered. I am not criticizing the artists, but the pace that is set for them for turning out a job to fatten the pocketbooks of the capitalists in back of the project.

I myself feel the spirit of the times and am swayed to work as carelessly as some of the others, not from choice, I assure you, but to keep up with the procession, to give the present generation what it is getting from others and what it is accustomed to digest. Commenting on the way quantity production has affected my technique, cartoonist Walt McDougall says in his autobiographical book, *This Is The Life!:* "As years went on, ZIM altered his style, growing funnier, if less artistic."

Readers can observe this alteration by comparing my earlier cartoons with more recent ones. The latter are drawn more hastily and with fewer lines. The same change in technique applies to the work of many other artists, such as Charles Dana Gibson, F. B. Opper, and T. E. Powers.

If you wish to know why I left the "regular grind" of New York City—well, the early days of *Judge* were so strenuous that I soon found my health slipping away, so I got out of the Big City and settled here in Horseheads where I had spent a few years before my advent into cartooning. I made semi-monthly trips to the *Judge* office, doing my work at both ends. My connection with *Judge* covered a period of about thirty years.★

★Whether Zim did, in fact, stay "dry" or not is now only conjecture.

★Shortly after moving back to Horseheads, ZIM became a regular contributor to several of the nation's major magazines, including *Lippincott's, Scribner's,* and *Collier's.* For *Collier's,* ZIM drew the illustrations for Bill Nye's weekly articles. However, with the death of

I might say that I am now getting the most out of life that circumstances and conditions permit. I don't crave for anything that I can't afford. I have come to the conclusion that craving for wealth and luxuries is either a false appetite or a bad habit. We don't give sufficient consideration to our health and happiness. No doubt I made the big mistake of sticking too long to *Judge* when more alluring prospects with dailies offered themselves but, like a good sailor, I hung on to the sinking craft 'till it became necessary to lighten her burdens by jumping overboard and taking to freelancing. Meanwhile, I worked out a correspondence course in cartooning and comic art [1923].

Irvin S. Cobb once pointed out that a shoe manufacturer could give you a pair of shoes and not feel it, for he retained the last and could soon make another pair of the same kind. When a writer gives away a story, however, he can't dispose of a similar manuscript to a publisher. An idea and a few hours of pen scratches mean more to the magazine writer than a whole case of shoes mean to the manufacturer. The same applies to a cartoonist.

If one's admirers would only realize that making a drawing is not merely a careless wiggle of the hand! Time is as valuable to the artist as it is to anyone else. Once I gave a local merchant considerable publicity by drawing a caricature of him which was published in a newspaper of 20,000 circulation. My work on that caricature consumed three or four hours, for which I charged nothing. To show how much the fellow appreciated my efforts on his behalf, I must relate what happened when I stepped into his store to buy a pound of bacon.

"Do you want it sliced or in chunk?" the merchant asked.

"What do you charge for slicing it?" I wanted to know.

"Two cents a pound extra."

So I paid the extra two cents, which he assured me was in accordance with the daily market reports. If ever I am called upon to do another job for that man, he'll surely have to pay full market price.

When the paper comes out, and my work is in the critics' hands, the feeling I experience some-times is akin to stage fright. A cartoon never looks as good to me when printed as it did while in course of construction, for usually I labor in a white heat of enthusiasm which grows cold by the time I gaze upon a reproduction of the finished product. The result is often disappointing, for I can discern, when too late, how the cartoon could have been bettered in composition and more interest injected in various ways. The layout of a cartoon is the part that fills one with anxiety; after that is settled, the drawing of it comes easy.

On many occasions I have hurried out of the city rather than face my cartoons on the newsstand. Had I dared to make such a confession to my employers, I might have been given my walking papers, but by ingeniously smothering my own doubtful thoughts I managed to "get by." I believe every artist has his dull days when it seems impossible to do anything right. At such times the wastebasket receives more attention than does the publisher.

Newspaper art has taken wonderful strides since *Puck*'s balmy days, and I wonder sometimes where on earth it will stop or to what it will eventually lead. Every kid welcomes the daily strips and Sunday supplements. They are as familiar with the numerous comic characters as some of our great grandfathers were with Scripture. I believe the comic supplement is a big factor in shaping character. Wherever those funny pictures enter a household, there is a perceptible cheerfulness in the nature of the youngsters. A lack of grouch, you may call it, and doubt if a paper could omit its comic section without affecting its circulation.

The world may not be improving morally, but some of the sting that dominated the old time cartoon and the venomous abuse of public officers seems to be a dead issue. I believe the spirit of the present day cartoon is more friendly in comparison. It does its work, not by force of the ax or the dirk. Politicians are ridiculed but not in a vulgar, vicious manner. The old-fashioned method of campaigning made men of the opposite political beliefs bitter enemies and campaigns were akin to slugging matches. This feeling was likewise evident in the early political cartoon.

National politics give me no great concern. Let those at Washington worry it out.* But I do feel

---

Bernhard Gillam in 1896, ZIM reduced his outside assignments to concentrate on art for *Judge;* Grant Hamilton, Emil Flohri, and ZIM provided the bulk of *Judge's* cartoons after Gillam's death.

*ZIM was one of two Republicans—the other was Bernhard

deeply interested in local civic affairs and the advancement of the youth of the community. Among several features in which I am just now interested is a Community Boys' Band. This supplies a bit of diversion, besides enabling me to study their characteristics. It is not a bad idea to fasten onto a worthy hobby as a side line. It helps one to forget his rheumatism if he has any.

Though I was born in Switzerland, I consider myself nevertheless a one hundred per cent American, for I arrived in this country at the age of seven. I believe in law and order and the constitution of the United States. Through no fault of mine, I have escaped the draft of several important wars. You see, when the Rebellion broke loose, I was yet in arms in a French Alsatian village. In 1870, the Franco-Prussian War chased me to America and I was beyond the draft limit when the World War happened, so I have missed that which might have changed my entire life, for it must be rather difficult to concentrate on comics in a hail of shrapnel. Instead of being an alleged comic artist, I might now be directing troops from a desk in Washington, D.C., or better still, retired on a pension.

During the past fifty years, I have learned it is remarkable what one learns about himself from reading the newspapers. For instance, my photo was published in the *Syracuse Herald* on March 24, 1910, in connection with this news:

> The Ann Arbor Railroad has been sold. Positive announcement was made here today by Eugene Zimmerman, of Cincinnati, who, with H. B. Hollus & Co. of New York controlled the property.
> Mr. Zimmerman, father of the Duchess of Manchester, refused to disclose the identity of the owners of the property.
> "I'm not interested in who got the road," he said. "What I wanted was the dust."
> Another announcement was made by Mr. Zimmerman, when he said the sale of the Ann Arbor was the first step in his plan to dispose of all his railroad interests and retire from active business to enjoy his millions. He is in the seven-

ties, but is as active as most men of fifty.

There were a few "minor" errors in the above item. I was not yet in my seventies, my daughter was not the Duchess of Manchester, I never lived in Cincinnati, I never had any millions to enjoy, and the only railroad I ever owned was a horse and buggy. Otherwise, the details are correct.

Nevertheless, there *was* a railroad magnate named Eugene Zimmerman, and when he died some time later the report got abroad that I had cashed in, causing a flow of condolence to my supposedly bereaved family. Flattering obituaries were published in London papers, and various art clubs were about to draw up resolutions of regret when I put an end to the celebration by declaring myself alive and well.

Many years ago, in Atlantic City, I was mistaken for Arthur Zimmerman, the leading bicyclist of that time. More recently, a Civil War veteran greeted me with: "I usta see you drawin' pick-ters on the sidewalks with chalks when you was about knee-high to a grasshopper, an' I said then that you'd make your mark some day." As a matter of fact, the incident was purely legendary, but I never contradict an admirer when he recalls events in my early life. It is tragic to shatter romances that have been cherished for years, so I let it go at that.

A supposed old acquaintance once came up to me with outstretched palm denoting welcome, then dropped my hand with an exclamation of astonishment and contempt.

"No, sir! I'm looking for ZIM the cartoonist."

I assured him that I was the man he sought.

"There is some mistake," he protested. "You're not the fellow I met down along the Hudson who said he was ZIM, the cartoonist, and lives in this town."

Another mythical account of my early days appeared in the *Leader* of Corning, N.Y., about twenty miles from my home:

> Eugene Zimmerman, whose name is known wherever humor is known, was a student at Corning Free Academy and in his school days showed exactly the same traits which were later to bring him fame.
> An old school mate in conversation with a *Leader* reporter Saturday recalled an amazing incident of ZIM's school days in Corning. Professor Slocum was then the presiding genius of the school room and ZIM spent a great deal of his

---

Gillam—on *Puck's* staff in the early 1880s—but even this didn't cause him much concern, for he drew "human nature" drawings, letting others do most of the biting political satire that helped Grover Cleveland become president.

time "making pictures." One day when he felt a little more daring than usual he put up a very striking and life-like caricature of the professor which, as those things sometimes do, fell into the hands of the instructor himself. Professor Slocum gravely looked at the grinning caricature of his countenance and invited ZIM to remain after school. The youthful ZIM saw visions of a packed school bag and a return home.

After the big school room was empty and the footsteps of the last pupil died away in the distance, Professor Slocum beckoned ZIM to his desk.

"My boy," he said, "I am not going to suspend you, although I must tell you out of fairness to yourself that the school room is no fit place for you. A boy with your talents should be on *Puck* or *Judge*."

A few years later ZIM took Professor Slocum's advice. He became the feature cartoonist of *Judge* and one of the best known comic artists in the world.

The truth of the matter is: I did not attend school at Corning, I never saw Professor Slocum, and I was never kept after school for making caricatures; however, T. E. Powers once told me that he had been forced into lithography and then the cartoon profession by being discharged from the clerkship in a hardware store in Kansas City when the proprietor came upon a caricature of himself which young Powers had dashed off.

In 1902, an imposter using my name was entertained for three months in Seattle, Wash., even by the Seattle Press Club. I learned of it from a lady resident of that city who had written the fellow a letter which naturally failed to find him and was forwarded to my home address. I asked the lady for further information, whereupon she sent me a clipping from the Seattle *Times*. Immediately I wrote to the editor:

My attention has been called to an article in *The Times* of October 12, 1902, in which I see that I have been spending part of the Summer in Seattle. As I have never had the pleasure of visiting your city, I have reached the conclusion that the story must either be a mistake or that some one has been impersonating me.

My letter was turned over to the reporter who had written the story, and the facts came out. The reporter, covering horse races, struck up an acquaintance with a handsome, well-dressed man of about thirty-five who introduced himself as "Fran-

cis B. Huston, better known as ZIM, the *Judge* cartoonist." Huston had plenty of money, his pockets were fairly lined with twenty-dollar gold pieces, and he showed a pass he had received from the Northern Pacific Railroad as a compliment to his work. He maintained a suite of rooms at a fine hotel, where he spent many hours drawing and painting. To the reporter he glibly told this story:

I was born in a little Methodist town in Kentucky. My parents were poor and I was early farmed out, as it were, to a baker by the name of Zimmerman. I used to pass the time drawing pictures in the dough, and one day Mr. Zimmerman suggested that I draw a picture and send it to *Judge*.

I was afraid to do this, as my people were Methodists and looked upon such frivolities as the work of the Evil One. My father had repeatedly threatened to ship me if I persisted in cartooning all his old-time friends and neighbors. But Mr. Zimmerman persisted, so I finally drew a cartoon, borrowed his name, and sent it under the nom de plume of "ZIM."

And that's how I came by the name. I soon received an offer from *Judge* and have worked for them ever since. See that pencil? Well, that little bit of silver, I suppose, has netted me $75,000, all told. I did my first work with that for *Judge,* and I hope I'll do my last with it.

About two years ago I went back to my boyhood home, and for the life of me I couldn't help drawing cartoons of some of those old Methodist people who had known I was going to the bad as soon as I commenced to draw. Honestly, when the copies of *Judge* containing those pictures began to get back to Kentucky I almost had to run for my life. No, I don't think it will be safe for me to go back there again.

Huston was a most accommodating person. He drew water color pictures, signed them "ZIM" and presented them to his acquaintances in Seattle. Suddenly he was tipped off that there was trouble in the wind, and he disappeared, leaving no forwarding address. Meanwhile, I had sent the Seattle *Times* photographs of myself and original drawings, together with a complete disavowal of the whole affair, in which I said:

I admire Mr. Huston's nerve, but I have no kick coming, as he has proven himself a good fellow, with lots of dough, and best of all, he did not leave your city with orders to send all bills to the *Judge* office, New York, so I will do nothing toward bringing him to justice.

The fact of his having $300 on his person at one time is sufficient, however, to mark him as a fraud of his profession. Did you ever run across a really true newspaper man with such a bundle? If you have, you ought to be numbered among our American discoverers.

Chapter 1

[ON MAY 26, 1862, IN BASEL, SWITZerland, a country that would maintain its neutrality against the armies of Louis Napoleon's France and Otto von Bismarck's Germany, Eugene Zimmerman was born. His father was Joseph Zimmerman, a baker born in Alsace; his mother was Katherine Amelie Klotz Zimmerman, a Swiss. An older brother, Adolph, was born in 1864, hours before her mother died at the age of thirty-two from complications in childbirth.

Unable to care for his children properly, Joseph gave Adolph and Amelie to relatives in Switzerland and took Eugene to live with relatives named Ehret, in Thann, in Alsace. In his notes, Eugene recalled that "Alsace was separated from Switzerland by a rail fence so low that one could almost jump over it, and yet, as I look back now in memory, it seems that I crossed a Rubicon when, at the age of two and a half, I took those few steps into a foreign country."

Joseph found employment in Mulhausen, near Thann, but with the approaching Franco-Prussian war and the almost certain prospect of a draft of young men, Joseph took Adolph and emigrated with him to America, leaving three-year-old Eugene at a school in Thann and one-year-old Amelie with relatives in Basel.

Eugene was brought up to avoid conflict, yet as a child he was torn between a set of pacifist values, and the colors and flamboyance of the military.]

For five years, until I was seven. I resided at Thann, attending a French school, beneath the pale blue mountains of Alsace. Those years before the hordes of mighty Bismarck ripped asunder that prosperous and peaceful French valley, installing German *Kultur* in its every corner, were glorious to me. If there is anything dear to a boy's heart it is a soldier suit, and in that turbulent but decidedly interesting period, even a child could sniff war in the air. In America, to which my father and brother emigrated, the Great Rebellion had just ended; and in Europe, Garibaldi's troops were fighting around Rome while martial activities were rife all over Louis Napoleon's Empire, notably at Thann.

Like many other youngsters old enough to waddle, I wore a minature Zouave uniform of red baggy pants and blue coat, with tin accoutrements at the side. Bright hues have always captured my fancy, especially on uniforms. If I had been older at that time, and more war-like, I would have enrolled under Garibaldi's banner, chiefly for the thrill of wearing a red shirt! (That was the very reason why I became a volunteer fireman at Horseheads, New York, many years later.)

Yes, I love colors. I remember how I doted on a small box of paints which Santa Claus put in my stocking at Thann before I was five years old. The daubs I made with those pasty pigments constituted my first venture into the art world. For-

Eugene Zimmerman, right, with brother, Adolph, and parents Joseph and Amelie. This photograph was taken in 1862 in Basel, Switzerland; Mrs. Zimmerman died shortly after childbirth two years later.

tunately, they have not been preserved for posterity. Another factor which helped to bend my juvenile mind toward a future career was the artistry of my cousin Eugene who was about eighteen when I was five. He used to amuse us by giving Punch-and-Judy shows in the attic of his home, carving the puppets' heads out of wine-barrel bungs from the shop below and touching them up with color. The whole process fascinated me very much.

When I was seven and a half, the war clouds had become so dark and ominous that my aunt decided to ship me to America in care of a friend of the family. (I never again saw my sister Amelie who remained in Switzerland, eventually married, and died in 1930; thus do paths diverge!)

Just before embarking from Havre, my guardian decided to show me the life and color of Paris. A military atmosphere hung over the entire city. Attachments of troopers of every variety of uniformed splendor were galloping about the streets, but as I was hardly of an age to comprehend the seriousness of the times, and the scene before my eyes assumed the aspect of a carnival, the memory of which is vivid to me this very day.

It would be less than a year that Alsace-Lorraine changed, and thousands of loyal French families left the region rather than submit to Prussian rule and taxation, moving to French possessions or to America. (To this day when I am asked why I have never worn a military uniform, I point out that I was born in a neutral country and was taught to keep peace with the world. If other nations saw fit to indulge in bloody conflicts, that was a matter all their own, and so far as I was concerned, I don't believe in or intend to stick my nose into other people's business. I am the offspring of a country that has lived in peace with mankind of all nations for several centuries; she has stood immune and independent in perpetual surroundings. Why then should not the gentleness of such a nation be instilled in the heart of its children?)

I left France as a steerage passenger aboard the *Paraguay,* one of those slow but sure French steamers that agreed to deliver its cargo of human freight anytime within one year of the date of sailing. There was no attempt at privacy by means of curtains or partitions of any sort, and the nights were made hideous by the rumblings of trunks and

boxes of passengers. The air, as I remember it, was foul and nauseating, and the heavy odor of chloride of lime seemed like poison to my nostrils. Our meals were served amidship on the kitchen deck. One day, the sea was rolling high and ill-behaved, and a huge wave swept over us and cleaned our plates of the midday meal, in consequence of which we had no dinner on that day. One cannot imagine the melancholy environments of the early emigrant ship and the dark forebodings of its weary voyagers seeking new homes, with no particular destination in view. We arrived only twenty-

The Paraguay, *drawn by Eugene Zimmerman when he was about seven.*

one days after leaving France. (After landing in this country, I have confined my ocean voyages to the Brooklyn-Manhattan ferries and an occasional rowboat on the Chemung River, though I freely admit having navigated many a schooner across the bar in prohibition days along the Bowery.) When we arrived in New York harbor, all bedding was ordered cast overboard to prevent any infection.

In those days immigrant ships docking at New York deposited their human cargoes at the Battery in Castle Garden, a prison-like edifice which had been erected in 1807 and used successively as a fort, a cabaret, a music hall, and an opera house. Between 1855 and 1890 that structure was an overnight terminal station for housing future American citizens. There, they were given health inspection and were tagged for further transportation to their respective destinations. Incoming foreigners were crowded like sardines into that famous circular building, which finally gave somebody the brilliant idea of turning it into a fish-house—and that's what it is today.★

Visitors to the Aquarium now gawk at sleepy crocodiles in the very spot where a grand ball was given for LaFayette in 1832 and a reception for President Tyler in 1843—where soldiers were recruited for the Mexican War and where General Booth organized the Salvation Army—where the Swedish Nightingale, Jenny Lind, brought tears to thousands of eyes by singing "Home, Sweet Home"—and where Thomas Nast, Bernhard Gillam, Joseph Keppler, and I, as well as other future American cartoonists arrived from foreign countries, and were deodorized, pasteurized, and certified before being turned loose on the New World. And on that day in 1869, the day I stepped off the ship, I became an American!

Chapter 2

[FOR ALMOST A YEAR, YOUNG ZIMmerman lived with an aunt and uncle [Surname: Stucker] and their two sons on Fourth Avenue, just off First Street on New York City's East Side. He seemed to be happy, yet missed his father, so one day he decided to go to Paterson, New Jersey, and surprise him; his father did not know that Eugene had left Europe.]

Even with the hair trunk, father was delighted to see me again. And when I moved over to Paterson, New Jersey, after spending a few months with relatives on New York's East Side, my father found bed and board for me at the bake shop in which he was employed.

Father was too poor and toiled too hard to give me much attention as the days lengthened into weeks, months, and years. For a while, he sent me to a French tutor in the hope of salvaging as much

as possible of my native tongue, but the humiliation I endured from having been an Alsacian—for which I was dubbed alternately "Frenchy" and "Dutchy"—spurred me to acquire the language of my newly adopted country, and soon I forgot all the French I had ever known.

Gradually, I became less and less of a foreigner in speech and mannerisms, because a young boy will pick up the customs of a strange land much quicker than his elders will. Compulsory education was not yet in vogue, so most of my knowledge of the New World's ways was gained from daily contact with the street urchins and through occasional schooling.★

I attended the Van Houten Street Public school, located just across the street from Cataract Hose No. 2, the only blue-shirted fire company in the city [other companies wore red shirts]; it was another factor in my early environment which, years later, influenced me to become a volunteer fireman.

Manual labor was required for the less fortunate boys such as myself, and I worked during the years which should have been devoted to play and book learning. By carrying a full dinner pail some miles distant from my home, I managed to earn fifty cents a week, and, with another quarter earned for polishing my father's shoes every Saturday, I had sufficient capital to keep me comfortably in chocolate taffy and butterscotch—two standard confections at Aunt Polly's tiny lollypop store.

On election nights, I and other boys would hang around the office of the *Paterson Daily Guardian,* eager to get my papers and skip about the city at 4 A.M., adding my melodious voice to theirs in singing the anthems, "Extrees! Full 'count of de 'leckshun!"

Once I discovered a five-dollar bill which seemed to be roaming about the neighborhood without a claimant, and thus it automatically became my property. Such a vast sum, however, was too much to trust to Providence in so worldly a city as Paterson, so I invested seventy-five cents of it in a small cast-iron bank, into which I placed twenty-five cents for a rainy day; with the remaining four dollars I availed myself of a lot of needed

★It was originally known as the South Battery. In 1896, it was converted to an aquarium-museum. It has now been restored to look like the original fort and is currently a museum.

★Zimmerman spoke only French and German when he came to America but, according to his notes, "soon learned to cuss and swear as perfectly as my American associates."

"The Hair Trunk"
Drawn by Eugene Zimmerman about 1922

knick-knacks; then a financial crisis came along and it was necessary to close accounts and declare the institution insolvent.

Clearly, Nature had not patterned me to be a financier; I was not given to hoarding; I believed in keeping my legal tender in circulation, a habit to which I have faithfully adhered until the present day.

It is natural for a boy to form a co-partnership with some trustworthy buddy and share with him the tips realized from doing odd chores about the neighborhood. Such an alliance I formed with a chum named Jimmy Dumphy. It started with a capitalization of one dime, which was thrust into my palm by a generous gentleman whose horse I had held for half as hour before a place where vile beverages were dispensed. I had been in business for myself prior to this incident, but when Jimmy cast his eyes on the coin and yelled, "Fifty-fifty!" I found myself involved in compulsory co-partnership. From that moment, we declared daily dividends on all cash transactions, according to the ethics of our clan. Although we reposed perfect confidence in each other's integrity, we deemed it more prudent to move about together in the channels of commerce and thus be sure of an honest accounting of each day's business. All melons were cut at the moment the fruit of our labors ripened. Our biggest harvest resulted during snow-shoveling time, when the firm's receipts often reached the enormous sum of forty cents a day; since most of it was collected in the big copper cents of an early

"The Firm of Felix and Dumphy"
Drawn by Eugene Zimmerman about 1922

coinage, you may believe that each partner had a fair sized pile when the day was done.

There came a time, however, when it became absolutely necessary to dissolve the firm, and each of us go his own way; that time was when the day's receipts were but nineteen cents, and a third party, a bigger lad, had to be called in to decide which of the partners should get ten cents and which to get only nine. "In order that this matter will assume an aspect of perfect fairness," said the umpire, "I'll give you each nine cents and I'll keep the odd one," thus closing the books of the firm for all time.

As a youth I was an ardent swimmer, and during the warm weather I could have been found at least two days a week with other boys along the Passaic River, below the gas house, at a point where the water had been enriched by the oily overflow of that institution and by city garbage.

There, one might bathe amid watermelon rinds in season and come up anointed with the output of the gas house. We never caught our death of cold because the delicate film that formed over the skin as we emerged closed the pores to all outside dangers.

I well remember how we used to play hookey from school in order to visit this hallowed spot, sling mud at one another, tie in knots the clothing of the weaker fellows and engage in other kind deeds. My father used to gaze suspiciously at my damp hair, as if he were wondering whether or not that were part of the curriculum, but he never got so far as attempting to delve into the cause of perpetual dampness.

Once, while I was swimming in the raceway of a cotton mill along the Passaic River, a husky mill-hand with bushy red hair tied a knot in my shirt. Believing it to be another fellow's garment, I advised "Reds" to tie it good and tight, which he did, to my supreme delight. Later, it dawned upon me that I also had a shirt in that pile, and proceeded to investigate. I was amazed to find that the one Reds had tied was my own shirt, of which I had but two to my name! This was truly a calamity, especially as the burly brute grinned and gloated over my humiliation. A plank bridged the raceway over which I was obliged to pass after dismembering the mutilated sleeve with my jack-knife. Tearfully, I dressed myself and started to cross the plank, meanwhile offering some genealogical observa-

tions about Reds which infuriated the brute so much that he made a dash for me. While dodging, I fell headlong into the stream, full dress, learning a bitter lesson that the little amusement one gets out of such actions does not compare with the misery it causes and the enemies it makes.

Playing "Big Injun" was one of my early pastimes, and the heroes of the plains were my ideals of vigorous American manhood. Although I never read the Deadwood Dick type of literature [dime adventure novels], which had fired the youth with ambition to perform desperate deeds, I was, nevertheless, on the job when there were Indians to scalp and wild buffaloes to kill.

I wish I could feel as important and big now as I did in the days I had two cheap powder pistols stuck in my belt, and was called "Texas Jack." We played Wild West after school and on Saturdays in what legend says was an abandoned Indian cave on the outskirts of Paterson. The Passaic Valley is a

"Texas Jack and Buffalo Bill"
Drawn by Eugene Zimmerman about 1922

busy part of the state, far enough removed from the Western frontier to make Indian hunting a safe and desirable occupation. However, I learned that it was neither safe nor desirable when, in an unguarded moment, one of my pistols discharged prematurely, and shot some powder into the painted cheek of a "big chief" who proceeded to kick Texas Jack off the face of the earth. It is remarkable how a well-placed kick will cool a boy's ardor for Indian scalping, saving me from dying with my boots on in later life.

When I was old enough to attend Sunday school, I learned of the marvelous phenomena of Bible days, such as Noah and his floating menagerie, an aggregation which, in these modern times, would require three sections of railroad trains to shift about the country. On each trip to Sabbath worship I was given two cents to pay for my salvation, but I had to pass Aunt Polly's lollipop establishment where Satan pulled me in and compelled me to divide, giving me a stick of candy in exchange. Hence, the house of the Lord got only half of the amount that was coming to it. But I had been taught that God was ever kind and merciful to sinners and would pardon my giving way to temptation.

Once a revivalist came to town to disinfect the moral atmosphere and rescue those who had skidded off the road to Glory. A big, burly, reformed drunkard was asked to relate how he had caught the life-line.

Dramatically he strode forward, regarded his audience with knitted brow, and belched forth:

"Ladies and gents, I've allus been a holy terror and a miserable drunken bum till now, and what I've got to say about this here thing they call religion is: If any man here loves Jesus better'n I do, just trot 'im out."

This simple bit of rhetoric went down in history as an outstanding feature of the campaign. Some years later, however, he stumbled off the narrow path of righteousness and was found dead in the lap of a friendly cellarway after a periodical debauch.

My schooling was at a very low ebb, for, to the mind of my father, a practical baker, education was an unnecessary acquisition. Geography did not tell him how far it was from the bakery to the doorstep of his farthest customer. Arithmetic helped to pre-

"Away to the Westward"

MRS. QUARTZ—"Injun?"
HANK—"Ya-as."
MRS. QUARTZ—"Git him?"
HANK—"Dead 'r winged; one 'r t'other."
MRS. QUARTZ—"Jest look over'n see if he's got any blue beads on his moccasins. I need 'bout a thimbleful more fer that 'Peace 'n Good-will' motter-card I'm workin'."

vent short-changing on collection days but it didn't state how much flour to the pound of sugar and how much raisins and molasses were required to make gingerbread, nor how to overcome the odor of a foul egg that accidentally slipped into the cake dough.

Boys of that period were obliged to think more seriously of *vocation* than *vacation*. Every lad of my acquaintance left grammar school before finishing the course in order to take up a job or become apprenticed to some tradesman.

In that busy little bakery at the corner of Broadway and West Street there were only two workers besides myself—the boss, Joseph Bourseleth, and my father—and none of us was given an opportunity to become sybaritic. Many times I was obliged to assist with the night work, in addition to the delivery job. On such occasions, I would snatch "forty winks" now and then by slipping out of the hot basement and casting my slight form upon a cool and inviting pavement, there to dream of better days to come. But the cruel, gruff voice of the boss would ring out upon the prevailing calmness

"At the Bakery"
Drawn by Eugene Zimmerman about 1922

of the immediate neighborhood to arouse me from blissful slumber.

As soon as I could shoulder a basket of bread, I began delivering the loaves (which my father baked) to the homes of the multitude of wage slaves in the vicinity of Paterson. To do this, it was necessary for me to arise at 5 A.M. and avail myself of a hurried breakfast, for, regardless of weather conditions, the staff of life must be delivered to its destination. Every customer was considered a precious asset, so it behooved me to be courteous and forebearing in the face of almost perpetual adversity.

Frequently, I had run the gauntlet of a much hated element called the Sandy Hill gang. Paterson, in the early days, was divided by the double tracks of the Erie Railroad, the hostile deadline between the downtown or business section and Sandy Hill, the rather tough residential section. The latter could be compared with the old Harlem of New York, where goats ran at random and the delicious fragrance of garbage prevaded the air.

When winter set in, hostilities cropped out between those two unfriendly local factions. All the bitterness of their hearts was wrapped up in soaked and frozen snowballs, and a flag of truce meant nothing but a rag to either side. You had to be one thing or the other, and as I was a downtowner delivering fresh bread through the Sandy Hill sec-

tion I necessarily became a target for the enemy. Nevertheless, there were two things in my favor; I was sheltered by an ample basket and my avoirdupois was so sparse of meat that there wasn't much territory to hit.

Frequently, I cussed the bakery industry in general, and Bourseleth's sweatshop in particular. I grew to spurn the pies and cookies to which I had access, for the sight of molasses, brown sugar, raisins, currants and putrified store eggs rendered themselves obnoxious by their incessancy. Place a privileged youth in a candy shop and he will soon eat himself out of his desire for sweets. Such was my case. I was fed up on the delicious product of the baker's art and for me the romance of the bakeshop had withered and died.

However, I attribute much of my success as an artist later in life to the experience gained in the cellar of that bakery. There, during the small hours of the morning, by lamp-light, I used to execute marvelous designs in frosting, or model in dough such realistic images that people, after purchasing, would hate to destroy them. When customers wanted food they went elsewhere.

Among the mural decorations and frescos of the nineteenth century were many wonderful creations by eminent artists, but one I have in mind was painted by my own hand at the age of eleven, the first piece of mine to attract any attention at all.

The subject was a very popular skit of the day, Harrigan and Hart in "The Mulligan Guards." One reason why it did not elicit wide applause was the mediocrity of its surroundings. There were no tapestries or batiks, no marble statuary or bronzes, to suggest the presence of an aesthetic temperament; just a plain bakery of the primitive type, with a setting of flour barrels, pans and yeast tubs.

In the early 1870s, whenever Harrigan and Hart put across a new song hit, it would appear in a ten-cent "songster" with a lurid colored cover; every boy deemed it a privilege to possess one and learn the lines by heart. At the height of "The Mulligan Guards" popularity, the idea struck me that a fresco of those burlesque characters in their ill-fitting military uniforms should adorn a whitewashed wall of the bake-shop where I lived and labored, so I produced a rather startling enlargement of the song-ster's cover design in a medium of kerosene oil, illuminated with vermilion and lampblack.

This premier masterpiece was allowed to stay on exhibition until the background gave way to the elements and a fresh coat of whitewash became imperative.

I had made quite a number of drawings, which my father frowned upon as a waste of time. He had no liking for caricature; more than once he threatened to chastise me unless I cast aside the troublesome crayons. The original of the first cartoon I drew in this country—showing a youthful pickpocket closely followed by a cop—is still extant. (I have not yet determined whether to present it to the Smithsonian Institution or the Metropolitan Museum; hence it is still in my possession.)

On one occasion, I was whacked over the pants with a cane while decorating a neighbor's high board fence with caricatures—a decidedly unfavorable reaction which almost killed my desire to continue the pursuit of art. The neighbor who did the whacking was a rich old codger with a hawk-beak nose and a soul without sentiment. As a result of that castigation I refrained from public display of my talents until such time as I could find appreciation.

Chapter 3

[ON A BEAUTIFUL MIDSUMMER'S DAY at the age of twelve, I suddenly wearied of the bakery with its cloying aroma of cakes and pies. My father, being a night worker, could give me very little attention, so I was at liberty to shift for myself and since my home environment was not of a desirable sort, I did so.

Hearing that a farmer named Bill Marshall desired to engage a chore boy and give him a good home, I sought out the tiller of the soil while he was making purchases in the city. After a brief interview I climbed into his old wagon with a tiny

"The Mulligan Guards"
Drawn by Eugene Zimmerman about 1922

bundle of wearing apparel and bade good-bye to the city's heat and stifling odors.

His farm was located at Totowa, just outside of Paterson. In addition to the house and a small acreage, he had many chickens, ducks and geese; a pious wife; red side whiskers; and a carmine nose showing the effects of occasional "benders." During my first few weeks on the farm I was so green it's a wonder somebody's cattle didn't eat me up.

Nevertheless, into those surroundings I fitted well and was treated like a son. Whenever the neighbors referred to me it was as "that there Marshall boy." I was hired to do chores at the stipulated income of three meals a day and a place to sleep. No mention was made of coin or other consideration, and when I ran shy of ample garments with which to face the wintry blasts I had to look to my father for such comforts. Folks were not proud in those days, however, and the necessary apparel for covering a lad my age was by no means extravagant. Except in cold weather, a shirt and overalls constituted my entire wardrobe. Shoes were almost unknown.

Bill Marshall's fame was based partly upon reflected glory. His wife was a chronic complainer and flattered herself that she would have become First Lady of the Land had she acceded to proposals made by Ulysses Simpson Grant at Galena, Illinois, before the Civil War, but she jilted the future general and married my employer instead. Grant probably forgave her; Bill never did.

I learned that my duties as chore boy required me to arise before the rest of the household, build a kitchen fire, fry the potatoes, and make tea. Two or three lessons equipped me with sufficient culinary knowledge to be entrusted with the task of preparing the nutritional meal. There was never a change in the bill-of-fare because the solemn faces and sour stomachs that graced the festive board every morning did not demand it.

The ax was always nearby, and numerous barrels and boxes were available for fuel. Bill scorned this part of the day's activities as beneath his dignity; so, from dissecting lumber, I gradually developed a right arm that would have done credit to a blacksmith.

Although many lads of my age would have regarded such environment as depressing, it was an innovation for me to find anybody at all interested in my stay on earth. Instead of prowling around at

"Lucky"

RAGGEDY—"What's troublin' yer, Sloppy?"
SLOPPY—"Indigestion."
RAGGEDY—"Yer lucky dog!"

night, making mischief with the gangs of the neighborhood, I was given patchwork to sew for quilts and the preparing of material for rag carpets as my regular evening's entertainment.

This proved a novel experience for me. My winter days were spent at public school, where I received such meager education as the times and conditions afforded; the rest of my training I was obliged to acquire through practical experience and contact with the outside world.

In those days we had no radio, no picture shows, no parties to break the dreary monotony of the daily routine, day in and day out. I was never permitted to remain overnight at the home of an acquaintance nor allowed to invite any to share the night with me. During those long dull years, life's joys seemed only for others. It is a marvel to me how I ever developed a humorous instinct in such an atmosphere of mediocrity, heart-hunger and sadness. Mindful of the tender love bestowed upon my playmates by indulgent parents, I was often given to silent prayers in the seclusion of my lonely attic bedchamber, prayers as only a kid could invent, for the gloomy people with whom I dwelt evinced little interest in my spiritual welfare.

Agriculture was not at all exciting. It was a relief each week when Thursday and Friday rolled

"The Fish Monger"
Drawn by Eugene Zimmerman about 1922

around and we turned to itinerant ichthyology. Bill Marshall had a brother who was part owner of a large and prosperous fish market in Paterson, and he permitted Bill to dispose of the perishing refuse of his store, embracing fish, clams, mussels, vegetables and all the unsalable week-end remnants, to the foreign elements in the suburbs.

We also peddled fish throughout the poorer settlement of Paterson, known as Shantytown. There is a passage in the Bible which authorizes the selling of bad [non-kosher] meat to foreigners, and in that respect, my employer and his brother were quite orthodox.★ On Saturday nights we sold fruits and produce on the curbside market.

I used to hail those excursions with glee, because of the vacation from farm labor and because they put me in touch with more varied phases of life, a constant change of faces and characters which, years afterward, I transmuted into comic art and cash.

Bucephalus, the farmer's nag, was attached to the caravan and away we went. I tooted the horn that heralded our approach. This was our chief form of advertising, unless an appeal to the olfactory sense could be included in that category, for the kind of sea food we toted around would not have received Board of Health sanction, however

★"Ye shall not eat of any thing that dieth of itself: thou shalt give it unto the stranger that is in thy gates, that he may eat it; or thou mayest sell it unto an alien: for thou are a holy people unto the Lord thy God."
Deuteronomy, 14:21

valuable it might have been as fertilizer.

The only part of peddling I disliked was crying out the merchandise for sale, which the boss insisted I should do, since my voice was younger and less harsh and raucous than his.

Bill Marshall was a business genius who could distinguish bigger money in his neighbors' crops than in those sown by the sweat of his own brow. Thus, he lived almost exclusively on the profits of his fellow-men's products.

One day he said to me, "Gene, put them sideboards on the buckboard an' hitch up the old hoss an' we'll go over to neighbor Wilkenson's an' make him an offer for a load of watermelons."

Ten minutes later he yelled, "Wilkenson, I'll give you just a dollar for a load of your melons, an' I'll load 'em on myself."

There was not a vacant inch of space left in that load, and since the deal was made on a Friday, Bill and I took them to market Saturday, cleaning up fifteen dollars for a day's work. The exploiting of unsavory fish and home-grown melons requires real ingenuity.

Bill Marshall's steed, Bucephalus, had served numerous masters before taking up his abode at Totowa. In time, he became so decrepit and so utterly useless as a motive power for the huckster's wagon that it was decided to dispose of him forthwith. A plan was devised whereby the animated bag of bones might return to its maker by a slow, easy process. Winter was near; to save the "hoss" from eating his own head off before the spring plowing commenced, it was deemed more profitable to let the crows do it for him.

In those days there was no demand for superannuated horseflesh, as Paterson had neither a menagerie nor a combined chewing-gum and sausage foundry. Besides, there were many crows in New Jersey and, since the Legislature had made no provision for such, they had to depend upon the obsolete, cast-off creatures of the neighborhood, especially in the season when no corn or cherry crops could be raised.

Final judgment having been passed upon Bucephalus, I was selected to perform the last rites of escorting him to his doom in the wilderness some miles distant. As the solemn funeral cortege proceeded up the dusty road, the sight to a beholder might have been a sad one indeed, but the procession encountered no beholders. There was not even a traffic cop to bid the travelers "keep to the right and don't break the speed limit." No historic pageant was more impressive in its simplicity than the passing of this once noble beast to his ultimate resting-place.

The spot designated for this ignominious climax to a useful life was now reached. The crows had gathered and were giving vent to a joyful requiem in anticipation of the feast.

I, an unwilling but humane executioner, climbed down from my burlapped elevation, then removed the steed's bridle, the last vestige of his lowly but honorable calling, I patted his head an affectionate farewell and "left him alone with his glory."

Turning away tearful eyes, I ambled off, sad and sorrowful. To erase the memory of that scene as speedily as possible, I journeyed homeward by cross-lots, glancing back now and then from a distance for a final glimpse of the ghastly stack of bones.

I saw the vanishing skate still located there, nibbling the flora that grew at his feet as the shadows of eternal night darkened around him, and it made me think of the last meal vouchsafed to a condemned man just before his execution.

Thus I let Bucephalus settle the matter with the crows as best he could. Tired and footsore, filled with freckles and stone bruises and remorse, I retired that night to dream of the miserable task that had befallen my lot.

Early the next morning my boss awoke me with this greeting "Young man, I thought I told you to turn that nag out to die!"

"An Unreasonable Offer"

STRANGER—"Fifty dollars, eh, fur the nag? Does the lot go with it?"

RURALITE—"Sartinly not; what do ye want the lot fur?"

STRANGER—"Why, to bury the hoss."

He led me to the barn where Bucephalus was standing in his accustomed stall, grinning from ear to ear and full of the pep of former days!

There he was, sure enough, his "innards" well stocked with delicate shrubs and lovely wild flowers acting just like a kid back from a day's outing—a treat he had never before been permitted to enjoy!

The change had made a new horse of him, and from day to day the critter continued to improve in looks and actions, so that when he was bid off under the hammer, some months later, he brought the unbelievable sum of thirty-five dollars in cold cash.

Chapter 4

"Returning to the Bakery"
Drawn by Eugene Zimmerman about 1922

THERE WAS AN EMPTY BED ONE morning in the little room under the eaves where I slept for many months. I possessed a sensitive nature and was resentful to harsh treatment, and when Bill Marshall's wife boxed my ears one day for slamming the kitchen door and obliged me to close it quietly, it ruffled my feathers, and I registered a solemn vow to quit the farm where such liberties were taken with my frail body. As the night grew dark, and the moon played peek-a-boo behind the cloud, my little attic window gave forth a mild squeak of protest over the disturbance at such an unseemly hour. I had already packed my belongings; now was the time for action and a safe get-away, leaving no tender note of apology, nothing to indicate whence or why I had vanished. A friendly grape arbor nestled beneath my window, and I descended and let myself to the earth below. Fortunately nothing gave way to lead to my detection. Kissing my hand to the slumbering neighborhood I turned toward Paterson, and to the bake shops of my former days. There at 3 A.M. I found my brother at his task of kneeding dough for the morning's baking. My father greeted me in the usual way that parents do who feel no particular interest in their offsprings. "Well," said he, "back again? What's wrong now?" After spilling my woes into my father's ear, I was directed to a bed. In the days ahead, I made myself useful to the baker by greasing pans and again delivering bread to the outlying customers, and never returned to the farm; only once or twice did I see that martyr, Bill Marshall, for truly if ever a man deserved a gilded crown it was he. I used to wonder why some men are driven to drink, but that was no longer a puzzle to me after a few years contact with such a dreary household as that turned out to be.*

*The preceding appears, with only minor changes, in the autobiographical novel. However, in a later autobiography, Zimmerman refers only vaguely to his leaving the Marshall household and not at all

[Shortly after returning to the bake shop, Zimmerman left again.]

When my brother, Adolph, died some time ago, I fell heir to his personal effects, including the letters I had written him as far back as 1873, before I was completely Americanized. A typical letter follows:

My Dear Brother:

as i thought i would write and tell you that me and father are very well and i am getting now 175 cents and soon will get 2$ Dollars father has a stidy job and me to and i hope you the same. i have only one good suit and that i ware at every day but i have a fine job and i will stick to it i will get a new suit next week or the week after and i will try to come over to New York and you tell Paul that i have not got any good cloth to have my likeness taken and have no more from the other time

The Complements of your brother

Eugene Zimmerman

The "stidy job" I had then, and for more than a year, was office boy to a real estate broker. [Edward M. Weiss was a former clergyman and, according to Zimmerman, "a pompous, good natured man."] As an employer, he was perfect, always treating me with kindness. My duties were to sweep out the real estate office, wash up, and shine the boss's shoes. I was still boarding with the Bourseleths and sleeping in a little room above the bakery, for which I was obliged to pay my entire income, $1.75 a week.

For the upkeep of the property entrusted to him, my employer always carried a goodly supply of house paints, to which I had constant access. Since he often needed "To Let" and "For Sale" signs, he regarded me as a handy utensil to have around. Occasionally, I painted "Beware of the Dog!" signs for owners of poodles and dachshunds who lived in continual fear of burglars. While my remuneration seems slim as compared with salaries of today, I felt amply compensated by the opportunity those paints afforded me in art advancement, for they

opened an avenue which led ultimately to my cherished goal, the sign shop.

I was with Mr. Weiss about two years when the call of the wild again possessed me.

I still harbored a craving to be a sign-painter. Near my home had lived a little old lady who sold homemade crullers and apple turnovers. I kept her supplied with showcards, for which I was paid in trade. The market value of a showcard [a poster advertising a show or product] according to local standards, was one doughnut.

Fired by success with doughnuts, and a craving to be a sign painter, I decided to seek employment at one of Paterson's leading sign shops. I was only eleven, but at that age I knew considerably more than I know today.

Jimmy Dumphy followed my star.

"You ask 'em first for a job, Gene. Then if they say 'yes' I'll tackle 'em for a job too."

With this understanding, we proceeded to the place chosen for our artistic debut. Confronted by the propietor himself, William P. Brassington, Esq., I opened negotiations thus:

"Mister, do you want to hire a boy to learn the trade?"

The man sized me up, smiled, and lit his pipe. Presently he spoke: "Can you sandpaper a church steeple?"

Jimmy and I looked at each other dubiously, then raced toward the door, which we had left ajar for reasons of personal safety. In three jumps we reached the sidewalk, our sign-painting star suddenly dimmed. Being nearer the exit, Jimmy beat me by at least two inches.

On another occasion, I was passing a small sign emporium located in a dingy basement on a side street and desired to explore the mysteries within, so I entered and addressed the seedy-looking proprietor:

"How about a job?"

"Sure!"

He put me to work at once on a lot of unfinished board and tin signs laying about the place. At noon I was invited to "dine" at his abode, which was over a truckman's stable in the rear of a row of ramshackle warehouses. We sat down to fried tripe as the main course of the menu. I might have forgotten the fellow had it not been for that sumptuous repast in which tripe cut such a figure.

---

to his meeting with his father. Perhaps in the years between writing the novelization and the autobiography, he may have decided that either he was too harsh on Mrs. Marshall and his father, or that by eliminating discussion of a part of his life, he could try to eliminate the unpleasantness.

At the close of the day, having discovered that I had no capital to invest, the boss adopted me as a silent partner and I fell for it because I needed sustenance. We waived all formality of contracts and written agreements.

Thus things ran smoothly for two weeks. Then I deemed it about time for a meeting of the stockholders to discuss and declare dividends. I was informed that the signs I had completed were already traded out, but as soon as all the old debts against the shop could be wiped off we would make a fresh start upon the basis of equal division.

Thereupon I dissolved the partnership with as little ceremony as it had been formed, and I put down those two weeks of unremunerative toil to practical experience. That was more than fifty years ago [about 1873 or 1874]; never since have I allowed an ounce of tripe to pass my lips.

I quickly returned to my former position as an office boy where I made many more "For Sale" and "To Let" signs.

One week's experience tending mules in a cotton mill was sufficient to satisfy me that the Lord never intended me to be a hostler. I had heard that boys my age were earning as high as six dollars a week in that occupation, which inflated them with profound feelings of independence. This aroused in me a spirit of mild jealousy and spurred me to the desire for a similar job in one of those plants.

I had tended horses on the farm but as for mules I admit I was a bit green. However, I was weary of the bakery and desired another change, so I ventured into a mill office and made my wishes known.

"I'll give you $3.50 a week to take care of mules," said a burly foreman, and I accepted. He thrust a bunch of wiping waste into my palm, directing me to lie on my back beneath the machines and wipe up the grease that had slobbered over them. I demurred, on the ground that I had been hired to look after the mules. The foreman grinned, eyed me from head to foot, then exploded:

"I'm a simple son of a sea cook. Is it possible there's such damn fools in the world as can't tell a mule when he sees one? *Them's* mules, yuh idiot!" He added, pointing to the greasy machines filled with whirring bobbins which moved back and forth on light trackage, "Git busy er out yuh go!"

"Illustrated Ad"
"Wanted—A man of experience with horses."

I remained there exactly one week, and collected $3.50. Once more I chose the dusty flour and sour-smelling yeast tubs of the bake-shop. However, the breadstuffs industry held no glamour, so I soon drifted away again. This time I went to Haledon, another suburb of Paterson, where I hired out to George Spangenmacher, a wine-and-beer merchant. His place of business was a very orderly saloon and billiard room in the old arcade building on Ellison Street. Attached to his home was considerable farm land, with a limited number of pigs, horses, cattle, chickens, ducks, geese, and bees. The place was enveloped in an atmosphere of rural luxury. Because of my experience as chore boy I fell into it quite naturally.

I had the care of a team of Arabian mustangs and frequently drove the boss back and forth to business; when not at the city establishment assisting in bottling wine, I helped at the chores of the farm. This home was very agreeable, however, and the work not irksome. I painted the farm buildings and whitewashed fences, and helped in the fall pig killing and sausage making. It was an ideal home farm, with always plenty to eat. A fresh cornhusk mattress, amply filled, formed the basis of many happy dreams.

When farm work was slack, I was obliged to help in the wine establishment—washing bottles and steins, bottling wine and delivering them to the houses of customers. Among the important lessons I learned was business deception. When a keg was not emptied before closing hour, it was condemned as too stale to serve over our bar, so by adding a pinch of powdered sugar to each bottle, wiring the corks securely and placing fancy labels on them, we served the best home trade at fifteen dollars a dozen, a fancy price in those days. Although constantly in the midst of wines, beers, and other liquors, I had no desire to avail myself of them. In fact, I experienced a keen dislike for such beverages. Those were days when bar-rooms were palaces, and one was not regarded as a vile sinner for entering them. Often I toiled 'till closing time, midnight, then drove home with Mr. Spangenmacher and returned again at six o'clock the next morning.

[An undated letter he wrote his brother, Adolph, in 1876, explains his life.

Dear Brother:

You must excuse me for Disappointing you in writing as I had no time. I am working out in the farm now and we have to work from 5 o'clk in the morning until 10 and 11 o'clk at night and then i feel so tied out that I can not write. I have Received 1 letter before this one father told me to write but i had no time we have summer Boarder's from New York about 25 or more.

Your's truly,

Eug. Zimmerman]

[Other letters he wrote to Adolph indicated that his father was having "hard sledding" on about twelve dollars a week, occasionally being out of a job.]

My correspondence to my family faithfully chronicled the news of each much-needed article of clothing which my father purchased for himself or his two sons. My brother must have given more trouble than I did, for dad frequently was obliged to send money to Adolph, where I contributed a little now and then toward his support.

My life on the farm was as close to nature as the climate would permit; I slept in the barn with the farm-hand and the horses during warm weather and on a corn-husk mattress in the winter. I dined at the second table upon food that was often cold and lacking in quality. Nevertheless, the hired man was a dear old fellow of about seventy summers who looked after my interests. Then milking time came around, and I could depend upon a liberal draught of the warm lactic fluid, besides having access to the honeycombs stored in the cellar and the fruits of the orchard. I dwelt, therefore, in "a land flowing with milk and honey," as the Bible says, just as my previous existence had been Biblical in another sense; I distributed loaves and fishes like the fellow in the parable.

One of my joys was the collecting of eggs from the various nests. It was an everyday function that had to be attended to regularly in order to keep the hens on their behavior and discourage them from setting. Hens are notional in that respect. If eggs are allowed to accumulate in the nest, the producer of those eggs is apt to decide to start her annual housekeeping and go brooding, so I was very methodical in gathering the hen fruit. Oftentimes, a hen might have arisen late and been delayed in her domestic affairs. During those anxious moments of expectancy, I refrained from disturbing the patient, but listened with keen interest outside the maternity chamber for the thump of the egg and the hen's cackled announcement of the new arrival.

Being a future cartoonist (although I didn't know it then), I was always bubbling over with exaggerated ideas which appeared to other minds as positively absurd; nevertheless, some of them have since matured and are now being employed with profitable results. For example, fifteen or twenty years ago, I wrote a rather ridiculous treatise on the hen and her output, for *Cartoons Magazine* of Chicago, in which I advocated the use of mirrors and electric lights in hen coops to speed up the laying and thus get more work out of the hens by supplying artificial daylight.

Rural newspapers copied that article and, to my surprise, farmers took the idea seriously; a multitude of hen-coops that formerly were shrouded in darkness at night are now illuminated, which is said to have increased the output of eggs in those coops.

The mirrors have not yet been installed. Where hens are numerous, the looking-glasses, said the farmers, would give a crowded appearance, embarrassing the hens who prefer privacy in their delicate occupation. However, where only a few hens are housed under the same roof, they may be relieved of loneliness by introduction of mirrors set against

"The Chicken Entrepreneur"
Drawn by Eugene Zimmerman about 1922

the wall. What the radio will do for the future of hendom, I leave to a better brain than mine to forecast.

I am glad I lived in that more or less primitive period before the charms of farming were dulled by modern science, for I believed those were the happiest of all my days. The farmer lives no longer next to nature. The canning factory supplies his needs in fruits and vegetables, and many who still churn the sweet clover butter fetch it to market and return with oleo and cow feed. When we think of the farm in these modern times and the high cost of things, it produces a deathlike shudder. Those children whose misfortune it is to be born in such healthy environments are educated at the city high school and prepared for college after which they marry and settle in a big city where pleasure and comfort are obtainable.

Chapter 5

ALL IN ALL, I HAD FARED PRETTY well in the wine merchant's employ, but Destiny was grooming me for a less bucolic job. One after-

noon while I was washing bottles, the startling cry of *"fire!"* rang out. Smoke was pouring from the cellarway. We saw at once that the place was doomed, for we had no means of subduing the flame until the volunteer fire department could arrive. It gave me quite a thrill, for there was only one exit and the blaze originated beneath that lone exit; I escaped by dashing madly upstairs through the smoke and flames. The fire lasted a night and a day, consuming, in addition to the wine establishment and billard parlor, a large grocery, a furniture store and a factory.

The fire damage was eventually repaired, and I began to reletter my employer's name and business on the new windows of the wineshop. A passing sign painter, William P. Brassington, noticed me putting on gold leaf in a murderous fashion, and stopped in to talk. He desired to know if I had ever thought of entering a sign-shop to learn the trade, and offered me an apprenticeship. Not being bound to the wine merchant by unbreakable ties of affection, I accepted Brassington's offer and eagerly launched into a connection destined to last for three years. [This is the same Brassington who had several years earlier inquired about Zimmerman's ability to sand church steeples.]

Whether Spangenmacher had regarded my departure as a loss or gain to the place I have never fully determined, but I do know that I retired from the liquor traffic with colors flying, long before Carrie Nation started on her famous hatchet crusade, and nearly half a century ahead of the Volstead Act!

During the next three or four years, I shared in all of Brassington's changing fortunes—I say *changing,* for at that time sign-painting was an uncertain industry with only a meager livelihood as compensation. However, I absorbed a great deal of technical knowledge, thus preparing for a more lucrative career.

Brassington reminded me of a circus manager; he was forever trailing the band wagon, would pull up stakes and go wherever excitement and business let him. Once, his attention was drawn to Deckertown, New Jersey, where General Kilpatrick had invited the Grand Army of the Republic and the state militia to feast and frolic upon his vast acreage. My boss happened to be a Civil War veteran, so he and I tagged along like sutlers after an army. With an ample supply of cheap muslin, paints, and brushes, we settled right beneath the muzzle of the sunrise gun. There, we set up our sign shop and for seven days we arose at reveille and plunged into sign work. Since we were the only representatives of our profession on the job, we became sign monarchs of that remote locality. Our tents and display banners, signs and flags, gave the place a side-show atmosphere, and the charges we levied for the very commonest black lettering on five-cent bleached muslin was truly scandalous. We were many miles from the nearest base of supplies and the concessions must have

"Civil War Veteran"

signs regardless of price—and must have them at once.

In September, 1878, Brassington journeyed to the County Fair grounds at Elmira, New York, while I remained behind to run the New Jersey shop. [Zimmerman was sixteen at the time.] Elmira, with about 20,000 population, looked quite healthy for a sign-painter to settle in, so upon his return to Paterson he decided to move there. The truth is that Brassington found it more convenient to migrate than to liquidate his heavy indebtedness.

At any rate, between dusk and dawn we left New Jersey miles and creditors behind us.

We arrived at Elmira with one big packing-box containing all our assets. Our combined wardrobes we wore on our respective backs. The box, when emptied, served as a dining-table, and for six months our frugal meals were spread upon it. To the packing-box were added a few second-hand chairs and a coal stove of like quality. Our quarters contained a parlor, but the only object of interest in it was a half-bushel of onions, taken in exchange for sign work.

Brassington was tremendously resourceful and soon had his family housed, provisioned, and in shape to extend its humble hospitality.

For want of bedsteads, we slept on the floor and the whole surroundings resembled a picture of rugged pioneer days. That half-bushel of onions formed the basis of the family larder. Salt pork and dried beans were brought in and became standard commodities. Due to his wonderful ability for holding off merchants, the boss' bills were collectable only in sign jobs, which kept me constantly busy satisfying accounts in that manner.

Thus, I became further inured to hardships, sharpening my wits and strengthening resistive powers which were to stand me in good stead later in life. During my apprenticeship to Brassington I scarcely knew the feel of a dollar. [Zimmerman's pay was three meals a day, a room, and used clothes. Although he doesn't indicate it, he probably received gifts—perhaps even some money—from time to time.]

By the end of the first year at Elmira, we were in pretty fair condition and the shop itself, located at the corner of East Water and Railroad Avenue, even bore an aspect of prosperity. As time went on, my boss advanced so far in public favor that he moved his family to a more desirable section of the city and lived quite comfortably. At first, none of the customers knew my name, for I attached Brassington's imprint to my work, but gradually I achieved recognition as one of the city's up-and-coming sign artists.

In those days, I frequently saw Mark Twain on the streets of Elmira. His bushy hair was still dark, with a sprinkling of gray. He lived at Quarry Farm, on the outskirts of Elmira, and eventually was laid to rest in a humble grave in that city.*

Another celebrity I knew in the late seventies was David B. Hill, for whom I painted a sign, "D. B. Hill Law Office," little dreaming that I was working for a future governor, senator, and presidential aspirant.

During the Garfield-Hancock campaign [1880], my boss obtained an order from the Elmira Republican headquarters for a net banner to be swung across the main thoroughfare. He had salvaged from a previous campaign a large painted figure of the Goddess of Liberty. Her head was somewhat mutilated, but we managed between us to fit another female head to it, with miserably mismatched colors.

The original painting was the product of an experienced artist of campaign heads, so you can imagine the finish our dastardly work put to the fair lady's body. However, the boss was so proud of it that he painted his imprint almost as large as the names of the candidates. This was a cue to the Democratic press for vitriolic attacks.

"Is the sign-painter running for the Presidency, or is Mr. Garfield?" they wanted to know. "And what washerwoman posed for the head of the Goddess of Liberty?"

For a while that banner was the most talked-of piece of art in the county. No circus parade, I dare say, ever drew more attention than that thing did. But my boss had wrestled with hard luck too often to feel the sting of such base, though just, criticism, so he merely added an extra twist to his military mustache, expanded his chest a few inches and said, "Let 'em think what they think. It's the only political job in this town that's caused any commotion!"

I was really the humiliated one, for I had a better appreciation of figure drawing than my boss, who had absolutely no talent along that line. Remorse seized me every time my eyes fell upon our great opus, and no one felt more relieved than I when that campaign ended.

I often envied Brassington's brass, and thought that if I had only half as much nerve I might some day amount to something. I remember the time he persuaded a poor bone-headed Dutch proprietor of a delicatessen emporium to consent to having his portrait painted on the front of his brick block. With a boastful air, my boss remarked, "Why, sure, Mr. Schnickerlfritz, I'll put your photograph over that front door in eighteen colors and so lifelike that your friends will tip their hats to it when they pass your store." I was detailed to commit the crime. You may believe me when I say that that portrait looked as much like the original as George Washington looked like Horace Greeley. [Greeley (1811–1872) was one of the greatest editor-publishers in journalism history.] The photo given me to copy was of a period some twenty-odd years past and all I had to do was bring it up to date.

My great surprise came when the man paid the bill without a word of objection. He even patted me on the back and complimented me on my success, saying he hadn't had a picture taken in twenty years that made him such a fine looker.

Whenever my boss suggested a pictorial sign to a prospective customer, it gave me the creeps, so that my teeth chattered 'til the job was over and I had slunk out of sight of the prying gaze of passers-by.

When a cub branched out for himself he immediately started landscape gardening on his upper lip. This gave him a dignified appearance. The importance of wearing a mustache had struck me quite forcibly one day.

Brassington had sent me to do a gold-leaf job on the window of a small bank in the suburbs. When I spread my stepladder and was about to mount to its apex, a haughty clerk with a fringe of virgin down upon his lip "sacheyed" from his cage and inquired what I was doing.

"I'm going to put gold-leaf letters on the transom," I explained, mentally bewailing the

*Twain and his family are buried in Woodlawn Cemetery, Elmira. In his original manuscript, Zimmerman referred to "a million-dollar hotel bearing [Twain's] name." This was probably built in the 1920s, at the corner of Gray and N. Main, and is now known as the Mark Twain Apartments, housing the elderly.

beardless face which gave me a callow appearance.

"Well, you'd better clear out with your pots and kettles," the clerk said lofily. "We hired a man to do that job."

"Yes, I know," was my reply. "I'm six miles from the shop where I got my orders, so the best thing I can do under the circumstances is go ahead with the job. If you don't like the effect, I'll gladly erase it."

I wasn't requested to erase it.

Twenty years later, when I became a depositor in that institution, fragments of my lettering were still visible.

The job was let originally for twenty dollars to a common house-painter who in turn had sub-let it to my employer on a fifty-fifty basis, while I, the dub, was detailed to do the actual labor.

Fifty-odd years ago, a sign-painter was recognized chiefly by the brush marks on his clothes. When an apprentice started out on his wild and colorful career, he began to decorate his outer garments with the spatter work of his calling. I spent the better part of two years trying to make myself look like a regular painter by daubing my working clothes—pants, coat, cap, shirt, shoes, and socks, and a conspicuous Windsor neck-tie—all of which claimed part of the splashes from my clever brush.

There were times when a smock would have been handy, but it wasn't fashionable for sign-painters to wear such effeminate folderols. Besides, a boy's bespattered suit was his individual press agent and made him a distinctive figure against the ordinary run of humanity.

I don't remember whether I had more than one working suit during my term of apprenticeship, but judging from the decorated condition of the one in which I graduated, I must have had only one in all my three or four years of shop life. The pants could speak for themselves, for they contained enough paint to make them self-supporting. No pants rack was needed when I retired at night; I simply stood them up in the corner of the room like two lengths of stove-pipe, where they did sentinel duty over the less fortunate shirt and socks. (When I later left that shop to take up a new lease on life, it was with a tear-stained face that I bade the old suit farewell and left behind a friend which had stuck to me through many vicissitudes.)

Electioneering in that period was done with torches, hickory clubs, cabbages and stale eggs, so that after each gorgeous political pageant our shop was filled with solemn bearers of optic discolorations. In those days it was as fashionable for men to camouflage black eyes as it is today for womenfolk to rouge pale lips and cheeks and to dab red noses with rice powder.

Disguising blackened eyes to give them a natural appearance was a thriving feature of the sign man's profession during the late 1870s. It linked with sign work as smoothly as mayonnaise fits into potato salad. Frequently, I was called upon to match up flesh tints and rescue my patrons from the humiliation which accompanies such a situation. For this form of art we charged a fee of fifty cents, regardless of the extent of the bruise or the depth of flesh tone to be covered. At times it called for two or three priming coats as a substantial foundation for the artistic touches that followed.

I have seen fellows carry around their eye sockets as much as a quarter of a pound of white-lead glazed over with baby pink that attracted far more notice than the original black eye itself, but that mattered not.

I remember one fellow who came in with the prettiest pair of lamps I ever had the pleasure of treating. He didn't mind paying fifty cents for one blinker, but he said seventy-five cents was a reasonable price for the pair, inasmuch as the material had to be mixed for one eye, and it would serve for two without adding greatly to our overhead expense. His argument sounded plausible and we agreed to his terms after he had promised to turn all his trade in to our shop; his wife, he assured us, was occasionally afflicted in a similar manner.

I am reminded of a local merchant named Bob Sims. Bob had made quite a bit of money at "hoss swapping," had just married a grass widow [A "grass widow" can be a discarded mistress; a lady with a child born out of wedlock; a divorced or separated woman; or a woman whose husband is temporarily away.] with a candy store, and was ordering a sign to be placed above its door, informing the populace of the new co-partnership. He was a man of keen business instincts and a far-away look into the future. I discovered this when I asked how he'd prefer the sign to read—"Mary Sims" or "Mrs. Robert Sims." The bridegroom replied with a nasal twang, "Well, make it read 'Mrs. Robert Sims,' an' ef Mary dies, I'll jest rub out the 'Mrs.'

and go on with the business so nuthin' had happened."

I believe the most annoying place to paint a sign is on the outside of a window right off the sidewalk where you can overhear the conversation of spectators. It is hard to shut your ears to the close-up comments while you are trying to keep your mind on your work, yet it is absolutely impossible to concentrate on lettering and listen, too.

If your audience happens to be a group of school children, the jabber will run something like this: "Oh, I know what the next letter is gonna be!" "Aw, who don't?—dat's easy, it's gonna be an *H!*" "Naw, 'tain't neither; it's gonna be an *N*," and so on.

Then you find yourself making an *H* that should have been an *N*. "There now! I told you it was gonna be an *H!*" I have often left such a job at that stage and sauntered leisurely around the block to give my audience a chance to fade away while I pulled my scattered wits into place.

Sometimes the comments of the curious bystanders will fill you with uncertainty, and you sneak back to the shop to consult the ancient paint-besmeared dictionary. I have witnessed the short-changing of victims by first getting them "Discomfuddled." Well, a rattled sign painter is in about the same fix.

One, at the dizzy height of thirty feet above the bed of a surging spring freshet, my boss swung a scaffold for me to cleave to, while I lettered the side of a brick wall with the words, "Kennedy, Live and Let Live Grocery."

I was never intended to be a circus performer, but this scaffold called for unusual skill and adhesive qualities. Its component parts embraced one twelve-foot ladder, one ten-foot plank and four bricks borrowed from a neighboring chimney. The plank was laid on the roof, the bricks placed at the end to counterbalance my weight, and the ladder was hung on the projecting plank. At the bottom of the ladder was a small platform so arranged as to keep the foot of the ladder from the building.

The wind arose before my task was completed. It fanned me and the ladder in an alarming fashion, while I held on like an aeronaut to an unruly balloon.

A crowd which had gathered below cheered me and yelled, "Hang on!"—quite unnecessary advice, for I did not intend to let go as long as life lasted.

When that job was finished, I registered a solemn oath against my boss' scaffold construction. The poor man is dead now, and with his passing my ire subsided. He was in every other way a good fellow, but I hope he'll never erect scaffolds for those with whom he is associated.

Incidentally, several years later, Mr. Brassington lost his mind through business reverses, and died in Buffalo. (He was not content to remain in one place long; consequently he was often poverty-stricken.)

After reaching my eighteenth year [1880], I was recognized as a full-fledged sign-painter and was offered the handsome salary of nine dollars a week to head the pictorial staff of a rival concern, the Empire Sign Company, J. C. Pope, proprietor—an offer I quickly accepted.

I was suddenly raised to absolute affluence from my former humble and impecunious state. I could now reside at a real boarding house, the Platt House, where at table I met jovial spirits who laughed and joked at adversity.★ The whole world seemed changed. A silver lining at last was skirting the dark cloud of other days.

On its letterheads, the Empire Sign Company bombastically announced itself as "The Only Establishment in the World where Pine Lumber is Bought in the Shape of Logs and Manufactured on the Premises into Board Signs." The concern had its own saw-mill, planing mill and sign shop, situated in the historic village of Horseheads, an Elmira suburb to which it moved shortly after I was hired.

Mr. Pope had a remarkably versatile disposition. He would fly to pieces and just as quickly scrape himself together in a docile mood. My work was largely designing and cutting stencils upon oiled manila paper. One day, the boss observed that I had omitted a letter from a word. Instantly he exploded with rage.

"What's the meaning of this carelessness! Don't you know, sir, that you are deliberately putting your hand into my pocket and taking out the

★The Platt House was one of the most famous hotels in the Elmira-Horseheads area; it was also the site of numerous political and cultural events. After it was torn down, a Marine Midland Bank branch was built on its site.

money I need to buy my family's bread!" Then, wheeling about, he left the scene and I felt as good as fired. With heavy heart I made the necessary repairs to the stencil which had caused such havoc.

Ten minutes went by and he returned, whistling a merry tune. He slapped me on the back and shouted genially, "Well, old scout, how do you feel?"

I never knew another man with such a kinky temperament, yet Pope's outbursts were less harmful than flea bites. Eventually he failed in business [late 1882 or early 1883] and my last sign-painting days were spent in the employ of Joe Densmore, of Elmira.

My labor was more interesting than irksome. I invented designs and cut the stencils, which were then turned over to stencilers to be transferred to signboards. All this time, however, I was aware of a growing ambition that made me discontented with my job. I wanted to be a comic artist . . . and the best place for a comic artist was on *Puck*.

Chapter 6

IN 1938 FRANK LUTHER MOTT, THE leading American journalism historian of the time, looked back on *Puck* and noted that the magazine during the 1880s and 1890s was "an institution *sui generis*. American journalism never had anything else quite like it, and this in spite of imitations. Its boldness, its incisive cleverness, its robust comedy, its real literary and artistic values made it a factor in politics and in social life" (*A History of American Magazines,* vol. 4, p. 532).

[There had been several earlier attempts at humor/satire magazines in America, most of them based upon *Punch* of London; all had failed. among the non-*Punch*-like attempts were two German-language weeklies founded in Saint Louis in 1870 and 1871 by Joseph Keppler; the second was named *Puck*. Both magazines failed in less than a year. In the mid-1870s, Keppler went to New York, teamed with Adolph Schwartzmann, a printer and businessman, and revived *Puck*, again as a German-language weekly. It quickly caught the attention of playwright Sydney Rosenfeld, who convinced Keppler and Schwartzmann to publish an English language edition.

[The first edition was dated March 14, 1877, with Rosenfeld as its editor. During the next year and a half, Rosenfeld, as editor, brought to the magazine sharp, biting satire that complemented Keppler's incisive lithographs. In 1878, Henry Cuyler Bunner became editor and thoroughly expanded the sixteen-page weekly's coverage of social politics. Bunner served as editor for the next eighteen years. Shortly after Bunner's death, Brander Mathews, writing in *Scribner's,* one of the most important magazines in America, noted that Bunner:

poured [into *Puck*] an endless stream of humorous matter in prose and verse. Whatever might be wanted he stood ready to supply—rhymes of the times, humorous ballads, *vers de societe,* verses to go with a cartoon, dialogues to go under a drawing, paragraphs pertinent and impertinent, satiric sketches of character, short stories, little comedies, nondescript comicalities of all kinds. . . . The average was surprisingly high, and the variety extraordinary [*Scribner's,* September 1896, pp. 287, 289].

[By 1883, *Puck's* circulation had topped eighty thousand, making it one of the strongest political forces in the country, a force that got its energy from vehement opposition to the monopolies and political corruption, probing and cutting hard at all forms of scandal. But in its March 8, 1882, issue *Puck,* the magazine's caricatured mascot, lamented:

He has seen about him death and defeat, injustice and incompetence, all forms of wrong and tyranny; he has seen the wrong triumph over the good; he has seen hope grow weary and courage fail. The merry laugh which he brought to earth with him has been checked now and again while tears of sorrow or sympathy ran down his rosy cheeks [*Puck;* March 8, 1882.]

[The driving force was Keppler, who quickly achieved a national reputation as one of the best of the cartoonists; and it was the political cartoon upon which *Puck's* fame would rest. In 1879, Keppler hired James A. Wales; two years later, Frederick Opper; a year after that F. Graetz and Bernhard Gillam. Then, in 1883, he hired a twenty-one-year old former sign painter, Eugene Zimmerman.

Wales, Opper, Graetz, Gillam, and Zimmerman would all earn national reputations surpassed only by that of Keppler himself. They were not the only artists hired by *Puck* to become nationally known.]

I had been fascinated by comic art as far back as I could remember, and the coming of comic weeklies increased that fascination. My strongest desire now was to get on the staff of an illustrated periodical. [On December 4, 1881, ZIM wrote his brother: ". . . I am quite well thank you but feel homesick as the devil, for the past 2 or 3 weeks. If I could get a job in the "Puck" establishment I would come down there to work. There isn't life enough in this place, & I want a change."]

In the early days of my sign-painting apprenticeship, I received merely board and clothing; consequently, I had no funds with which to buy the illustrated weeklies—*Puck* and *Harper's Weekly* were my favorites—and I could look at them only through the windows of the book stores.

Thomas Nast had just passed the peak of his fame, while Joseph Keppler's work in *Puck* was beginning to attract much attention. About the same time, an artist with rather crude technique, Thomas Worth, was producing a series of lithographed comics depicting the activities of the Darktown Fire Brigade. Worth's originality, although absurd in many respects, accentuated a desire to develop my own latent talent along that line.

There were no mail courses available in comic art, and newspaper artists were rare. The dailies had not yet gone into the cartoon game to any great extent. Syndicates were not even dreamed of. Under such conditions, progress was necessarily slow.

Brassington had encouraged my budding ability by advertising "Pictorial Signs" on a placard hung outside his shop. Having no talent himself beyond lettering, he was uncritical of my faulty drawing. As I look back now I pity those customers who were obliged to accept my productions as works of art.

Pope had given me further encouragement, and my last sign-painting employer, Joe Densmore, added the crowing touch. I made a collection of the comic art of the period, which I would study and copy laboriously on evenings and Sundays. When I had filled a sketch book with a variety of drawings of my own in wetcolor and other media, I was quite elated.

One day, I visited New York City to spend a holiday and took along the sketch book, which relatives persuaded me to leave with them for a few days. Later, I learned that it had been mysteriously brought to the attention of Joseph Keppler, the famous cartoonist and co-proprietor of *Puck*.

The man who really obtained my first audience with Keppler was a Mr. Schreiner [or Schreimer] in whose diamond-setting shop a cousin of mine [Andrew Hoch] was employed. Schreiner had asked to see a book of my drawings which I was carrying under my arm when I called on this cousin at the shop and, after examining them, said he desired to show them to Keppler, a close friend of his. I loaned the book to Schreiner for that purpose. A few days later I received a letter inviting me to call at the *Puck* office.

Evidently Mr. Keppler scented talent in my amateurish watercolors, for he wrote requesting that I call upon him at the *Puck* office, 21 Warren St., New York City. Having a rather bashful nature, I was tempted to pass up the opportunity as too severe a shock to my nervous system; and it could be a wild-goose chase. But, to meet a man of the superior attainments of Joseph Keppler was something I had prayed for, but now feared to undertake. Besides, my finances were at a peculiarly low ebb, and the cost of train fare made the journey from Elmira look as prohibitive as a trip to the moon. I discussed the situation with Mr. Densmore. When I showed him that letter of glowing possibilities, this fatherly person remarked, "My boy, don't worry, I'll get you the money to pay your railroad fare. I don't like to see you go, but there is something better in store for you than you can ever hope to find in this sign business, so go to it and God bless you." The poor man was always hard up, but his friends were legion and a request for assistance always met with ready and immediate response, so he left me with my brain in a whirl. Soon he returned with a $10 bill in his outstretched palm and a broad grin on his countenance. "Here it is," said he, "enough to see you to the Metropolis at least." It was all he could raise, yet it was enough. I thanked him and soon afterward set out for the great metropolis.

On May 28, 1883, at the age of 21, with precisely fifteen cents in my clothes, I draped my lanky form over the rear end of a horse-car enroute to meet Joseph Keppler, debating fearfully with myself—should I assume a jaunty air, or should I

"Awaiting an Appointment"
Drawn by Eugene Zimmerman about 1922

approach the distinguished cartoonist in a spirit of humility?

Down the Bowery jogged the horse-car, with me weakening rapidly as fate drew nearer. I walked across City Hall Park from "Newspaper Row," my legs fairly wobbling, meanwhile wishing every second that a calamity would occur to supply a plausible excuse for breaking the appointment. But nothing happened, and I was forced to proceed to 21 Warren St., a dingy building a half-block off Broadway.

Outside, the structure was gloomy and depressing; within, I found a cheerful bustle of clerks at desks. Somewhat relieved, I breathed my name and business into a receptive ear. The message was wafted through a speaking tube to the great Keppler, three floors above, whereupon that high and mighty personage came down and met me.

Heaven's gates opened to me when I discovered that Mr. Keppler was merely a human being, kind and considerate, albeit a bit pompous. He was a typical artist of the old school—a commanding

figure with iron-grey hair, mustache and a goatee of the Louis Napoleon type. His partner, Adolph Schwarzmann, was short, jolly, full faced, with similar hirsute adornments. After some discussion, a contract was drawn up in pen-and-ink and we all signed it; I was hired for a period of three years at five dollars a week the first year, ten dollars the second, and fifteen the third. [Zimmerman had been earning nine or ten dollars a week with Brassington; within months of joining *Puck,* however, he would be earning ten to fifteen dollars a week.]

Before I was presented to Keppler, my imagination pictured his studio as a gorgeous show place like an Arabian Nights dream. I expected to find the master cartoonist surrounded by medieval armor and tapestries, Chinese jade and incense burners. It never occurred to me that such a museum would be unsatisfactory as a workshop. Keppler occupied a small clean enclosure in the *Puck* art department; a similar adjoining one was used by his lieutenant, Bernhard Gillam. The studios of those titans were about as imposing as the stalls of fine racehorses, yet in such unpretentious compartments were created the wonderful cartoons that made political history during the big presidential campaigns of the 'seventies and 'eighties.

Emerging from the *Puck* office, my eye caught a sign on Greenwich Street:

Pork and Beans and a Big Schooner for/5¢

which prompted some mental arithmetic, the result being I selected that place as my future Delmonico's. For seventeen weeks, I subjected myself to monotonous fare of beer and beans, until the very thought became anathema—like the tripe of sign-painting days. It was a godsend when my income was increased and I was able to sit down to luxuries like Hungarian goulash and Horton's ice cream.

Fifteen cents a meal was my usual limit. To save a nickel in pleasant weather, I used to hike to the office from my hall bedroom on East Eighty-second Street—a distance of about five miles. At that time, the Yorkville section of Manhattan was out in the wilderness, with more vacant lots than there were houses, and whenever I started on a pilgrimage to City Hall Park I felt like a country yokel bidding good-bye to the farm. Many a man would like to live his youth over again; so would I, if I could forget that Greenwich Street beanery and those long, long walks.

"Scanning the Menu"
Drawn by Eugene Zimmerman about 1922

I recall when daily newspapers could not afford to publish illustration, except for a few small advertisement cuts or, very rarely, a single-column map or a political cartoon reproduced from one of the weeklies. However, from 1873 to 1877 New York did have an illustrated *Daily Graphic,* which was of standard newspaper size and consisted almost entirely of pictures, and very little advertising.

At this stage in the history of illustrated papers, the system of engraving was undergoing a radical change from the tediously slow woodcut method to the rapid zinc plate process by which acids performed the work formerly done by the engraver. Many of its political artists, whose names have since become famous for their work on contemporary publications, are Miranda, Auscacks, W. A. Rogers, James A. Wales, Grant E. Hamilton, and Louis Dalrymple. To these political artists was given over the entire front page of the old *Graphic.*

Prior to that, only such weeklies as *Harper's, Frank Leslie's, The Police Gazette, Saturday Night* and *The New York Family Story Paper* were able to illustrate their pages with wood engravings. The well-pawed *Police Gazette* displayed sketches of females in short skirts, exposing much less of their anatomy than we see in today's society rotogravure section, and yet it was continually hounded by Anthony Comstock's Society for the Suppression of Vice.

Keppler, Gillam, and Nast head the list of nineteenth century cartoonists in America. All three were foreign-born—Keppler from Vienna; Gillam from the nursery-rhyme town of Banbury, England; and Nast from Bavaria.

Nast was America's first outstanding cartoonist. For about ten years he monopolized the center and both sides of the stage with little opposition. His part in overthrowing the Tweed Ring [Tammany Hall] has become a saga, and his Republican elephant, Democratic donkey, and Tammany tiger will outlast the parties they symbolize.★

Nast drew most of his famous cartoons on wood blocks, working rapidly. A slab of boxwood large enough to accomodate a double page was made of a group of smaller blocks bolted together and smoothly surfaced and coated with a white preparation to the finish of modern bristol-board. After the cartoons were drawn, they were engraved by skillful artisans. The whole process was considered a week's labor—nowadays it takes but a few hours.

At the time of my debut on *Puck,* Nast was still performing creditably for *Harper's Weekly,* but was getting ready to retire, while Keppler and Gillam were gaining popularity week by week. Unlike Nast, Keppler was painstakingly slow. There are no extant originals of his masterpieces, for the reason that Keppler drew directly on the lithographic stones from which they were printed, and since the stones were always ground off for succeeding issues of the magazine, the original drawings were necessarily effaced. The lettering

★William (Boss) Tweed of New York City complained that it wasn't so much the articles and editorials opposing him—"The people can't read"—but Nast's cartoons that finally destroyed the Tweed Ring.

"Posing for Keppler"
Drawn by Eugene Zimmerman about 1922

was done in reverse, which led to some amusing mistakes.

For nearly three years I occupied a desk near Keppler's compartment and assisted with his color-stones. Being considerably in the boss's confidence, I had the opportunity to know him as well as anyone on the staff. Keppler's aim was to make *Puck* the best paper of its type—*Puck* was not merely a comic weekly, it was a very influential political journal—and as long as it published his and Gillam's cartoons, *Puck* had no rival.

Mr. Keppler was an artist of unusual ability, and his cartoons were more than that name implies. They were real works of art, both in drawing and coloring. Keppler's latter day cartoons were rendered by means of three-color stones and one black—though, by a clever process of distribution of colors in the press founts and blending, as many as eighteen tints might be introduced in a cartoon. Keppler was an Austrian, and his conversation was much of Vienna. With wavy iron grey hair, mustache, and goatee, one would pick him on sight as a true artist of the Old School. Some have called him pompous, but he did not impress one as such when

in daily contact with him. *Puck* was fearless in its attacks on religion. A paper taking a decided stand against the Catholic or Jewish faiths today in the manner of *Puck*'s early onslaughts would be signing its own death warrant, yet *Puck* did it with impunity. However, those who originated the ideas and submitted them at conferences of editors and artists were careful to select subjects that were being discussed in the newspapers and by the public in general, for in the event of threatened libel suits, it could be shown that *Puck* was not the first offender. [Nevertheless, the art was racist, portraying Blacks and Jews in the most stereotyped terms possible. It was Keppler who gave ZIM the base for the grotesque distortions that characterized some of his work.]

Most of Keppler's cartoon subjects were originated by his colleagues; for Keppler, although an expert draftsman and well informed, was a man of few ideas. His genius lay in vitalizing those subjects, giving them the imprint of his own personality.★

★Although Zimmerman questioned Keppler's ability to develop ideas, and it is quite possible that Keppler may not have been an "Idea-

Keppler was most interesting when he talked about his past. I remember him telling me of the humiliation he endured when he was down at the heel and was eking out a living at portrait painting. "I had finished a water-color picture of which I felt tremendously proud," he reminisced. "It was my masterpiece—the portrait of a rich lady—and I had figured on getting a nice piece of change for it. You can imagine my feelings when the lady told me the picture didn't look a bit like her. I spat on it and rubbed the palm of my hand over the face before she had a chance to protest; then I said to her: 'Madam, you do not wish a portrait which doesn't resemble you,' and I threw it in a scrap heap."

Keppler was an actor as well as an artist—a vaudeville comedian, I judge, for he showed me some early photos of his act, a "sneezing song." The scene of his earliest art efforts was St. Louis, where in 1871 he first published a German edition of *Puck* for one year. [*Puck: Illustries Wochen-Schrift.*] Then he moved to New York and drew funny pictures for *Frank Leslie's Weekly* for fifteen dollars a week, fell out with Leslie over a five-dollar increase and announced his determination to start a humorous weekly of his own. "If you do that," Leslie warned, "I'll start one just like it and drive you out of business."

Nevertheless, Keppler collected $1,500 capital, took Adolf Schwarzmann, the foreman at Leslie's printing plant, and in September, 1876, revived the German *Puck*—with a new sub-title, *Illustrires Humoristisches Wochenblatt*—which ran for exactly fourteen years. (Now and then, big-chested Prussians with gold medals on their bosoms would strut into the office to visit Keppler who was a leader of the German element in New York. The editor of the German edition was Karl Hauser, a lovable humorist who was kind to me. Some years later, after he had left *Puck* and was publishing *Deutsches Kalendar* magazine, I gave him many drawings out of gratitude for that kindness. I believe he died in poverty.)

F. Graetz was another unfortunate German with whom I became quite friendly. Graetz could not speak English, which made it difficult for him to understand American humor, so I shared his stall in the art department and acted as interpreter. All ideas assigned to him had to be translated into his native language, a rather slow process for getting out cartoons! Graetz was an elderly gentleman with short-cropped hair and abundant red whiskers. He was an excellent pen-and-ink artist but too careful in detail for an American comic paper. Evidently, the publishers did not wish to renew his contract, for they cut his salary in half and obliged him to resign. Broken-hearted over the humiliation, Graetz returned to his former home in Vienna. I felt almost as sorry as did the old fellow himself.

There was a German poet, Leopold Schenck, whose self-esteem was ludicrous. Schenck was a big fellow, physically as well as poetically, but when he sat in his dingy seven-by-ten cubicle, with its low partitions, at the rear of an equally dingy building, he looked about as meek and unimportant as a shaggy prize heifer at a county fair. Whenever his concentration was disturbed by anything—such as the irritating squeak of a pump busily lifting water to lithographers on the third floor—the art and editorial departments took up his cry for the janitor, which turned that usually peaceful haven into a den of roaring lions. I dared not roar with them, for I had not reached an eminence which would entitle me to a voice in the matter. So I sat back and trembled until the bedlam ceased and the animals were pacified.

The *Puck* venture was so successful that in March, 1877, Keppler established an edition in English, which remained a feeble bantling until he published in it a startling picture of a scene on Fifth Avenue following the death of a certain fashionable abortionist. Thereafter, *Puck*'s circulation rose rapidly and more colors were added to its cartoons, although no other sketches of that nature appeared.

Keppler was well informed on both American and European politics, but preferred international subjects for his cartoons because the pomp and ceremonial of the Old World afforded opportunities for more vivid color effects. His pictures were too refined to be classed with political cartoons; many of them were in the category of great paintings. Familiarity with the canvases of the early masters made it easy for Keppler to utilize them to fit modern conditions, which he often did.

man" in the classic sense, several authors think otherwise. Frank Luther Mott, in a definitive history of American magazines, noted that "Keppler was a man of remarkable energy and fecundity of ideas" (*A History of American Magazines,* vol. 4, p. 522.) The noted cartoonist W. A. Rogers, in *A World Worth While* (1922) pointed out that Keppler's mind "was in a constant state of eruption" (p. 1284).

When Keppler stepped out of the grotesque, he became sublime. His allegorical scenes, in which sorrow and sympathy were expressed, were models of color and composition. Keppler was a past master of lithography and understood how to get results in color by avoiding the harsh treatment of the less skilled draftsman. His cartoons compelled one to study them from an artistic point of view long after their political significance had been assimilated.

Gillam's technique, on the other hand, made a stronger appeal to the general public, which grasped only the idea and not the subtlty of its artistic qualities. His work was strong in lines and more forceful in spirit as a cartoon, and impressed me as being the pictured thoughts of a great student, which in truth he was.

Gillam was never more contended than when he was occupied on Shakespearean subjects, for he knew that field. Historical situations twisted into modern politics was his big hobby. When Gillam ran short on ideas for the next week's cartoon, he would delve into Shakespeare, Dickens, Robinson Crusoe, or even the Bible.

Gillam had a peculiar manner of proceeding with a cartoon. He would make a complete layout, then trace only the portraits upon the lithographic stone minus the bodies, and finish them in crayon. Finally he would add the bodies. Keppler always completed each figure or group of figures separately, beginning with the face and proceeding downward with a finishing stroke and shading his figures as he advanced. Keppler's lines were soft and rollicking; Gillam's were firm and decided as if carved from stone.

I used to study Keppler's work. The grace and ease of his strokes captivated me. It was well adapted for lithographic cartoons, but I did not copy his style in comic drawing. L. Hopkins, once of the *Daily Graphic* and later of the *Sydney* (Australia) *Bulletin* also had a great influence on me. Something in his pictures hit me forcibly, but I discovered in time that I was drifting into another man's technique, so I swung away from it, unconsciously creating a style of my own.

Keppler set me right on composition; I learned to balance a drawing by watching his method. Whenever he detected defects in my draftmanship, he suggested changes, which were always valuable. Gillam's technique was far apart from my own. I never knew him to comment on my style, nor did I ever discuss his style with him, although I used to help both Keppler and Gillam on their tint-stones.

As one of the proprietors of *Puck*, Keppler could have insisted upon monopolizing the center double-page—the most important cartoon location, but preferred to pass it around so his associates might share in the glory. I was given a chance at it once, and depicted President Cleveland and his cabinet making a "Civil Service" fire about the Capitol to eliminate the grasshopper pest (office seekers). I also remember doing a front-page cartoon for *Puck* showing David B. Hill (for whom I had once painted a sign in Elmira) as a plumber trying to connect the pipes of the various disturbing elements in the Democratic party.

It often happens that a cartoon must be under way prior to election day and appears on the stands after the result is announced. This puts the artist to a severe test of foresight in which he is just as apt to guess wrong as right. In 1884, Hill ran for the governorship of New York State. In the closing hours of his campaign such an error was made by one of *Puck's* artists who pictured Hill as the defeated Democratic candidate when in reality he was elected. There is no help for such a situation if one forecasts election results, but a cartoonist doesn't always miss. During the Cleveland-Folger gubernational campaign of 1882, Keppler drew a cartoon a week before election for the issue of *Puck* which would appear on sale the day after election. It showed Folger, wearing clumsy shoes labeled "Forgery" and "Fraud," walking towards a ferryboat landing, from which a craft had just pulled out with Grover Cleveland aboard. The cartoon was entitled "Left," and created a powerful impression.

Adolf Schwarzmann was a good natured soul who enjoyed the success his financiering brought to *Puck*. He seemed proud of the fact that he was one of the publishers of a famous comic paper. Every morning he would pause before each of the artists' cubicles and utter the same remarks: "Vell! Got Someding? No? Yes?" and would chuckle heartily if a joke were related to him.

Members of the *Puck* staff used to put their heads together to devise subjects and captions for the following week's cartoons. Occasionally, Eugene

Bisbee, an itinerant vendor of cartoon suggestions, peddled his wares in our office. Bisbee sold ideas at a dollar apiece, and Schwarzmann would bring a few of them into the art department and scatter them around as largess. Frederic Burr Opper, the recognized comic artist on *Puck,* generally had first pick of this material, in addition to his own original ideas. Opper had always been a prolific worker. His hours on *Puck* were 9 to 4; during that time he pounded out enough art work to occupy a big share of the paper. The Opper of those days was a round-faced young chap with mild gray eyes and sandy mustache who kept largely to himself.

Like most of the men associated with him, Opper was of German descent, but was born in Ohio in 1857. He had been connected more or less intimately with *Wild Oats, Frank Leslie's Budget of Fun, Phunny Phellow,* and other humorous papers, all now extinct, that preceded *Puck.*

Opper obtained wide popularity through his famous characters, "Happy Hooligan" and "Alphonse and Gaston." Possibly the best lampoon he ever did for *Puck* was based on a remark by the Rev. Dr. Thomas DeWitt Talmage in a sermon preached at the Brooklyn Tabernacle, of which he was pastor: "What races shall we run when we are celestal athletes?" The cartoon, published in 1883, represented Dr. Talmage as an angel sprinting down a cloud bank, while a large audience of heavenly beings watched with eager interest. One fat angel, acting as time-keeper, held a big watch in his hand. Another, seated on a bench, was serving as judge. Underneath were the words:

> "Talking of celestial races,
> here our artist tries to sketch
> Talmage as he'd look a-cutting
> down the sacred quarter stretch;
> Don't you, O religious reader,
> lift your hands in holy awe—
> If 'twaw right for him to say it,
> 'tisn't wrong for us to draw."

The genial clergyman chuckled over that cartoon and later added a copy of it to his collection. Talmage was one of the most picturesque characters in the American ministry. His Brooklyn Tabernacle, seating four thousand, had been burned down in 1872 and rebuilt. In 1889 it was again destroyed by fire and rebuilt. A third time, in 1894, the edifice was reduced to ashes but this time it did not emerge phoenix-like. Talmage's sermons were best sellers in book form, besides being syndicated regularly to three thousand newspapers in this country and abroad.

Talmage frequently selected news themes for his sermon topics, which he treated rather sensationally, and he enjoyed a very wide popularity. Naturally he was a shining mark for the cartoonists. His sermons and lectures were filled with challenging statements which comic artists found hard to resist.

In 1900, two years before his death, the venerable Dr. Talmage, then editor of *The Christian J*
ald, placed an order with a news dealer in Washington for copies of all of the cartoons of himself published during his palmiest days, for which he paid a good price.

Why the clergyman wanted these pictures has never been explained, for many of them were crude and bitter. The cartoons of the 'seventies and 'eighties followed the fashion set by Nast, being merciless rather than merely funny. Nevertheless, Talmage ordered and bought them all, humorous as well as malicious. One of his pleasantest traits was a willingness to enjoy a laugh at his own expense, and perhaps in his declining years he appreciated those reminders of the days when his novel style of preaching was calling down upon him fierce denunciation all over the country.

A cartoon that Keppler printed of him in *Puck* after his visit to the Tenderloin district was one of the most savage bits of work ever done by an American caricaturist and it is hard to understand how even Dr. Talmage's sense of humor enabled him to look at that picture with any pleasure.

For eighteen years, Opper stayed with *Puck;* then in May, 1899, he went over to William Randolph Hearst's *New York Journal.* When an organization known as The Cartoonists of America gave a banquet at the Hotel Astor on March 18, 1927, Opper was one of three veteran cartoonists who were guests of honor, the other two being Gibson and W. A. Rogers. I was also invited, but was unable to be there.

Rogers began his career on the New York *Daily Graphic.* He was best known as staff cartoonist for the *New York Herald,* and was decorated with the *Chevalier de la Legion d'Honneur* for his cartoons reproduced in the Paris edition of the *Herald* during the World War. When Frank A. Munsey bought the

A scene in front of a bakery, perhaps reminiscent of ZIM's early life as a baker's apprentice.

For these, who fought, the War is done:
    For them life's evening sky
Grows tender o'er a setting sun
    Where fires of anger die.
Toward the mountains of the west
    They look with peaceful sight;
The storm they braved has sunk to rest,
    Into forgetful night.

From foe to friend—from foe to friend!
    O consecrated years,
How have ye worked toward this end
    Through myriad doubts and fears!
The hand that laid the sword aside
    Now seeks the conqueror's hand—
Friends? They are sharers in one pride,
    And lovers of one land.

O meaner folk, of narrower souls,
    Heirs of ignoble thought,
Stir not the camp-fire's blackened coals
    Blood-drenched by those who fought;
Lest out of heaven a fire shall yet
    Bear God's own vengeance forth
On those who once again would set
    Discord 'twixt South and North.

FORT DONELSON, 1862.   GRANT AND BUCKNER.   MOUNT McGREGOR, 1885.
A Rebuke to the "Bloody Shirt" Patriots.

"A Hunter and His Dog"

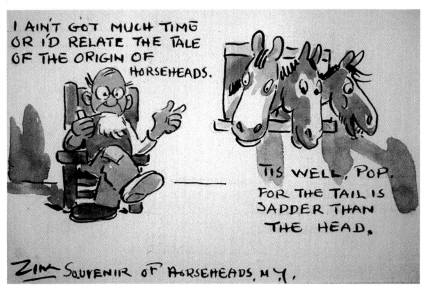

I AIN'T GOT MUCH TIME OR I'D RELATE THE TALE OF THE ORIGIN OF HORSEHEADS.

'TIS WELL, POP. FOR THE TAIL IS SADDER THAN THE HEAD.

ZIM SOUVENIR OF HORSEHEADS, N.Y.

WELL PUT.

GROWING EVERY DAY.
YOUNG SAMMY CROWDS THEM ALL AT THE GATEWAY OF COMMERCE.
(NOTE—Exports during the fiscal years '97–'98, $1,200,000,000. The largest ever recorded.)

VOTED TO A MAN.

VOL. 44 NO. 1117   MARCH 14 1903   PRICE 10 CENTS

WHY NOT?

JUDGE (*to Uncle Sam*)—"Everything we have is big except our navy. Why not build a navy to correspond?"

VOL. 49 NO. 1249   SEPTEMBER 23 1905   PRICE 10 CENTS

A GOOD HAUL.

The T.R. on the sleeve refers to Teddy Roosevelt.

COMPLIMENTS OF THE DAY.

VOL. 49 NO. 1246   SEPTEMBER 2 1905   PRICE 10 CENTS

Judge

"YUM, YUM! BUT I DOES LOVE WATAHMILYUN!"

PARADOXICAL, BUT PERTINENT.

Mrs. Goode—"I hardly know which of you two men's misfortunes is the most worthy of charity."
Blind Organist—"Mine is, mum. Not bein' obliged to hear his organ's music makes de deaf man's misfortune a sort ov blessin'."

WEIGHTY REASONING.

VOL. 51 NO. 1304   OCTOBER 13, 1906   PRICE 10 CENTS

Judge

WHAT MAY HAPPEN IN CUBA.

The President—"If that pot boils over I'll have to put the lid on."

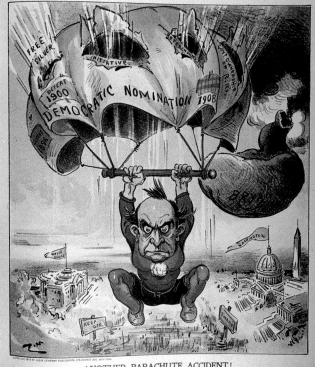

VOL. II NO: 281

MARCH 5, 1887. PRICE 10 CENTS.

Judge

ENTERED AT THE POST OFFICE AT NEW YORK AS SECOND CLASS MATTER, COPYRIGHT 1887.

THE FORTY-NINTH CONGRESS BREAKS-UP AND TAKES THE SURPLUS WITH IT.

VOL. 48 NO. 1226

APRIL 15 1905 PRICE 10 CENTS

Judge

ENTERED AT THE POST OFFICE AT NEW YORK AS SECOND CLASS MATTER, DECEMBER 1904 BY JUDGE COMPANY. TITLE REGISTERED AS A TRADE MARK.

THE GREAT AMERICAN TOBACCO HOG.

The way to kill it is to follow the example of Wisconsin and Indiana, which have made it unlawful to sell, give away, or import into the state cigarettes or cigarette material. Let all the states do likewise.

SEVEN AGES OF THE WHEEL.

THE HOME GUARD.

Let Spain or any other country beware when Uncle Sam calls out his deadly reserves.

WAS ON TO HIM.

Financier—"I told me boss I couldn't afford to work fer t'ree dollars a week."
Merchant—"What did he say?"
Financier—"Said he hadn't noticed me tryin' to."

KNEW THE BREED.

Fattened Fagan (with a childish sigh)—"Well, I'm surprised! After dat you can't tell me dat insects ain't got sense. Dat little feller knows we won't move."

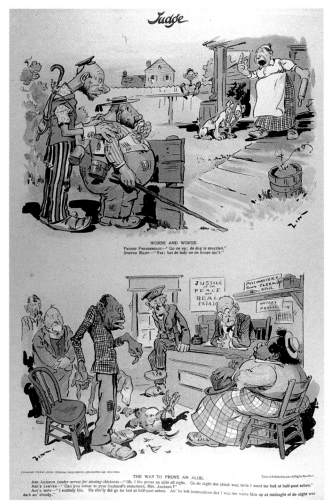

WORSE AND WORSE.

Faded Prendergast—"Go on up; de dog is muzzled."
Stewed Riley—"Yes; but de lady uv de house ain't."

THE WAY TO PROVE AN ALIBI.

Abe Jackson (under arrest for stealing chickens)—"Oh, I kin prove an alibi all right. On de night dat chick wuz stole I went ter bed at half-past seben."
Abe's Lawyer—"Can you swear to your husband's statement, Mrs. Jackson?"
Abe's Wife—"I suttinly kin. He sho'ly did go tur bed at half-past seben. An' he left instructions dat I wuz ter wake him up at midnight of de night wuz dark an' cloudy."

Herald from the estate of James Gordon Bennett—Munsey had an antipathy to cartoonists—Rogers switched over to Edward B. McLean's *Washington Post* where he remained until his death, October 20, 1931, at seventy-seven, the dean of American editorial cartoonists. His formula for success was to "Let your method be humorous but your purpose serious." Rogers specialized for years in sketching news events and was the only artist permitted to sketch the dying President Garfield at the bedside. At various times he was on the staffs of *Harper's Weekly, Harper's Magazine, St. Nicholas, Century,* and *Life.*

Gibson's tremendous popularity is due mainly to his contributions to *Life,* which at first included political cartoons. One of them showed the Democratic donkey and the GOP elephant as pugilists squaring off for the quadrennial championship bout. The country lost a promising political cartoonist when it acquired the "Gibson Girl." [The Gibson Girl was a series of drawings of outstandingly beautiful American women drawn by Charles Gibson.]

Perhaps the most careful draftsman in the annals of cartooning was the tall, gaunt A. B. Frost, an occasional contributor to *Puck, Harper's Bazaar,* and other papers. Frost lived in a luxurious home in a suburb of Philadelphia with an unpronounceable name. Although he is said to have been color-blind, he executed many watercolor paintings. In his youth, Frost was very poor, but his fortunes turned when he married a wealthy lady.

Most of the Tammany politicians of that period were men whom reputable citizens would not invite into their homes—loud-mouthed, heavy-handed ward heelers with coarse bloated features and big black mustaches, bearing the unmistakable stamp of the slums. Working as I did in the vicinity of City Hall, I saw plenty of them. One of the finer types was "Nick" Langdon, who usually could be found in close proximity to a certain saloon on Nassau Street. Jim Wales was a great friend of Langdon's and always saluted him with the complimentary title of "Alderman." One day, Wales drew a clever caricature of Langdon from memory, fearfully exaggerating his elephantine ears, wrinkled visage, and beady eyes. The picture was published and was keenly relished by the ward leader's friends and foes alike. "Nick" himself,

"A ZIM Self-Portrait"
Drawn by Eugene Zimmerman about 1922

however, did not take kindly to it. Next time the cartoonist greeted Langdon on the street with, "How are you, Alderman?" the politician growled, "Go to hell!"

"Why, what's the matter?" Wales inquired innocently.

"When yer drawring elephants," was the angry retort, "why don't yer drawr elephants?"

Caricature is a distortion of the features and retaining a resemblance. In many instances Nature has taken the initiative and produced living caricatures in the human race. An unfortunate thing about caricaturing is that your subject is seldom willing to admit a resemblance, because he cannot see himself from the artist's point of view.

Foreign caricaturists usually exaggerate the ugliness in facial expression, whereas the American, relying largely on the humorous qualities in a face, stops short of the grotesque. I don't believe in hideously distorting the face of a subject. A caricature can be rendered ludicrous yet pleasing, and by such sketches one makes friends rather than enemies.

Studio photographs usually are not desirable to work from because the very characteristics which the caricaturist wants to emphasize are toned down or eliminated. This, of course, is done to gratify vanity. Men in the public eye desire publicity and, whether they admit it or not, are delighted when caricaturists notice them. (Jose de Leon Toral, who assassinated President-elect Obregon of Mexico, gained access to him by posing as a caricaturist.) Some of the lesser lights deliberately throw themselves into the way of the pencil distortionist in the hope of appearing in print. I suppose that every cartoonist in the country could confirm this statement in ways that would be unflattering to certain well-known citizens. Many celebrities save cartoons of themselves in albums just as small boys save postage stamps. Congressman "Sunset" Cox remarked that he would rather be kicked than not noticed at all, and this applied to nearly all of us.

There were no tricks of the trade in the *Puck* office; the whole matter of producing was simple—all it required was drawing ability. To draw on stone required practice, as the use of a grease crayon was more difficult than lead-pencil or pen-and-ink rendering. Most of my early sketches were crude in technique, as I realized when I compared them with the professional work of my colleagues, but I labored diligently to correct my faults and as I improved, I began picking up commercial art jobs which I handled as a side line after office hours. Eventually, I acquired a large clientele of advertisers using my drawings at prices most gratifying to me, so that hardly a week passed in which I did not earn from fifty to seventy-five dollars besides the regular pay envelope.

Early in life my long name became a burden, so I threw two-thirds of it overboard, thus saving time, space and India ink, and providing a *merman* for any sea nymph who cared to salvage. A friend, a very successful business man, noticed that my signature, "zim," had a downward slant. Said he, "Never sign your name downhill, always uphill, it looks more prosperous." From that moment, I have always signed my drawings uphill, for I believe there is truth in his assertion.★

I must confess that I rarely see anything funny in my own drawings and am continually seeking bet-

ter results, while the humor of other artists fills me with a sort of envious delight. My finished work always appears defective and, as I look back upon it, I am not far from incorrect in believing thus. At first any unfavorable criticism almost rendered me ill. In later years I learned to pay little attention to criticism because I found it impossible to please so many different minds.

Doing the best I knew how to serve and to please my employers, there was no time to linger over the cartoon pages. Everything moved by schedule and every stage of the week's activities was planned; any delay in carrying out those plans might prove fatal by delaying the issue—which was as unthinkable as holding up a show would be among theatrical folk.

If an artist can produce a momentary laugh, he has earned his money, no matter in what manner he did it. A comic cannot be drawn tediously and yet contain the mirth which it is possible to put into a quick sketch. In the latter case you get the spontaneous thought and humorous action, most of which you unavoidably destroy in polishing up the work for presentation to the public in a finished manner. The artists who drew for *Puck,* from Keppler down to the humblest contributor, sincerely tried to combine good draftsmanship with cleverness of ideas.

The sketch-book which had given *entrée* to *Puck* kicked about my premises for many years afterward, finding its way into the cellar, where it reposed in dust and mold. One day it turned up at a spring housecleaning and the drawings looked so uncouth that I promptly cremated them; the volume had served its purpose and deserved exemption from further scrutiny.

Chapter 7

THE BLAINE-CLEVELAND PRESIDENtial campaign [1884] was characterized by more muckraking and mudslinging than any other Presidential contest I know. The Republicans attacked

---

★In one of his "Phoolosophy" columns, Zimmerman wrote that the first change to his name occurred when a final double-*n* was reduced to one *n*. None of his personal documents indicates such a change; it is possible the change was made by his father years earlier.

Grover Cleveland's morality and backed up their charges with statements purporting to have emanated from Mr. Cleveland himself. Democratic newspapers such as the *New York Evening Post* (which today is conservative Republican) argued that even if the charges were true, Cleveland's morality was no worse than that of George Washington, Benjamin Franklin, Thomas Jefferson, Alexander Hamilton, and other national heroes.

The Democratic press, particularly the *Indianapolis Sentinel* of August 8, 1884, was unreasonably bitter in its aspersions upon the moral character of James G. Blaine, which brought forth the threat of a libel suit against its publishers in response to a scathing attack of a sensational nature dating back to March 25, 1851.

The incident is not mentioned in history books or Blaine biographies although it influenced a Presidential election, possible even turned the tide, for the popular vote was very close: Cleveland, 4,874,986; Blaine, 4,851,981. The Rev. Dr. Burchard's unfortunate reference to the Democrats as "the party of Rum, Romanism, and Rebellion" also cost the Republicans many votes, despite Blaine's desperate efforts to smooth things over. [When Burchard, a Republican, spoke of "Rum, Romanism, and Rebellion," Blaine was in the audience, but remained silent in response to Burchard's oratory. It is believed that Blaine's silence cost him much of the Irish-American vote.] Blaine himself blamed the loss of New York, the key state, on the cartoonists—notably Keppler and Gillam in *Puck* and Nast in *Harper's Weekly.* He was especially upset about a *Puck* cartoon which showed him in the role of a tattooed Belshazzer at the famous feast where the Hand wrote on the wall; Blaine was represented as wining and dining plutocrats in exchange for their support.

The "Tattooed Man" cartoons which figured so conspicuously in the campaign made their "tenstrike" by the merest accident. The idea was originally intended to be a comic satire, not a personal stab at the Republican standard-bearer. Bernhard Gillam was racking his brain for a subject for a center double-page in *Puck* when Karl Hauser [editor of the German-language edition of *Puck*] entered his den and suggested a national dime museum. At first the idea did not appeal because it seemed too commonplace, Gillam being inclined toward more scholarly subjects, so it was shelved

for about two weeks. Gradually, however, it took shape in his mind, and Gillam drew a picture of the museum in which some of the leading aspirants for the Presidency and other notables were represented as side-show freaks. Most prominent of the group was Baline's figure arrayed in trunks and tattooed *cap-a-pie* with such incidents in his career as the Mulligan letters, Little Rock bonds, *etc.,* transactions which had been assailed by the Democratic press as acts unworthy of a great statesman. [In 1876, Blaine had used his influence to preserve a land grant for the Little Rock and Fort Smith Railroad Company. He later profited from selling some of the railroad's bonds. James Mulligan was a clerk of the Boston stock company where Blaine got the stock. Mulligan had letters that apparently incriminated Blaine and showed them to Blaine, who asked for, and received, the bonds for one night with the promise to return them the next day. He failed to do so.]★

The cartoon was published April 16, 1884, over the title, "The National Dime Museum—Will Be Run During the Presidential Campaign." It scored a tremendous success. The demand for that issue of *Puck* became so great that extra editions were required and 300,000 copies were sold.

General John A. Logan, who later became Blaine's running mate, issued an indignant statement that such cartooning was unwarranted; whereupon Gillam made a second "Tattooed Man" cartoon, showing Logan and other loyal partisans attempting to sandpaper and scrub off Blaine's tattoo marks behind a curtain in the dime museum. It was published May 7, the caption "Love's Labor Lost."

The following week, Keppler used the provocative symbol in a double-spread entitled "More Than She Can Carry." The Republican party was seen staggering under various swindles and corruptions, while Whitelaw Reid was placing on top of the burden the tattooed Blaine partially wrapped in a sack labeled "Roteen Record." This was an allusion to the fact that the *New York Tribune,* of which Reid was editor-in-chief, was boosting Blaine for the G.O.P. nomination. The cartoon angered Reid, who editorialized:

★Although Zimmerman, and common opinion, credit Gillam with the idea for the "tattooed man," it is probable that the idea originated with Karl Hauser.

Washington was a great and good man. Yet he was a tattooed man for all that. No man ever held or was named for the exalted office of President without becoming for the time being more or less a tattooed man [June 13, 1884].

Such comment naturally inspired another Gillam cartoon, and the fight was on. Blaine was shown gazing at his reflection in a quiet pool; around him were lily pads bearing the ecstatic faces of his admirers, including Reid. The caption was: "Narcissus, or the Man who was Mashed on Himself. —J.G.B." The remarkable resemblance to George Washington is what strikes *me!*

Gillam did not realize how big a hit he had made until the opposition press, led by the *Tribune,* began to rake him fore and aft with broadsides. A *Tribune* reporter named Lake wormed his way into Gillam's studio and, under the guise of friendship, obtained an interview which, when published in distorted form, infuriated Gillam. Then the *Tribune* commented editorially:

It appears that the caricaturist Gillam who made the picture of Mr. Blaine as "the Tattooed Man" is an Englishman. Evidently neither the native-born, imported nor hired Englishman can ever forgive Mr. Blaine for his American ideas [June 14, 1884].

What especially enraged Gillam was the fact that he had been a victim of unethical journalism, and he made it known that under no circumstances would he extend a similar courtesy to representatives of the opposition press; all such interviewers would be treated to bare knuckles and boot leather. Thereafter, Whitelaw Reid was very much in evidence in Gillam's vitriolic cartoons, beginning with the "Narcissus" already mentioned.

The *Puck* vs. *Tribune* battle continued until election day. On August 10, just after the *Sentinel* had published its sensational charges, the *Tribune* editorialized on the "decadence" of American cartooning:

The question is often asked, "Why is there no American Punch?" The reason is that political partisanship has broken the edge of satire and converted caricature into defamation. . . . "With charity for none and malice toward all" seems to be the motto of certain cartoon-makers.

Then someone remarked that Blaine's "purity of character" and "personal magnetism" were suffi-
cient refutation of the slanders against him, which prompted another *Puck* cartoon—a burlesque of Gerome's famous painting, "The Trial of Phryne," wherein the beautiful courtesan displays her nude charms to the Athenian judges. This was modified to portray Blaine, naked except for trunks, exhibiting his tattoo marks to the Chicago *Tribune,* captioned thus: "The Trial of Phryne (with Apologies to J. L. Gerome). —Ardent Admirer: "Now, gentlemen, don't make any mistake in your decision. Here's purity and magnetism for you—can't be beat!"

There were many other variations of the "Tattooed Man." A well-known advertisement of Pear's Soap was parodied to represent the Republican candidate as a naughty schoolboy exclaiming, "Hurray, soap to remove tattoo!" In another picture, Blaine was a tattooed Egyptian mummy; then Gillam made him a tattooed "Plume Knight" and later a tattooed Negro at a fancy dress ball. Keppler produced a very striking cartoon entitled "He Can't Beat His Own Record," in which the tattooed Blaine was running the Presidential race against his own tattooed shadow. Still another one showed even a curtain tattooed.

Opper also adopted the "Tattooed Man," using it at least once, in his conception of Blaine as the Pied Piper. The idea's effectiveness lay in its reiteration of the weak spots in Blaine's record, the tattoo implying that such scandals were not eradicable. These cartoons were all well drawn, brilliantly colored, and printed on *Puck's* center double-pages or front or back covers. Thus, we see that a cartoon which at first was drawn largely in the spirit of fun and was not intended as a vicious assault, became a powerful factor in a national campaign. When its effect was realized, *Puck* decided to keep the "Tattooed Man" alive, and the luckless James G. Blaine was forced to appear in that unlovely guise as long as he remained in public life. Nothing helps a paper's circulation or a cartoonist's prestige as much as lively controversy, for the cartoon is essentially a weapon of attack and the cartoonist is at his best when he has a fight on his hands. It is only in times of prosperity and contentment that his crusading impulse dies and the cartoonist slumps into the status of an amusement vender.

In the meantime, Thomas Nast was crucifying Blaine in *Harper's Weekly* with some of the old vigor he had used to dethrone "Boss" Tweed more than ten years before. Nast's activity provoked the *Tribune* to another outburst:

> At no period in our political history have the abuses of caricature been more conspicuous than in the present campaign; and on the other hand, never have political cartoons possessed so little influence in affecting man's judgements. The attempt made to defeat Mr. Blaine's nomination by the circulation of foul pictures was a single failure; yet the cartoon makers have not been discouraged and are still employed at the same despicable trade of misrepresenting facts and assaulting established character. The effort to defeat the Republican leader by means of highly colored and indecent pictorial lies has only tended to increase his popularity and to bring reproach upon the degraded art of caricature. . . .
>
> In an old file of *Harper's Weekly* is a cartoon showing Lincoln in 1861 on the eve of inauguration, tippling with drunken loafers and cracking jokes, while outside is a horse bearing the Union and the Constitution to the grave [August 3, 1884].

The *Tribune* also said that a paper which had defamed the immortal Lincoln could not be trusted to treat Mr. Blaine more fairly, and Whitelaw Reid followed up this attack by reprinting some of the *Harper's Weekly* cartoons which had belittled Abraham Lincoln. On October 26, the *Tribune* commented:

> Most of the cartoonists who had been engaged in lampooning Blaine and Logan are foreigners. Gillam is an Englishman. Nast is an Englishman also. Frederick Opper is a German.

The *Tribune* was wrong in regard to Nast and Opper, and it neglected to mention that cartoonist Jacob De Grimm, of the *New York Telegram,* who had been pitching into Blaine rather mercilessly, was a recently imported Frenchman. It also overlooked Keppler's foreign birth.

Then, certain Republican journalists tried to fight fire with fire; they published a campaign magazine entitled *Jingo,* to which the *Tribune* gave a long and favorable review. One of the cartoons in *Jingo* showed a tattooed white elephant, labeled "Cleveland & Hendricks," which was being scrubbed by Henry Ward Beecher and Carl Schurz. [Carl Schurz—lawyer, newspaper editor, civil war general—was a leader of the Reform Republicans who opposed the nomination of U. S. Grant for

the presidency. In 1876, he had been appointed by Rutherford B. Hayes as secretary of the interior.] This cartoon proved to be a boomerang because readers refused to accept Barnum's *white-elephant hoax* as a symbol of the Democratic party.

Election day came November 4, 1884. For two days the result was in doubt, then the *Tribune* announced in bold headlines: "BLAINE ELECTED! . . . New York for Blaine by a Small Plurality . . ." and began publishing jubilant editorials. For a full week the *Tribune* stood its ground, while the whole country waited tensely for a recount; finally, even the staunch *Tribune* broke down and conceded that Grover Cleveland had won.

Nevertheless, it is barely possible that Mr. Blaine was elected after all. The result was very close and hinged on New York State, which reported a scant margin of 1,100 for Cleveland, thus deciding the election. Some years later, John McKane, Tammany boss of Coney Island, was convicted in court of having stolen 8,000 votes from Blaine—more than enough to have changed the result in New York State and to have sent the "Plumed Knight" to the White House! For that crime of ballot-box stuffing, McKane served a term in Sing Sing, which, to my way of thinking, automatically invalidated the Cleveland victory!

As I look back to the Presidential contests of the eighties, I marvel at the lack of interest surrounding those of today [1920s]. I used to watch the inspiring torch-light processions, miles in length, and was dazzled by the gaudy oilcoth capes and regalia of the paraders. Each delegation endeavored to outdo the others in military splendor and brass bands. Many of those uniformed bodies were carefully drilled to perform evolutions while on the march. In Patterson, New Jersey, alone, there were, as I recall, the Garrett A. Hobart Guards, the Blauvelt Battery (with cannon), Phelps Guards, Boys in Blue and many others, all appealing strongly to the youthful voter. Before I became of age I enlisted in one of such brigades in the city of Elmira, New York.

I remember witnessing numerous mix-ups when the rival political parties happened to meet on dress parade. Men were excited almost as though hostile armies had met in battle array. I have seen the streets littered with broken torches and tattered uniforms after one of these delightful spectacles.

This method of campaigning was still in evidence, although in a very mild form, as late as the first [Theodore] Roosevelt regime. It must have cost enormous sums to run Presidential campaigns in those times, yet money was not so plentiful—or rather, so concentrated—as it is today.

During the stirring 'eighties, an Independent Party was born to national politics, composed largely of malcontents from the two stronger groups. [The Independent party was also known as the "Mugwumps," the name believed to have originated from an Indian work meaning "chief." The party was organized mainly to defeat James G. Blaine in the 1884 election.] It became necessary to invent a figure to typify the new organization's good qualities (but not its bad ones), so *Puck* offered as an appropriate symbol, a vigorous-looking voter in red shirt, boots and hat, bearing a new ax labeled "Reform." During an entire season's campaigning—cutting and slashing into current politics—the ax never had its luster tarnished nor its blade nicked, and the "Independent voter" was a clean-shaven and handsome at the end of his hard-fought battle as on the day he started his clean-up.

The figure answered the purpose for which it was intended—it lent fresh color to the campaign and, on the whole, was a new plaything for the cartoonists. *Puck* did its best to prolong the life of this muscular and well-intentioned youth, but, like the Greenback Party and others of more recent date, he succumbed to the inevitable, only to make room for similar hobbies in campaigns to come.

I do not remember Bernhard Gillam ever having employed this figure in his cartoons, possibly because Mr. Independent Voter was not his own invention; although, as I have stated, Gillam's "Tattooed Man" was adopted by both Keppler and Opper; and Nast's elephant, donkey, and tiger have been accepted by editorial cartoonists all over the country.

Bernhard Gillam was a perfect type of Americanized English gentleman. It was a pleasure to chum with him, for Gillam's knowledge, acquired from good literature, seemed unlimited. He was a stranger to slang and never once did I hear him relate a vulgar story. We met often in the evenings at Gillam's home in Brooklyn, a stately old brownstone residence of three stories and base-

ment. The top floor was given over to lounging and recreation, of which penny ante was the limit.

Squire Gillam, the father, was a fine old fellow with a full beard, who liked his bottle of Bass ale, was seldom without it, and was ever ready to sit down to a game of cards. Bernhard rarely sat in, because his mind was forever seeking ideas for *Puck* cartoons, yet in a fit of abstraction now and then he would jump in, throw down his book and call for a hand and a stack of chips, but never tarried long at the game. He would withdraw as abruptly as he entered, and would again knit his brows over some literary classic, surrounded by hilarity and cigar smoke and the players' arguments, which never seemed to disturb his meditation.

If you can visualize a man in environment so opposite to his natural bent and yet able to concentrate on books, then you have Bernhard Gillam. He remained modest to the very end, and fame never turned his head.

Gillam once journeyed to Washington with a score or so of Saroni's photographs of national celebrities to compare them with the subjects themselves. [Saroni created "living pictures," reproductions on stage and later in photographs of famous masterpieces. Many of the reproduction photographs were published in 1894–95.] Gillam made many preliminary studies of Blaine's physiognomy before he drew the "Tattooed Man." His method was hard and firm. His drawings were never done with a rush, but with a carefully studied English style (he was a great admirer of Tenniel, of *Punch*) which was admirable for driving home political arguments.

But Gillam took too serious a view of life. The scholar in him and his constant search for information with which to develop his cartoons destroyed the lighter pleasures most of us indulge in. When Gillam endeavored to draw a funny picture he dissipated most of its humor by unnecessary refinement or meticulous technique.

One Saturday afternoon I persuaded him to see Neal Burgess in a funny play. While the rest of the house was in convulsions of laughter, Bernhard sat scowling and muttering to himself "Rot!" I was actually afraid to grin for fear of giving offense to his superior judgement. When we emerged outside he turned to me with:

"If you ever dare take me to see such rot again I'll kill you!"

Bernhard Gillam

My friend was just as savage in his criticism of bad Shakespearean actors, because he knew how the characters should look and how their parts should be played. His cartoons were full of that spirit; they cut to the quick and caused unscrupulous politicians to squirm.

Outside of his scathing cartoons, Gillam would not offend anyone purposely, yet sometimes he was too wrapped up in his work to receive callers; the name had to be announced first and, if convenient, the visitor was admitted. On one occasion Bernhard was engrossed in work when the attendant handed him a card bearing the name of a particular friend. The artist remarked, "Tell him I'm out to lunch."

The attendant delivered that message.

"Is that so?" responded the friend. "Well, tell him for me, he's a liar. When Mr. Gillam goes for lunch he'd better get away from that front window. I just saw him as I came across the street and I know he's there."

As soon as this statement had been repeated to him, Gillam rushed out and grasped the fellow in his arms, insisting that the attendant had misquoted him. The cartoonist was positive he had said, "Show him in."

Gillam once declared he owed his success entirely to the kindness of Henry Ward Beecher. As a poor English boy, Bernhard had become interested in portrait painting. He regarded General Grant and Beecher as the two greatest Americans, and decided to make a bold stab at fame by painting one of them. After deliberation, he decided upon Beecher, obtained a photograph and labored patiently until he had produced a creditable likeness of the Brooklyn clergyman.

Then, wrapping it carefully in paper and placing it under his arm, he visited Beecher's residence early in the morning. A motley crowd of early callers was sitting in the parlor. Mr. Beecher finally appeared at the folding doors and each visitor waited his turn to present his case. Young Gillam shrunk into a corner to escape observation until the crowd had gone. Finally his turn came. Mr. Beecher, with a pleasant smile, inquired, "What can I do for you my boy?" Bernhard's hesitant and trembling hands undid his precious package, and at the same time the youth explained as best he could that he was an artist in search of recognition and had come to Mr. Beecher for advice. The great preacher was impressed by Gillam's sincerity and was so pleased with the picture that he quickly arranged for Bernhard to exhibit it in the show-window of a popular Brooklyn store.

Beecher obtained this favor for Gillam from the storekeeper and also the privilege of receiving orders for portraits at the store. Within a few days Bernhard had gotten several requests for pictures at $15 each. Others continued to come in and he felt justified in raising the price to $25, to $50, and finally to $75.

This was the beginning of Bernhard Gillam's success. His talent attracted attention, and his conspicuous abilities, indefatigable industry and rare judgement soon brought well-deserved fame and fortune. He was a great artist—really great, a genius in his line—and he never forgot the kindness that Mr. Beecher had shown him.

At the age of eighteen, Gillam had decided to try his hand at oil painting and immediately set to work on a pretentious canvas depicting an early scene from American history, the gallant struggle of a body of Aztec Indians against a detachment of Spaniards. All around lay the bodies of dead and dying. *All Quiet on the Western Front* in its goriest moments never equaled such a scene of carnage. Gillam's picture was sent to the Brooklyn Academy of Fine Arts, and was numbered 93. No one ever called it anything else.

"The sensation of the hour," said the *Brooklyn Eagle,* "is number 93. There was never anything funnier than the dying men in 93, unless it is the men who are already dead. Don't fail to see it; it's the greatest show on earth!"

Crowds hung around the canvas all day. Gillam's dramatic effort provoked nothing but screams of laughter, even from a Brooklyn art audience, and the artist was advised to hire a hall or take it around the world. Tears came to the young man's eyes, and he was heartbroken at the failure of his first attempt at oil painting. He did not forsake art, however, but turned his attention to another field—cartooning.

A place on *Leslie's Weekly* was offered to him, but soon after he made this connection Frank Leslie died, the policy of the paper changed and Gillam went over to the *Daily Graphic*. During the Garfield-Hancock [1880] campaign, he drew cartoons for *Harper's Weekly,* working with Thomas Nast. His brilliance attracted Keppler's attention, and in 1881 the proprietors of *Puck* engaged him at what was said at the time to be the highest salary ever paid a cartoonist, except Nast.

An editorial cartoonist must have a keen perception of right and wrong, but not so keen that he can detect the political fallacies of his own party. He represents the only party of purity and reform. In the opposition he must see nothing but corruption and mismanagement—for which he is paid a good round salary. The more fault he can find with his political rivals, the better his salary becomes. The cartoonist has opinions of his own, of course, but these may be remolded easily by an offer of a more lucrative position on a newspaper of opposite political faith, whereupon the scales are lifted from his eyes and he immediately sees the unpardonable crimes of the party he has just deserted.

The "Tattooed Man" was one of the greatest cartoons of the Nineteenth Century—It not only assisted in sending Mr. Cleveland to the White House but virtually doubled *Puck's* circulation— and yet Gillam himself was an ardent supporter of Blaine even at the time he drew that masterpiece for Democratic *Puck*. Later, the cartoonist joined the staff of Republican *Judge* and gleefully attacked President Cleveland whom he had helped to elect.

Chapter 8

WHEN GENERAL SIMON B. BUCKNER came up from the south to pay his last respects to the dying General Grant at Mount MacGregor, N.Y., in July, 1885, I was asked by *Puck*'s editor, Henry C. Bunner, to accompany him to the Fifth Avenue Hotel for an interview and sketches of the Confederate leader who had surrendered Fort Donelson to Grant.

General Buckner, a fine type of southern gentleman, graciously submitted to the interview, after which Bunner and I strolled over to Brown's chop house, just off Broadway, where he treated me to a brace of the finest mutton chops I have ever tasted, with a bottle of Bass ale on the side.

Even during the period of his impoverishment and disgrace, Grant was a beloved figure. [Corruption pervaded the White House during Grant's last term, although there is no evidence that Grant himself was aware of or condoned any of it.] The honest old chieftain was no match for the wolves of Wall Street. Shortly after he had allied himself with Grant and Ward stockbrokers, with which his son was connected, the concern tried a stunt and failed to the tune of $14,000,000. Grant, white-faced and desperate, paid a midnight visit to his friend, William H. Vanderbilt, to see what could be done to avert the catastrophe. The millionaire loaned him $500,000, holding as security Grant's personal collection of souvenirs, including gifts and decorations from crowned heads and other admirers. Then, in a further effort to raise money for his creditors, the victor of Appomattox undertook the herculean task of writing his memoirs, completing them even while he was slowly dying of cancer. Fortunately, they brought enormous profits to the author. And Congress came to the rescue, four months before his death, by restoring Grant to the Army with the rank of General and retiring him on full pay.

My Grant and Buckner cartoon was printed on the back page of *Puck,* in the same issue with an appropriate poem by Bunner, which I illustrated. The *New York Times* commented:

. . . One of the simplest and most moving was a cartoon published in *Puck* by Eugene Zimmerman ("ZIM") just before Grant's death. It repre-

BASE BALL PARK. LEAGUE GAME TO DAY.

sented the feeble old General on his porch at Mount MacGregor, awaiting the approach of death. Buckner was coming up the walk, hat in hand, a look of respect and affection on his face, and Grant was feebly trying to rise from his chair and stretching out his hand to the man he had captured at Fort Donelson. Buckner had, in fact, called on Grant just before this cartoon was published. It was entitled "Another Lesson for the Bloody-Shirt Patriots."

Grant was the most persistently caricatured man of his generation. Shortly after his death, the General's widow assembled a collection of Grant cartoons which had appeared in various publications during a period of twenty years. Nast was General Grant's stalwart defender; all Nast's cartoons of him were friendly except one or two published at the time of the Garfield-Conkling fight, and those were in no way severe. One of them represented Conkling, after his resignation from the Senate, as having lost his head. Conkling was standing in pompous attitude, with his right hand thrust between the third and fourth buttons of his frock coat, à la Napoleon, while Grant stood on tiptoe with Conkling's head in his hands, trying in vain to put it back on the shoulders.

Most of the color cartoons in Mrs. Grant's collection were drawn by Keppler and were quite bitter. Keppler began his war on Grant in 1874 when he was cartoonist for *Frank Leslie's Illustrated Newspaper,* and kept at it after he founded *Puck.*

During Grant's trip around the world [1879], he published a cartoon wherein the population of Cork was shrieking defiance at the General, who, with an unmoved air, was pulling the cork out of the whiskey bottle. The significance lay in the title, "Grant's Consolation for Irish Insults—One Cork Always Open to Him."

The third-term propaganda in 1880 provided material for some of Keppler's keenest pictorial satire. During his second term, Grant had become very unpopular as a result of Government scandals at Washington. Wholesale frauds on public funds were committed and because some of the culprits were men closely associated with Grant, it was difficult for many to avoid the suspicion that the President himself was not guiltless. Thus, Keppler had plenty of ammunition of his broadsides.

Among the Keppler cartoons is "The Kind of Canal Business Grant is Going Into." It portrays the gentleman from Galena, Illinois, lazily direct-

ing the excavation of a ditch leading toward the White House and labeled "Third Term." Some of his political friends are easily recognized at work with shovels and picks, while in the dry ditch is a rowboat crowded with passengers placarded, "For His Uncles and His Cousins and His Chums," nepotism being one of the charges against Grant.

Another Keppler attack is captioned: "*Puck* Wants A Strong Man at the Head of the Government—but Not This Kind." General Grant is seen as a trapeze artist clinging to a "Third Term" as well as the "Whiskey Ring" and "Navy Ring." With his teeth he is supporting figures designated as Shepard, Robeson, Williams, Murphy, Belknap and Babcock, also heavy weights called "Nepotism," "Revenue Frauds," "Stock Speculations" and "Land Grabs."

At the Republican National Convention in Chicago, Grant's name led on thirty-six consecutive ballots, but Garfield was finally chosen. Keppler came out June 16, 1880, with a cartoon entitled "The Appomattox of the Third Termers—Unconditional Surrender!" in which Grant was represented as giving over to Garfield the third-term award marked "Imperialism."

At Grant's death, however, he published a masterful tribute to the great warrior, showing North and South weeping at his bier. Gillam, too, who had mercilessly caricatured Grant only a year before, published impressive pictures after his death, as did Frank Beard in *Judge,* and many others. (Frank, by the way, was one of four brothers connected with *Judge* at various times, the best known being Daniel Carter Beard, founder of the Boy Scouts of America.)

When General Grant lay in state in City Hall, a block from the *Puck* office, I was one of the multitude who gazed upon his calm features. The warrior who said, "Let us have peace," had himself entered the gates of peace everlasting. Twelve years later, as a press representative, I attended the dedication of the Grant tomb on Riverside Drive. It was a bleak day, April 27, 1897. The ceremony and parade lasted several hours. There was an air of gloom within that great purple-lighted mausoleum, just as there is today, which, added to the chilly weather at the time of dedication, was more than ordinarily depressing. The funeral cortege, moving up Broadway, was a magnificent tribute to a popular idol. At its head rode General Winfield

Scott Hancock, every inch a military man, on a black charger. Hancock received an ovation, against which he protested by raising a hand for silence.

Three other stirring and important events which I witnessed while on the staff of *Puck* were the opening of Brooklyn Bridge, dedication of the Bartholdi Statue of Liberty, and the blowing up of the Hell Gate rocks in the East River.

Brooklyn Bridge was open to traffic on May 24, 1883, which happened to be Queen Victoria's birthday. Nearly every shop in New York and Brooklyn declared a half-holiday; and a gala procession, headed by President Arthur, Governor Cleveland and Mayor Edson, wended its way across the world's latest wonder, as cannons roared their salute and a tremendous shout went up from the assembled populace. After that, the President, a future President and other dignitaries visited the bridgebuilder, Washington A. Roebling, who was then an invalid as a result of devotion to his work and had never seen, except through a telescope, the span whose construction he directed.

Two roommates of mine in Brooklyn were machinists at the Brady Manufacturing Company, where the wires were assembled for the Brooklyn Bridge cables, and through them I learned how the bridge had been constructed. This was the first time steel cables had been used on a job of such magnitude, and Roebling had to devise a new method of tying them together.

Frederic A. Bartholdi's Statue of Liberty, according to a news item in the *New York Tribune* of July 13, 1884, was originally destined for the Suez Canal under the title of "Progress," but, being refused by the Canal promoters, who sold as a job lot at reduced price to the French-American Union, which had it erected in New York Harbor as an inspiration for immigrants.

The cornerstone of the pedestal was laid August 5, 1884, in the presence of about 900 persons, after a big military parade headed by Bartholdi himself. The ceremonies had to be hurried on account of the rain.

At the time the huge figure of the goddess was placed in position, two years later, I was on the staff of *Judge,* which issued a special Bartholdi number embellished with a gold border in honor of the occasion. I prepared the frontispiece and

Gillam the center double-spread, while Grant E. Hamilton did the back-page cartoon. William J. Arkell, the publisher of *Judge,* was so delighted with the issue that he gave a banquet to the journalist fraternity in New York City.

I never viewed a more awe-inspiring spectacle than the destruction of Hell Gate in 1885, when dynamite was used to make the East River safe for navigation. One moment the air was filled, as from a great fountain, with water and flying debris; the next moment all was over. Whistles tooted, bells rang, and throughout the whole city was a deafening din of rejoicing.

Another memorable scene I witnessed was the return of survivors of the ill-fated George Washington De Long expedition, in 1882, combined with obsequies over the caskets of their comrades who perished in an ice jam off the Siberian coast. The expedition had been sent out for Arctic exploration by James Gordon Bennett, Jr., with the idea of providing news copy for the *New York Herald.* Seven or eight hearses were in line with a naval escort, and *Herald* star reporters covered the story magnificently.

The following year, when John Howard Payne's body was brought back from Tunis, I listened to Arbuckle's 22nd Regiment Band render his "Home, Sweet Home" from the steps of City Hall, and I am certain there was not a dry eye in the vast gathering, so touching was the occasion. Shortly afterward I witnessed the impressive funeral services for Peter Cooper, builder of the first locomotive in America, philanthropist, and one-time Presidential candidate.

In 1887, two years after I had left *Puck,* death called Henry Ward Beecher from the pastorate of the largest congregation in America. Gillam and I fell in line for a last view of his kindly face as the great minister lay in state at Plymouth Church, which was near my home and where I had often heard him preach. I realized what Mr. Beecher had done for Bernhard Gillam and I knew of at least one way in which my friend had shown his gratitude. Immediately after the 1884 Presidential election, Beecher was criticized harshly by Republicans of his congregation because he had opposed Blaine. Gillam saw a chance to repay in part the debt of gratitude he owed Beecher and at the same time to uphold *Puck*'s stand against the G.O.P. candidate. So he drew a cartoon entitled "Gulliver and the party Lilliputians—They Cannot Bind Him," which was published on a three-colored double-spread in *Puck* on January 7, 1885. It showed Beecher as a colossus towering above his puny critics, who bore placecards marked "Down With Him!" and "He Defeated Blaine" and who were slinging mud at the preacher and his Plymouth Church. I can easily believe Gillam took a great deal of personal satisfaction in creating that bit of pictorial satire.

Chapter 9

Eugene Zimmerman about 1885

At FIRST, *PUCK* WAS POLITICALLY IN-dependent but gradually listed toward leaving a gap for a Republican rival to slip in. James Albert Wales, cartoonist and former wood engraver, saw the opportunity and, with a surprisingly small amount of capital, launched *Judge* on October 29,

1881. By that time, *Harper's Weekly* had nearly spent its political force, and the nation's eye was focused on the newer *Puck* and *Judge*.

Then *Life* came into existence January 4, 1883, the same year I had joined *Puck*. [*Life* was founded by John Amos Mitchel as a picture weekly. Its biting satire was nonpartisan. There was no connection with *LIFE* founded in 1936.] At first, *Life* was a black-and-white publication, which, when compared with the less refined colored comic weeklies, did not show promise of the growth it has since attained. Nor did it cut much ice politically. *Puck* and *The Police Gazette* used to be the leading educational features of pool rooms and barber shops, and eventually lost ground with the rise of the safety razor, which allowed me to easily shave at home. *Life,* on the other hand, had played up to the elite, and the discriminating public came to recognize that whatever *Life* did was the proper course to pursue.

The illustrated journals of fifty years [the 1880s and 1890s] ago showed more individuality than those of today, for the reason that each maintained its own staff of artists who did not contribute to other publications. Besides, the readers in those days had fewer papers to choose from. They were not surfeited with movies and radio; hence they pounced upon the weekly offerings like a hawk pursuing a chicken.

Puck had been vicious in its attack on the Catholics and Jews. *Life* sidestepped religious prejudice, thus gaining the respect of all denominations, although its editor, J. A. Mitchell, with the aid of Charles Dana Gibson, F. G. Atwood, Frank P. ("Chip") Bellew, John Kendrick Bangs and a score of others who have since made journalistic history, led a campaign against the closed-Sunday policy of the Metropolitan Museum of Art. Keppler threw *Puck* into the fight also and helped to bring about the open-Sunday victory.

The "Tattooed Man" had increased *Puck's* circulation from 65,000 to 125,000 but it started internal discord in the *Puck* office which terminated disastrously for that paper.

Some years before the Blaine-Cleveland campaign, Keppler and Schwarzmann had made an agreement with Henry C. Bunner, editor, whereby he was to get $1,000 if the paper should ever exceed a stated circulation—which it did, on this occasion. Gillam, being largely responsible for that increase, felt he was entitled to a raise in salary from a $100 a week to $125. But his employers did not see it that way, so the creator of the "Tattooed Man" began looking around for new world to tattoo.

The American humor market was virtually cornered by *Puck* and *Judge;* if you didn't see it in either of those two periodicals, it wasn't funny. But *Judge* was a losing proposition of less that 14,000 circulation. It had entered the field of colored cartoons under the guidance of a former *Puck* cartoonist, James A. Wales, assisted by Grant E. Hamilton and two other artists of note, McCarthy and Ehrhart. (Wales' colored political cartoons appeared in *Puck's* earliest issues, and were clean cut and masterly. Wales had a technique which was deemed worthwhile imitating, and some of the artists of that day, in their work, clung closely to Wales' style. Wales, while on *Puck,* was the author of many powerful political cartoons. His handling of his subjects was always genteel and free from the bitterness that characterized the work of some cartoonists.) The combined efforts of these able men were of no avail against so powerful an antagonist as *Puck* appeared to be, and week by week the end seemed nearer.

Frank Beard had taken charge of *Judge* in its infancy, extricated it from a very deep mudhole with Grant Hamilton's help, and made the paper so attractive that Billy Arkell bought it in 1885, retaining Hamilton but not Beard. Indignant at losing his job, Frank declared, "I'll never resurrect another corpse," whereupon he went out and resurrected *The Ram's Horn.* [*The Ram's Horn* was almost dead until Frank Beard pushed it into fame with his cartoons, the first lithographs on religious and ethical subjects ever done in the style of political cartoons.]

(Dan Beard, sole survivor of the four brothers, all of them journalists, is widely known as an artist, author, naturalist, and founder of the American Boy Scout movement. It is not difficult to trace hereditary influences in the Beard family. The father, James, and his brother, William, were both successful painters, members of the National Academy, specializing in animal subjects. Dan was born in 1849. His art career began as a sign painter and map maker, but in 1878, he sold a few sketches of wild animals to *Scribner's Monthly* for $50, after which he took a permanent vacation from map making. He illustrated the original editions of

Mark Twain's *Tom Sawyer* and *Huckleberry Finn,* and numerous other books, besides contributing to so many magazines that he has lost count of them. He also wrote and illustrated numerous books. In recent years he has been running a summer camp for boys at Hawley, Pennsylvania. "Uncle Dan's" picturesque language is shown in this fragment of a letter I received from him, dated April 27, 1917:

I often think of the good old times in the Judge building, and of all the good fellows, including my three brothers, who were there and have since hit the trail over the Great Divide, where all pony tracks point one way. You did great work, and I still insist that you are by long odds the best in your line in this or any other country. I have one of your sketches hanging in my room along with one by Howard Pyle.

Kind regards, old comrade, and that the Great Mystery may put sunshine in your heart, is the sincere wish of

Your friend,
DAN BEARD

Nevertheless, I digress.) "Billy" Arkell was the son of the late State Senator James Arkell, of Canajoharie, New York. In youth, his face was burned terribly by a gasoline explosion; his life was de-

Billy Arkell

spaired of, but eventually "Billy" was saved by the grafting of literally hundreds of portions of cuticle, a complicated operation. Up to the time of his death he was living in retirement in California, after having promoted gigantic commercial and industrial enterprises which elevated a number of his fellow beings into the millionaire class.

Arkell in 1885 was well qualified to rejuvenate *The Judge,* as the magazine was named originally. Besides being proprietor of the Mt. McGregor Hotel and Railroad and part-owner of his father's paper-bag factory, he was publisher of the *Albany Journal.* (He had a flair for publicity and circulation-boosting. On one occasion he offered a prize of $100 to the new *Journal* subscriber who should guess nearest to the majority which the successful candidate would receive in the Blaine-Cleveland election. The winner turned out to be a clerk in the *Journal* counting-room. "This will never do," Arkell told him. "People will swear it's a put-up job, even though it isn't. I'll give you fifty dollars to withdraw your guess and let the prize go to your nearest competitor." The offer was accepted. By that expenditure, $150 altogether, the *Journal's* publisher had netted an increase of 18,703 subscribers.)

[To become editor of what was to be a rejuvenated *Judge,* Arkell selected I. M. (Ike) Gregory, editor of the *New York Daily Graphic,* a major American newspaper. Gregory had been city editor of the Elmira, New York, newspaper, and was able to combine his knowledge of art and photographic design with his ability to "sniff out" stories and dig beneath their surfaces. For art editor, Arkell wanted Bernhard Gillam. But Gillam was hesitant, so Arkell not only offered a salary of about $150 a week, one of the highest in journalism at the time, but also 20 percent of *Judge's* stock. Gillam still didn't jump to *Judge* until Adolph Schwarzmann, co-owner of *Puck,* refused him a raise; Gillam had correctly believed that he was a major reason for a substantial increase in *Puck's* circulation during the Cleveland-Blaine campaign a year before and believed that he should be rewarded.]

I was Gillam's only confidant in the *Puck* office,★ and we talked over prospects of such a move.

★Part of that friendship, undoubtedly, was because Gillam and ZIM were the only two Republicans on the Democratic *Puck.* In 1884, during their working hours, both had mercilessly satirized and caricatured James G. Blaine, Republican candidate for President against Grover Cleveland, but both probably voted for Blaine.

Bernhard put the matter up to me because he said he did not wish to go into it single-handed. I was then making $35 a week, which was rather good for a fellow of twenty-three in those days, particularly in view of the fact that the *Puck* artists were at liberty to do commercial drawing outside of office hours and my total earnings ranged between $40 and $90 a week. But in every concern will be found elements that stand in the way of somebody's progress. This was true in my case. There were more *Puck* artists than there was white space to fill in the paper, so that often one man would have to give 'way to make room for another's work. This was a serious obstacle to my artistic advancement, and I listened eagerly to Gillam's invitation.

Gillam promised me $80 salary, with other advantages over the old job, including unlimited freedom in selecting ideas, ample space in the *Judge* to play with, an occasional chance at the center double-spreads and an option on shares of stock in the publishing company, in addition to retaining the privilege of doing outside commercial work.

I sparred for time to consider his alluring inducements, hesitating because of *Judge's* uncertain future and my loyalty to *Puck.* [ZIM also was beginning to get better assignments.] Meanwhile, I sought out a venerable friend, Mr. Shaw, who was boss transferer in an adjoining lithographic shop.

"Mr. Shaw," I said, "I want advice and I don't

"Fo' de lan' sake, 'Rastus, I wish yo wouldn't chaw terbacker an' blow de flute at de same time."

know of a better man to come to than yourself. I have a tempting offer to leave *Puck* and go with *Judge*. I like the people and nearly everything else in my present position, yet I don't see much more than a clerk's wages for me on *Puck,* where even Gillam's fame can't bring him higher than a hundred dollars a week."

I told him the whole story, this man of seventy years, and here was his answer: "You are a young fellow and have many years before you reach my age. This may be your big opportunity. If you fail, what of it? You have at least made the effort and you can start again. But it's worth trying. Take it!"

"Now," he continued, "I'll tell you *my* story. When I was young I had a chance to better myself. I didn't grasp it because I was earning good wages and felt satisfied. That's why I'm still here, drudging at the same work, getting older every day and making less salary every year. *I missed my big opportunity—don't miss yours!*"

I thanked Mr. Shaw for those comforting words and decided to cast my lot with Gillam, who seemed closer than a brother to me. The three-year period covered by my contract had not quite expired, but that document was not binding on me because of an error in phraseology.

The hard task of breaking the news to our employers fell to me. It was decided that I tender my resignation first and Gillam would fire the concluding bomb into the *Puck* camp afterward as a compliment for his failure to receive just compensation.★ When I announced my intended departure from *Puck,* both Keppler and Schwarzmann tried to dissuade me. They put up very plausible arguments, and had it not been for the talk with my aged advisor, I surely would have weakened, for I held my employers in great esteem.

Gillam and I were regarded as ingrates for quitting the paper. One would have thought that two criminals were making their escape instead of law-abiding citizens tendering their resignations. No "good-bye" or "God bless you!" floated through the air. Nothing but failure was predicted for our venture, yet it was not many years thereafter that *Puck* began its decline and eventually gave up the ghost. Today [1930], it is an effort for the casual reader to recall that *Puck* ever existed, notwith-

★There are conflicting reports about who tendered the first resignation.

standing the fact that it was once the topmost comic paper in America.

Refusal to meet Gillam's demands eventually cost the publishers of *Puck* many thousands of dollars, for they employed several other artists to fill the gap and they were obliged to give the reader more for his money in the way of cuts in order to keep abreast of *Judge's* output. They took back Jim Wales and hired two new artists, S. S. Pughe and Louis Dalrymple, as well as two French cartoonists: DeGrimm, of the *Telegram,* and Giani, formerly of the *Daily Graphic.* The *New York Tribune* commented:

. . . both proved failures, and that has been the result of many other Frenchmen who bring their pencils to bear on American subjects. . . . French artists in this line are said to catch the ideas in every field except politics [July 11, 1886].

After leaving *Puck,* I went to Horseheads, New York, for the Christmas holidays, and Gillam's enthusiastic letters kept me informed on latest developments; at the same time he sent me material to illustrate for *Judge.*

[On December 18, 1885, Gillam wrote to Zimmerman:

Schwarzmann has engaged Wales again and at my request he comes to work on Monday. And I leave Saturday! Shake hands!! . . . Opper, at my instigation, made a kick to get a raise of $15. Would you believe it—he was getting only $70 a week? That is a fact. Now he is to get $80. Wales is to have $60 for 3 years. Bunner feels that you did not bid him good-bye—and Opper says he feels the same.

We have taken the whole floor underneath the present *Judge* office and are fitting it up for artists and editors. . . . Oh, by the way, don't advertise the going-to-be *Judge* owner's name, as Arkell wants to surprise the world with the announcement.

[On December 19, Gillam wrote:

I leave this morning from *Puck.* Schwarzmann thinks we shall both come back. I told him "NEVER!" It was money or nothing—and we were going in for money. Mr. Becker of *Leslie's* thinks *Judge* is a sure success. I'm certain of it.

[Gillam's leter of December 20 gives more insight into *Judge* and *Puck:*

I left yesterday! So that ends our connection with *Puck*. . . . I shall have to spend the greater part of next week in the *Judge* office and see how they work and who we shall have to get rid of. The place is in a terrible state. The foreman does not understand color, and when the artists asks for grey he gives them malory blue with a little black. And as they know no better, the paper has suffered. And, would you believe it, they have no yellow lake, no umber, no silk green, no olive—in fact, only the most primitive colors? We shall have to discharge the present foreman—that's settled. And besides, we must get another transferer, as Hamilton has shown me that he (the present man) has butchered their drawings. So you see, I shall have plenty to do.

I had the pleasure of being introduced to Wales on Friday. He is a great big stout man of 35 years—bloated and red-faced—and told me he weighed 225 pounds!

"Ah!" says he to me. "So time brings in its revenge. I went out of *Puck* onto *Judge,* and now come back to *Puck,* whilst you took my place, four and a half years ago, now take my place on *Judge*."

Opper hates him, and told me that he would never affiliate with Wales.

I had the honor of a private cable gram from James Gordon Bennett yesterday asking me to take DeGrimm's place on the *Telegram* at $10,000 a year! He said he had heard that I left *Puck*. I refused it, of course, but showed it to Schwarzmann before I left, to make him feel good.]

If my friend Bernhard had not been honorable, he could easily have double-crossed me by accepting the $10,000 offer. I believe, however, Gillam's salary and income from his shares in *Judge* eventually doubled that figure.

[On Christmas Eve, Gillam wrote:

. . . I had the pleasure of meeting several great and small politicians yesterday, and they all (with one exception) predict our success. We received $1400 of advertising for the new paper in one lump. And Arkell bet me a champagne supper and a suit of clothes that we, through taking up the Protection issue, should get $25,000 worth of advertising this year from Protectionists alone. I think that it is an excellent idea for *Judge* to be a Protectionist paper in opposition to Free Trade *Puck*.

We have had a great deal of free advertising all around; every paper in the city has given us a show except the *World,* and Pulitzer is too much a friend of Keppler's to give a notice to *Judge*. . . .*]

I feel sure that if *Puck* had paid Bernhard Gillam the salary he demanded, *Judge* would have been unknown today and *Puck* would still be sold on all the news-stands.

Chapter 10

[W]HILE ON *PUCK'S* STAFF, ZIM WAS IN competition with the nation's best cartoonists. It proved to be an excellent training ground, but also limited the amount of his work to be published, since there were only so many editorial columns a week to fill, and Keppler, Gillam, or one of the older cartoonists always got the covers, centerfolds, and back pages; ZIM got the black-and-white inside cartoons. He didn't fight for position and accepted his "lot in life" as a young man on a prestigious publication. In 1885, Friedrich Graetz left *Puck,* and ZIM was given the opportunity for his first published chromolithograph, an unsigned anti-Blaine cartoon that appeared in the May 11, 1885, issue. Color cartoons by ZIM appeared frequently the remainder of the year. Yet when the opportunity to go to *Judge* arose, he jumped at it, perhaps even eagerly sought it, believing that he could get "choice position"—and credit.

[*Judge* itself was undergoing a change, one that was eagerly looked at by the Republicans who would now have their own satiric voice, in opposition to the Democratic-leaning *Puck*.]

The Republican dailies, especially throughout the state, were generous in rooting for our success. More than fifty of them gave us pats on the back,

---

*It is difficult to believe that Keppler, whose comic weekly held Jews up to ridicule and who was accused of being anti-Semitic, and Pulitzer, a Jew, could form a bond of friendship.

such as this from the *Elmira Advertiser:*

The first member of the *Judge* under its new management is the finest paper of its kind ever issued in this country. It is a surprise even to those who knew the ability and skill of the men who compass the staff. The paper is new in every respect, even to the type and white paper, and at once takes a most prominent place in the illustrated journals of the world [January 14, 1886].

Said the *Rochester Democrat* and *Chronicle:*

The first issue of *Judge* under the new management exhibits a great improvement in every way . . . There is also an excellent specimen of the handiwork of Mr. Zimmerman, formerly from *Puck,* on the first page. It represents "Clothier Kelleefland" (Grover Cleveland) trying to fit civil service reform to the back of the Democratic party. Although the garment is several sizes too large, he exclaims: "Blesh mine soul! It fits you shoust like the baper on der vall." In the background, looking through an open door, stands "Mother" Beecher, holding little Carl Schurz in her arms. The effect of the cartoon is irresistibly funny . . .

At first, *Judge* was located on the first floor of the Potter Building on Park Row at Beekman Street. All the newspapers of account were on the Row, most of them in tumble-down structures. The *Tribune* Building with its tower was about the only imposing bit of lofty architecture in view. We would gaze with awe at the tremendous height of Trinity spire and wonder how the builders ever got the material up to such an altitude. Today, the Trinity spire is less conspicuous on Broadway than a push-cart vendor.

With *Judge,* I had absolute freedom to do as I wished and draw what I pleased. Mr. Arkell gave himself no special concern over our department, so I had a clear road ahead and no traffic cop to hold me up. It was the opinion of the *Puck* people that no paper but *Puck* could exist long. They predicted our early return to the fold, but with us it was a case of "make-or-break"; it was not our intention to return. Our aim was not to injure *Puck,* but to cover a field which that paper ignored. The Republicans needed an organ and, as that field of opposite faith appeared large enough to support such a paper, we were taking no big risk.

Naturally, we ate into *Puck's* circulation. For several years we worked like dogs, nights and Sundays included, and it was largely due to that determination and brotherly spirit between the *Judge* artists that *Judge* succeeded. We treated every contributor with due consideration and put him at ease in our presence. This welcome made the *Judge* art department a desirable place to visit, while the quick and just methods Gillam employed in dealing with newcomers and in passing upon their work had a wholesome effect.

In 1886, the year after I left *Puck,* Keppler and Schwarzmann bought land near Houston and Mulberry streets upon which to erect an imposing new *Puck* building. It seemed to me that the site hardly fitted the exalted spirit of the paper. That neighborhood has always had an unsavory reputation. Harry Hill's sporting place was nearby, and a jail gave Mulberry Street a creepy feeling. Nevertheless the new building was erected for *Puck* and eventually proved its tomb. [The magazine suffered after 1910 and died a lingering death between 1918 and 1921. Keppler had died in 1892 while on assignment at the Chicago World's Fair.]

"City and Country"

MR. JOHNSON (of New York)—"See here, yo' kintry niggah, doan' yo' gib me nun ob yo' sass or Ise'll kearve yo' wid dis yer razzer! See?"

COUNTRY DARKEY—"Whad's dat yo' say, niggah! Whad yo' say?"

My first two years on *Judge* were filled with anxiety, modified by bursts of exuberance. Fear that the venture would fail brought many sleepless nights to members of the staff.★ We toiled like beavers, with only an occasional Sunday off for rest and recreation. It was a constant uphill struggle to put out a weekly that would elicit favorable comment on the streets and at clubs, in opposition to *Puck, Harper's* and *Frank Leslie's Weekly,* all of which had been firmly entrenched for years, and *Life,* which had begun to develop into a strong competitor.

★There are conflicting reports about ZIM's status on *Judge.* Billy Arkell was accused of wanting to fire ZIM, frustrated at his "fondness of leisure." Arkell is reported to have noted that ZIM "never wanted to work when he had a few dollars ahead." However, Arkell is reported to have also said that he regarded ZIM as a "comic genius" and didn't consider firing him, but was questioned by Gillam, who had. Another report indicates that it was, perhaps, Gillam who thought of firing ZIM, for it is now known that Gillam did not appreciate ZIM's grotesque distortion of Blacks, Jews, and the Irish, and dumped many cartoons presented to him. One version states that Arkell strongly urged Gillam to run ZIM's work; another version says that Arkell didn't care one way or the other. Undoubtedly, during an intense campaign to raise circulation and dominate the market, numerous personalities came into conflict, and many ideas, suggestions, and possibilities were thrown in for discussion, some to be acted upon, some to "test the waters," others just from frustration.

"Superfluous"

JOHNSON—"Whad yer got in yer bundle, George?"
GEORGE—"Underclothes.
JOHNSON—"Why yo buy dem? Noboddy kin see um."

Our weekly editions were based upon reports from the news company which handled distribution. Before going to press, proofs of all cartoons were submitted to the news agency, and by these sample sheets the demand could be roughly estimated in advance of publication.

It was a gamble, of course, and many weeks the returns were discouraging. Nevertheless, there are tricks in all trades, including journalism. What appeared to be a dead loss in the way of unsold copies was really a benefit, for they were afterward bound into volumes and disposed of at good profit as premiums in getting new subscribers. [Within two years, *Judge*'s circulation increased from 14,000 to 65,000, putting it on a solid financial base. But the strain upon the staff was severe.]★

During those days when we were bending every effort toward success, my father became seriously ill and died in a hospital at the age of fifty-seven. Those were the most discouraging days I have ever known. More than once I felt an urge to resign, but I could not desert Gillam, and although I was a physical wreck, I stuck to the ship until it reached safe harbor.

By that time, the nervous strain had undermined my health, so I was compelled to relinquish my shares of stock in the Judge Company and go to Florida to recuperate. There, in the land of razorback hogs and orange groves, "Mrs. ZIM" and I luxuriated in balmy sunshine while New York was being lashed by the severest blizzard of its history.† I learned later that the East River had been frozen solid, thus forming a natural bridge which thousands of pedestrians—one of them being Al Smith—used in traveling between Manhattan and Brooklyn.

(I have always admired Mr. Smith. We were both born of humble parentage and we both sold fish for a livelihood. Not long ago he sent me an autographed portrait and a letter recalling the cartoons I drew for *Puck* and *Judge,* adding:

When I was a boy, these publications were to be

found in every barber shop, and I remember looking over them with a great deal of pleasure.)

While in Florida I was not on salary but turned out piece-work entirely. My income varied from $25 to $100 a week. Lacking prophetic insight, I passed up a perfectly good chance to become a millionaire. The yellow-fever lands through which I slashed in 1888, shooting snakes and alligators, have since been given fancy names and sold at so much per square inch. Florida today is a playground of the moneyed folk, a winter paradise for

WIFE—*"You haven't been inside a church since we were married—there!"*
   HUSBAND—*"No, a burnt child dreads the fire."*

★Although ZIM occasionally contributed several back-page color cartoons and a few cover and centerfolds, almost all the *Judge* lithographic art was originated by Bernhard Gillam, Grant Hamilton, and F. Victor Gillam (who signed his works F. Victor at first, then later Victor). ZIM contributed black-and-white line drawings, a large proportion of them depicting Blacks, who were involved with preachin', chickens, and watermelons; and Jews, who were trying to get a customer's last dollar.

†It is quite revealing that in an era when any mental problem was spoken of only in hushed whispers, and never "among company," that ZIM, both in the mid-1880s when he went to Florida and in the periods of 1910 and 1920, freely wrote of his trip, and told the world that he had had a nervous collapse, caused by overwork and tension. Another revealing aspect of ZIM is what he chose *not* tell in his autobiographical essays. On September 29, 1886, he married Mabel Alice Beard, daughter of Alvah Peter Beard, a master carpenter from Horseheads. Two years later he and his wife became parents of a daughter named Laura. He occasionally mentions his adopted nephew, Adolph Zimmerman, son of his older brother. ZIM and his wife adopted young Adolph, a six-year-old orphan, in 1889. The only reference he makes to his wife in any of his writings is when he discusses his trip to Florida. He occasionally mentions Adolph, but not Laura. There is no evidence that he ever wrote about his wife or daughter, or that he ever caricatured either in his cartoons, or even painted their portraits. ZIM loved his daughter and adopted son but, according to many who knew him or knew of him, was not happy in his marriage.

the plutocrat who owns many homes but enjoys none of them. Forty years ago all the swampy real estate within my vision could have been purchased at twenty-five cents an acre.

In one of these swamps, called the Little Hillsbarougho River, I was kicked backward six feet by an overcharge of powder in my gun. Those who saw me two-thirds submerged in mud and slime declared it was a funny sight, but I could not appreciate humor at that precise moment. While camping on the Gulf Shore I helped fetch in a stump to place on the fire. As the stump warmed up, a snake of ample size crawled out, causing our party to scatter hastily.

(A similar experience occurred some years later. I was camping near Big Flats, New York, hunting woodcock on a jungle island, when I encountered two rattlesnakes. The first one I shot dead. Then,

Adolph Zimmerman (ZIM's nephew) about 1901

Mr. and Mrs. Alvah Beard (Mabel Zimmerman's parents)

with an unearthly howl, I jumped clear of the second and kept on running until I reached the Chemung River.

A snake escaped from a reptile show on the Atlantic City boardwalk near Hotel Berkeley while I was a guest there. The locality was thrown into a panic and everybody seemed to be looking for the serpent. This prompted me to organize a snake hunt of my own. Purchasing a realistic *papier-mâché* snake from a Japanese curio shop, I flung it into a flower bed outside the hotel and intimated to a waiter that I had seen an escaped reptile. This rumor spread like an electric flash. Out came cooks and scullery maids with carving knives and rolling pins, while heads of guests protruded from windows above, but as soon as the excitement reached that point I discreetly vanished.)

For five long months my wife and I had remained in Florida, gazing upon an unbroken skyline of pines, pursuing fleas to and fro in and out of our boudoir, and keeping the too friendly woodtick from forcing its attentions upon us. Finally, the sun grew so hot that we went back to Northern civilization.

Laura and Adolph Zimmerman, mid-1890s

"The Nearest Thing Yet to Perpetual Motion"

Mabel Zimmerman, late 1880s (?)

Shortly after "Billy" Arkell took over *Judge,* Joseph Drexel, the millionaire banker, became interested in the paper and had part of its staff at his home for a formal dinner. The Drexel mansion and its gallery of rare art treasures were widely known, but not everyone was privileged to look upon them. It was the first time—also the last—that I had the privilege of sipping my coffee from a solid gold spoon of exquisite pattern. The feast was munificent, of course, but for real comfort I prefer a cold pancake and thin "silverware" on the bank of a creek where suckers are running on a lazy summer afternoon. At the table I sat with Mr. and Mrs. Drexel, W. J. Arkell, John A. Sleicher, Bernhard Gillam and Grant E. Hamilton.

The story is told about Billy Arkell that he approached a fellow publisher for a loan of $4,000 with which to meet his payroll. The latter advised him to "Think up a good excuse and go to a rich bank—but ask for $40,000."

Arkell had a modest personal checking account in an institution of which his father, State Senator James Arkell, had been a stockholder, so he went there and boldly asked for $400,000, according to this story, suddenly determining to consolidate *Judge* with *Leslie's Weekly.* It so happened that Mrs. Frank Leslie's *Popular Monthly* and her *Weekly* were published in the Judge building (which did not, however, belong to *Judge*) at Sixteenth Street and Fifth Avenue. At any rate, he got the $400,000.

Thus the Leslie-Judge consolidation is supposed to have come into being. I cannot vouch for the authenticity of that legend, but I did learn, on more reliable authority, that Leslie's widow received $200,000 out of that deal and invented it so wisely that she left an estate of about $5 million when she died a quarter of a century later.

By no stretch of the term could Arkell have been called "publicity-shy." On one occasion [1900] he visited the annual New York Horse Show, advertising the Arkell publications, *Judge* and *Leslie's Weekly,* in company with Grant L. Hamilton and myself.

Hamilton and I strolled around innocently to see what was going on, while Arkell pointed us out to the reporters with these words: "There goes Hamilton, *Judge*'s great cartoonist! And I declare, if that isn't Zimmerman with him!"

"Say," continued the energetic exploiter (I quote his fulsome praises *verbatim* from a newspaper ver-

Eugene Zimmerman about 1901

sion of them), "that fellow ZIM is a wonderful fellow! Always wants to be hunting and fishing. Wouldn't work more than a day a week if *Judge* were to give him a million dollars a minute. He lives up in Horseheads, New York, and now he's at the horse show. Horse show, Horseheads. That's a joke!" and Mr. Arkell chuckled a little at his own pun.

"I tell you what it is," he went on. "I don't know which is the more wonderful man, ZIM or Hamilton. They're both stars in their own particular lines, and as long as *Judge* has such men so long will it continue to be America's greatest cartoon and comic weekly. Hamilton is from Ohio, you know. Wonderful man, Hamilton. Strong cartoons—telling cartoons—forcible cartoons, and I am not far out of the way in saying it was his cartoons and Victor Gillam's that elected McKinley, And McKinley knows it! Ah, *Judge* is a great paper—a great paper—and so is *Leslie's Weekly!*"

Before the days of the Klondike gold rush [1898] Arkell financed an expedition to that locality in the interest of *Leslie's Weekly.* It returned, like the spies

"Extremes Meet"
MR. WHITE—*"Don't give me none of your lip!"*
MR. BLACK—*"Don't give me none of your chin!"*

sent out by Moses to investigate the Promised Land, with tales of fabulous wealth. Arkell's explorers even brought cans of nuggets and other evidence to back up their report, but the publisher was skeptical and admitted privately that such statements were too fishy for belief. However, the expedition, which was to have cost about $7,000 but actually cost much more, supplied good reading matter for the *Weekly,* and a lake in the Klondike was named after its sponsor. "If you hadn't been a skeptic," Arkell bewailed later, "I could have acquired a large slice of the Klondike for almost nothing!"

The $400,000 loan had proven to be a millstone around the Leslie-Judge neck; the publishers could not pay, so their bank sold the company [in 1901] to the Standard Oil Company, which is said to have secretly used *Leslie's Weekly* as a propaganda organ by means of an editorial page clip sheet mailed to newspapers all over the country.

The Leslie monthly was discontinued immediately by the combination which Arkell formed, and *Leslie's Weekly* was dropped [in 1932] by the present owners of the Leslie-Judge Company.

Even after he had sold his publishing business there were several times when Billy Arkell came

within an ace of making millions.

In those days, Billy lived on West 37th Street, maintained a large racing stable and backed his own horses heavily. He was reputed to have won a bet of $150,000 on a race, having staked his publishing business against the other man's money. In 1903, Arkell retired from racing at the request of directors of the United States Light & Heating Company, of which he had been elected president.

At one stage of his career [about 1905], Arkell tried to buy the old *New York Sun* from the W. M. Laffan estate, and hoped to obtain the services of former President Roosevelt as its editor. Arkell was told that executors of the estate had refused $3,500,000 and the negotiations ended. In the meantime he had carried on an extensive cable correspondence with Roosevelt, then in Africa on a hunting trip, in the interest of having the former President head the paper if the negotiations to purchase it were successful.

He was head of the G. Washington Coffee Company and an early promoter of the American Chicle Company, the American Locomotive Company, and other commercial or industrial enterprises. He also served as an officer of the Diesel Engine Company and of the American palace Car Company (organized to run sleeping cars on European railroads), and was a member of a syndicate which proposed to buy the New Orleans race track as well as the Union Jockey Club's track in St. Louis. In addition to all these ventures, he had extensive mining interests in Montana and Nevada, besides handling a real estate business in California, to which he moved in 1920 for his health.

When I last heard from him, the versatile promoter had become totally blind and was awaiting the final curtain. He died in Los Angeles on December 30, 1930, leaving his brother, three sisters, a son and a daughter. They brought him back to Canajoharie for burial, and William J. Arkell is sleeping out eternity there in the little town that had given him birth seventy-four years before—in the same cemetery with his gifted brother-in-law, Bernhard Gillam.

Thus the seven who had eaten from the golden spoons at the Drexel mansion dwindled to one since I began writing this book. I happen to be that one.

There were three Gillam brothers, all on the *Judge* staff at one time or another. Bernhard was the

"An Aid to Truthfulness"

JESSUP (GEORGIA) CITIZEN—"*You can get the story from an intelligent negro's own lips, sir. Caspar, is your race oppressed in this state?*"

CASPAR (promptly)—"*Nossir; we's comf'able as chipmunks, sah!*"

oldest. He was succeeded by Fred Victor, who had been employed as a portrait artist on the *Albany Journal* and who stepped into the harness with a technique similar to Bernhard's and continued to draw Gillam cartoons for *Judge*. Fred Victor died a few years later, after severing connections with *Judge*. The youngest brother, Charlie, worked for a while as Bernhard's office boy. He had a soft snap but never seemed satisfied. One day he resigned suddenly, giving various colleagues a piece of his mind. Afterward, Bernhard wrote me a rather touching letter expressing the hope that Charlie would "recover his senses and come back." I don't know what finally happened to Charlie Gillam.

Bernhard Gillam was thirty-two when he married Billy's older sister, Bartelle, and only thirty-nine when he succumbed to typhoid and brain fever at Canajoharie, January 19, 1896. His last cartoon was a sly dig at ex-President Harrison, whom it showed sitting on a sled atop a hill leading to the White House, with the inscriptions, "Please Push Me." Nevertheless, Mr. Harrison wired to his widow:

I am greatly shocked at news of the death of Mr. Gillam. Please accept my sincere sympathy in your bereavement.

BENJAMIN HARRISON

A week after Bernhard's pencil had been stilled forever, Mr. Arkell conferred with the surviving artists of *Judge* and his statement to the newspapers was characteristic of his flair for publicity:

You can say that the policy of Mr. Gillam in regard to *Judge* will be followed as nearly as possible and that the artists of his own selection will carry on the work. His cartoon assistants, who have been scattered, will be brought to the home office—Grant E. Hamilton, from Youngstown, O., Eugene Zimmerman, from Horseheads, N.Y., and Fred Victor Gillam, from Springfield, L.I.

It might be interesting to know that Gillam received a salary of $25,000 per year and a percentage of the profits from the paper. I have decided to divide this equally among the staff artists who have been with the paper ten years.

The loss of Bernhard Gillam affected me in three ways. It caused deep personal sorrow, it drew me closer to Grant Hamilton, and it obliged me to make more frequent trips to the metropolis, in accordance with Arkell's announcement, so that I spent two weeks out of each month at the *Judge* office while still doing considerable work at home in Horseheads.

[After Gillam's death, Grant Hamilton became *Judge's* art editor. He was a friend of President William McKinley; his most popular cartoon, "The Full Dinner Pail," gave McKinley a slogan for the reelection campaign in 1900. "One day," according to ZIM, Hamilton "suggested that we jump a train and drop in on McKinley," whom Hamilton had visited many times in the White House between 1896 and 1900. ZIM, however, wasn't ready to "drop in" on a President.]

"Nicht moglich!" said I. "If the President wants to see me, he'll probably send word, then I will go."

But apparently Mr. McKinley's mind was taken up with other matters, for no word was forthcoming. Then he was assassinated and Theodore Roosevelt took the reins. "Teddy" was the most caricatured man in the world's history—and relished it immensely. His teeth, glasses, mustache and "big stick" formed an irresistable temptation

Bernhard Gillam, left, *and Grant E. Hamilton,*
1889

to the cartoon fraternity. Since his death, Roosevelt's birthplace at 28 East 20th Street has been turned into a memorial museum, the most conspicuous feature of which is a permanent exhibition of the original drawings of cartoons featuring T. R. at all stages of his strenuous career. Nast, Keppler, Gillam, Hamilton—in fact, most of the artists mentioned in these pages, including myself—are represented in that collection. A friend of mine, Assemblyman Jones Van Duger, once showed me a letter which Roosevelt had written him before becoming governor, in which Teddy declared he was going out of politics; however, fate willed otherwise.

Hamilton believed it was a serious mistake for *Judge* to remain in the political field after the close of the Nineteenth Century and, with the connivence of its editor, J. A. Waldron, he persuaded Sleicher, the owner, to make *Judge* an all-humorous weekly.

Like most of the artists on *Puck* and *Judge* in their early days, Hamilton was a Brooklynite. His home was on Quincy Street; the Gillam brothers resided on Dean Street; Opper, on Kingston Street; and I lived on Herkimer Street before moving to Horseheads; Schwarzmann, Keppler's partner, picked St. Mark's Avenue.

Hamilton and I frequently ate at Luchow's on East Fourteenth Street, Manhattan, and on our way there from the *Judge* office we would pass the rank and file of stage folks sunning themselves in various pompous attitudes. High and low comedians in and out of jobs, wearing checked suits, spats and plug hats—a tempting assortment for the caricaturist's pencil. We felt flattered when they mistook us for a vaudeville team.

When the instantaneous camera [about 1888] was invented, the Judge Company bought one as an experiment, or perhaps took it in exchange for advertising. It was in the form of a stiff false vest front, covered with suiting, at the time fancy vests were in vogue. The camera was a flat nickel-plated circular affair with a revolving plate capable of holding eight pictures and which operated automatically when the shutter closed. The small lens peeped through a button-hole and was neatly disguised as a button. It was intended as a detective camera. You could approach a person and, with one hand in your trousers pocket, pull a string which led into the pocket, operating the shutter.

Hamilton and I were slumming for character studies one day and experimenting with the new little plaything. The first human to strike our fancy was an aged woman scavenger whose upper part

"A Little Rough"

MR. DROOLS (to himself)—*"Ah wondah ef dat southern gent ordered watahmilyun an' br'iled chicken jes' ter tantalize dis poor cullud waitah?"*

was buried in a barrel of rubbish, with the rear elevation conspicuously aimed at us. After taking a couple of preliminary shots, we desired a study of the face as well, so Hamilton told me to get ready, and let out a tremendous yell. The woman jumped clear of the barrel. I pulled the string, got her face and quickly left her neighborhood, followed by a whole paragraph of the most exquisite profanity that ever warbled from the throat of a filthy bird.

In his capacity as art editor of *Judge,* Hamilton once sent a telegram to Horseheads asking me to come to New York at once and "bring along all the black and whites you can scrape together." Ham meant black-and-white drawings, of course, but the local telegraph operator interpreted it otherwise and spread the rumor that I was getting up an excursion for the poor blacks and whites of the town, whereupon the station agent quoted me special rates on parties of from twenty-five to solid vestibule loads. I hope that with the adoption of Esperanto or Volapuk or some other universal language, [language will become simplified].

Hamilton was really funnier by nature than his drawings indicated. His humor was serious rather than flippant, but as a cartoonist, Hamilton was of the first water and a mighty fine fellow to tie to, else I would not have stuck to him in business for more than a quarter of a century. His letters to me were friendly and encouraging and full of good ideas. For instance:

Feb. 4, 1897

Zimmerman, Dear Boy:

Mr. William Chase, the great painter, was in here yesterday and said that he considered you the one and only comic artist in the world and that for good drawing you were the best, that every figure you draw seemed to have bones in it, etc., etc. He also said that E. A. Abbey, the artist, had nearly all of your stuff pasted in a book and that Abbey considered you in a class all by yourself and far in advance of any one on either side of the Atlantic.

As you know, Mr. Chase has the largest and most stylist art school in this country and his receptions to the public are very largely attended. Now, what he wanted to do is to give an exhibition of your work. That is, he wants to borrow 30 or 40 of your originals for that purpose. He will return them to us. I think it would be a great ad for you, and if he should sell any of them I would see that you get the dust. . . .

I remain Your Old Pal,
GRANT HAMILTON

I remember the time Hamilton and I were confidentially informed by Harriet Quimby—the first aviatrix to fly across the English Channel—that, in view of her connection with *Leslie's Weekly* as a staff writer, she was going to take us up in the air at Hempstead, Long Island, in the near future. I assured the lady that Mr. Hamilton would be unaccompanied by me on that delightful occasion. Subsequently her plane nose-dived into Boston Bay, killing both Miss Quimby and the president of the Boston Aero Club. That night the *Judge* staff were enjoying a fancy dress banquet in a New York hotel when the ghastly news was brought to Mr. Sleicher and fell on the merrymakers like a wet blanket, for the aviatrix had been a popular figure at our office.

Hamilton was chief of the Government's art bureau during the World War [1917–18] and later when he undertook to produce comic films at Hollywood, he put his entire fortune into it and failed. He died in Los Angeles, April 17, 1926, at the age of about sixty-four—"without a dollar," I was told by a close friend. My first inkling of his death came in the form of a request from Freeman H. Hubbard, editor of *Cartoons Magazine,* to write an obituary for that publication. The case is too sad to dwell upon. I have letters he wrote me that held out promises of fabulous riches in the movie field, each letter a little less enthusiastic as he saw his life's savings vanishing.

Chapter 11

IN A MOMENT OF ANGER, W. J. ARKELL resigned the presidency of the Judge Company and the job was taken over by Austin Fletcher, a wealthy lawyer, who was unpopular with the art staff. [Arkell may have been forced out in bankruptcy proceedings of 1901.] Hamilton quit as art director and joined Arkell in starting a new magazine, *Just Fun;* I was about to do likewise when *Just Fun* foundered on the rocks. Later, Fletcher was forced out by John A. Sleicher, editor of *Leslie's*

"Accommodating, Very"
PROFESSOR J—"Before the performance begins, will one of you gents be so kind as to hold this—

—chick-e-n!"

"Croquet Rules"

HE—"Yo' mus' hit me befo' yo' kin git anudder go,
Miss Linda."
MISS LINDA—"All right!"

Weekly, who assumed the presidency and brought Hamilton back again.

Sleicher's purchase of a majority of stock put the company's affairs under one-man control for the first time in ten years. But the company was losing money, and in 1909, Sleicher's management had to be financed by the Standard Oil Company of New Jersey, acting in the name of the City Real Estate Trust Company which took over the indebtedness of the publishing house and reorganized it as the Leslie-Judge Company. On behalf of the Sleicher management, there was floated a bond issue of $700,000, most of which was acquired by the printer, William Green. Standard Oil expected Sleicher to repay them by buying back the bonds with money from the Leslie-Judge earnings, but Sleicher's untimely death obliged the oil company to liquidate the bonds as best it could. Standard Oil withdrew its financial support, Leslie-Judge was thrown into bankruptcy in 1921, and Green was left holding the sack.

I had quit the *Judge* staff in 1912 for the life of a free-lance, so the failure nine years later cannot be laid to my door. I resigned because I did not have confidence in the Sleicher management and could not do my best work under those circumstances. In 1915, when Walt Mason, of Emporia, Kansas, was getting out a portrait, he wrote me confidentially:

Every time I open *Judge* and see the "illustrations" they disfigure my stuff with, I heave a sigh. Their artists are no doubt good draughtsmen, but they never had a humorous idea since they were born. A competent architect would do as well as an illustrator. How those *Judge* artists get away with it beats me. Two or three times I have felt like writing to Mr. Waldron and asking him why he doesn't fire the dreary bunch and try to capture a real comic artist, but I realize it's dangerous business betting in that way.

The letter refers to James A. Waldron, editor of *Judge* from 1912 to 1918, who died June 3, 1931. After Waldron retired, the Leslie-Judge Company coasted down hill with frightful momentum. In 1919, it lost $150,000 and in 1920, $300,000. In 1921 it was pushed to the wall. Liabilities were set forth as $2,210,000, with assets of $420,000, including *Judge, Leslie's Weekly, Film Fun,* and various books which were being sold on the installment plan. The collapse was attributed to the mounting cost of paper and Sleicher's failing health, together with office extravagance.

Eventually, stockholders came to the rescue, the concern was again put on a paying basis, and *Leslie's Weekly* was discontinued, although its circulation a few years before had been three times that of *Judge*.

Conducting an illustrated paper is like running a boarding house; all the scraps of the week go into a delicious hash which is enjoyed by everybody.

Sleicher, however, wasn't satisfied. He was forever asking his friends for opinions and criticisms, and was too easily swayed by them. One week he would tell me, "Your sketches lack the former humor. What we need is the kind of fun that will make readers laugh their buttons off. That's the suggestion I received from a group of newspaper men I met at dinner last night." Maybe a week later we'd be told that someone at a gathering of ministers or toxicologists or organ pumpers had objected to ludicrous sketches, and we had better lay off that type of art for a while. Sometimes Sleicher would say, "I asked the Reverend So-and-So what he thought of our pictures, and he condemned this and that."

In short, Sleicher turned down many good ideas for fear of offending personal friends or acquaintances; the advertising department hampered us still further. Any subject which displeased that august body was thrown out bodily, so it behooved us to hold ante-mortems over ideas and get the jury's verdict before proceeding with a sketch.★

Nothing like that happened under Billy Arkell's control; the art staff was allowed to decide what was best for the paper, and invariably got better results. And today [1930], if Sleicher were living, he would be aghast at the modern *Judge*'s frankness in handling religion, liquor, sex, and other controversial subjects. A lot of my drawings which were shelved twenty years ago because of business office objections would look tame enough now beside the pictures of bootleggers and "flaming youth" in the latest issues of *Judge*. Business department taboos are not always reliable. The safest rule is to

★It has been traditional in journalism for the editorial and advertising departments to remain aloof from each other. That *Judge,* a national magazine, would allow its advertising department to dictate "caveats" indicates a management that was afraid to take bold steps and possibly was in financial trouble.

give the public what it wants.

Mr. Sleicher should have canvassed barber shops and clubs—not the churches—to learn what was keeping his paper alive.

Chapter 12

ANSWERING THE QUESTION, "WHERE do you get your ideas?" W. A. Rogers says in his autobiography:

They might as well ask of a farmer, "Where did you get all that corn?" The farmer could tell you that he planted it and broke his back hoeing it; otherwise the crop would fail. The cartoonist plants his garden with carefully selected facts. No matter how dry these little seeds may seem, he knows that with proper cultivation they will produce a crop later on. There lies the whole secret of a cartoonist's bag of tricks laid bare.

Thousands of such "seeds" I have planted in leisure moments while off duty and have been rewarded in time by seeing them sprout, almost unexpectedly, on the soil of white bristol-board. Naturally, when a man takes an interest in his vocation, his mind becomes trained to discover in everyday life the seeds of ideas that can be utilized. For instance, as a youth I used to attend the horse-swapper's convention, because I was sure to find there abundant material for studies in vagabond horseflesh—studies which eventually appeared in the pages of *Judge*. The horse-swappers' convention, I may add, is now *passé*, even as a rural institution, and its successor, the modern horse market, has about as much "kick" as near-beer.

Once, while Bernhard Gillam, head of the *Judge* art department, and I were struggling for a back-page subject, a rap came at the door and a middle-aged lady entered with samples of her son's skill. My desk occupied a position from which I could scrutinize Gillam's features as he assured the persistant fond mother that her offspring was as good an artist as anyone in his employ—yet I read his mind differently. Innate sense of courtesy forbade putting his real thoughts into execution, much as

"The Professional Difference"

The barber.   *The tonsorial artist.*

he wished that lady elsewhere. At any rate, I was no longer in need of a subject. That interview supplied a back page and the work was underway even before the visitor left the office.

Another incident: Entering a barber shop, I noted a doleful expression on the proprietor's face.

"What's up?" I inquired cheerfully.

In reply, the barber pointed to a row of coat hooks along the wall. "Does that look like a lot of business?"

Thereupon, after divesting myself of clothing for a tonsorial operation, I observed that even the few garments I had distributed about the chairs and hooks gave the place a more prosperous appearance. That situation, with a slight change and added absurdity, shortly afterwards became a comic for *Judge*. Thus, a barber's lugubriousness stimulated my creative faculties.

The Jewish clothing industry of the 'eighties and 'nineties could always be counted upon to yield material for comic art. Whenever the fountain of inspiration ran dry, one had merely to stroll through the Ghetto and make true-to-life sketches of its long-bearded shopkeepers, which readers in the hinterland would regard as screamingly funny caricatures.

I remember being sadly in need of an overcoat, in the days when I knew very little of Manhattan

life. A cousin, Paul Stucker, now of the Bureau of Engraving and Printing at Washington, was living in New York then, and he said, "Come with me. I'll help you pick out a coat and save you money."

We walked down the Bowery toward Baxter Street early on a Monday morning. My cousin, knowing the tricks of the clothing trade, was aware that no Jew would voluntarily permit the week's first customer to leave his shop without buying anything—it was extremely bad luck. So I selected a coat which suited me and asked the price.

"Fifteen dollars," was the response.

"I'll give you just four-fifty for that coat," Paul bargained.

The Jew nearly passed out from shock, but reduced his price to ten.

My companion shook his head. "Four-fifty is all I've got and that's all I'm going to pay."

"Now, see here," wailed the merchant, "you don't vant to ruin me, do you?"

"No, I want to help you to sell that coat, but four-fifty is all I can give for it."

"Ach, my dear friend, maig is eighd tollars! Dat's de leasd I'll take for him."

"Four-fifty!" my cousin persisted, laying that sum temptingly on the counter.

The owner of the disputed garment almost wept with chagrin, for we had him cornered. To lose the

"Too Valuable to Cage Up"

POLICE JUSTICE—*"What's your name?"*
PRISONER—*"Jones, your honor."*
POLICE JUSTICE—*"What's your first name?"*
PRISONER—*"John."*
POLICE JUSTICE—*"You are discharged. Officer, take him down to Newspaper row. A man that can lie like that ought not be allowed away from a newspaper office."*

"Obviously"

SAMBO—*"Look heah! I doan' want none ob your lip."*

week's first sale would be a calamity, yet the sacrifice seemed too great to bear. Paul returned the money to his pocket and we were bidding the dealer good-bye when he yelled:

"Holt on! Take it for four-fifty und get oud off mine blace."

It was really a good coat and served me for two years, after which I unloaded it at a profit of several dollars.

Such incidents supplied many of my ideas for *Puck* and *Judge*. The most widely quoted witticism of mine was embodied originally in one of the first comics I drew for *Judge*. I pictured an excited pawnbroker running out of his shop and grabbing the arm of a policeman whose revolver was aimed at a fugitive thief. The pawnbroker was saying, "Shoot him in der pants. Der coat und vest are

"Making the Church Attractive"

VISITOR TO THE GABESVILLE CHURCH—*"I thought they usually had an eagle on the lectern."*
REV. MR. RIVERMOUTH—*"Dey does sometimes, sah; but I done thunk dat yer would 'peal mo' t' mah congergasion, so I had 'm made t' ordah."*

"Not up to Snuff"

mine." This expression attained vogue on the vaudeville stage and among professional story-tellers. William Jennings Bryan used it in a speech to illustrate his point that each man wanted protection for himself but free trade for the other fellow.

Forty or fifty years ago the comic papers took considerably more liberty in caricaturing the various races than they do today. Jews, Negroes, and Irish came in for more than their share of lambasting, because their facial characteristics were particularly vulnerable to caricature. Although most Hebrews enjoy jokes on themselves, the strictly orthodox do not take kindly to that form of humor. One time a Semitic society threatened to boycott *Judge;* and as our purpose was not to offend, and as the vital part of a funny paper is its circulation, we quickly put on the brakes—just as Henry Ford recently did with his *Dearborn Independent.*★

★A large portion of the American Jewish community organized an effective boycott of Ford automobiles because of Henry Ford's anti-Semitic policies. The pain and fury caused within the Jewish community was so deep that even in the 1980s some Jews refuse to buy Ford products because of Henry Ford's statements.

JOBE (professional shark)—*"I calls yo'! What yo' got?"*
PROM (novice)—*"I'se got foh aces."*
JOBE—*"Dat ain't no good, niggah. I'se got five sixes."*
PROM—*"No use mah playin' pokah. I allus git a good han' beat."*

On another occasion, a Negro preacher took exception to my darky cartoons; he wrote a very "sassy" letter to the effect that it was not only colored gentlemen who stole chickens, and cited numerous instances to prove it, so I had to let up a bit on the Ethiopians. Several issues of *Judge* were barred from Russia because we poked fun at the Czar, but our Russian circulation was almost nil and the publicity was not at all harmful.

Some years age, Horseheads had a colored barber, Charles Brown, whose head and face were adorned with an exceptionally large number of curves and odd bumps. He was funny, too, and—as is still my custom with interesting characters—I cultivated him. Bye and bye, the natives of Horseheads recognized caricatures of that gentleman in *Judge,* and the town paper commented:

"Quick-Witted"

COHEN—"Do you allow Chews ad dis hotel?"
CLERK—"No, sir."
COHEN—"Vell, I'm glad of dot. Me und my vife are
Irish und very barticular."

. . . Anyone who knows the colored barber referred to, knows that he has been the most extensively cartooned of any colored person on earth.

Perhaps a street scene may suggest something entirely different from the scene itself, according to the law of Association of Ideas. For example: After declaring he was so full of rheumatism that he could hardly move a joint, an old man inadvertently picked up a piece of hot iron that lay beside the anvil in a blacksmith shop. He jumped two feet when he made contact with the iron. I metamorphosed this situation so that the old fellow sat on a bees' nest while soliloquizing on the merits of Christian Science.

One noon, I sauntered through the East Side, with no particular purpose except to settle a rather heavily-laden stomach. It was a sloppy day, and noticing a horse and cart under the protection of a long single sheet of canvas, the idea struck me that the addition of another horse directly behind him would make a ludicrous picture. The original steed and his mackintosh supplied the suggestion, which had to be exaggerated to make it interest the fun lover.

The idea for the two Irishmen in the street repair gang came to me similarly. While passing up Sixth Avenue I had seen a burly laborer shift the heavier end of the burden upon a weaker comrade. This scene had to be doctored up ludicrously, of course, to make it suitable for publication.

I seldom jot down such ideas on the spot; usually I can remember them long enough to wait until I return to my studio. On many occasions, I even neglected to carry a pencil and I resorted to that hackneyed custom of tying a knot in the hand-

"A Shame"

GILBRAITH—Oi say, Gilhooly, phwat makes yez look so dhown in th' mouth?"
GILHOOLY—"Oi was afther thinkin' phwat a shame thot a foine counthry loike Ameriky should be discovered by a dirthy Oitalian dago."

"An Opportunity Not to Be Missed"

MRS. O'ROONEY—*"Now, droive by the McGintys',
Moike, an' we'll croosh their souls wid invy."*

kerchief as a reminder of suggestions that came to life in my wanderings. My friend, Hy Mayor, used to carry a small memorandum book for that purpose. Hy was most prolific in ideas. He could see possibilities in almost everything.

I had a funny experience with Hy Mayor the first time we met, at Atlantic city. We were sight-seeing along the boardwalk and indulging in various amusements, among which was a revolving tower. We stepped in, but as the balcony ascended, Hy became uneasy, imploring me to hold on to him lest he leap overboard, warning me that he had such an impulse. I kept a firm grip on Mayor's left leg and assured him that if he did jump he would have to jump without the leg which was in my possession. Well, I was worried and did not enjoy my surroundings in the least, though under milder conditions the experience would have been delightful.

As we approached the ground, "Hy" gave a deep sigh of relief and declared he'd never again go up in that affair, to which I added, "If you do, you'll certainly go without me."

Mayor is naturally a funny fellow. One day he walked into a German restaurant on 14th Street where Emil Flohri and I were seated at lunch. Hy had just returned from a European trip and, copying us, he hailed a passing waiter. "Here, vaiter, bring mein friends someding to eat."

"This is not my table, sir," the servitor responded haughtily.

"Vell, for God's sake," was Hy's impatient rejoinder, "giff me your abron and I'll vait on meinself."

Hy was a busy man. I met him often after nightfall on his way to his studio; sometimes I went along and watched him work on his Sunday page for the *New York Times.* A happy mortal he was—he would sing at his work. I never knew Mr. Mayor to be pessimistic or ill-tempered. He would say, "Don't you think I draw better than I used to?" and I would reply, "Oh, yes, you'll learn to draw some day." Then he would come back with, "Ach, Gott! Vat's the use of asking you anything? You always make a choke of it." Whereupon he would go right on whistling or singing merrily, putting into his pencil some of the joy that was in his heart.

Forever in search of new types to caricature, I visited the Bellevue Hospital one evening with a friend and peered through the iron bars of that delightful chamber of horrors known as the morgue. The attendant, who had a typical Tammany face, courteously tendered us the privilege of a stroll through that mysterious enclosure, remarking in a tone of apology that his supply of "stiffs" was rather low, but he could show us a few of the latest importations in an excellent state of preservation.

Pulling out a drawer-like slab which bore a label of identification and a still form with a coldly peaceful expression, he introduced us to, ". . . McCart'y; he was biffed on the dome wid a pick handle, which didn't agree wid his healt', so they sent 'im down here to board wid me till his folks came along an' claims him."

Then our guide ran his fingers through the whiskers of the deceased and informed us it was pure Irish lace he was fondling. This fellow, whose embroidered announcement on his cap marked him as keeper of the dead house, had a small but vivid nose which looked suspicious of having many dimes tied up in it, and a breath that suggested a handy bottle somewhere about the premises.

He prattled on jocosely from one shrouded slab to another, until I felt a dire need of fresh oxygen and a stimulant to hold my disturbed dinner in check while the process of digestion took place.

Since then, my search for experiences has confined itself to the land of the living, although I have run into death involuntarily several times. On one occasion I was returning from a bus ride to Coney Island when a small boy slipped off a bicycle and under the bus, where he was crushed to death. There was nothing I could do for the little fellow, so I slipped out of the crowd while the rest of the passengers were being rounded up by policemen and escorted to the station house. I had work to do on *Judge* which could not be delayed, hence my anxiety to keep away from the jurisdiction of the courts.

Chapter 13

I REMEMBER WHEN THE FANCY OMnibus was the only public conveyance on lower Broadway, although a horse-car line ran between Fourteenth Street and Central Park. Madison and Fifth Avenues had bus service, too. The floor of these buses was covered with straw in wet weather, and the interior was highly ornamented with various scenes; scenic artists must have been in demand for that class of work. The earliest coaches of the elevated railway also had landscape panels to ease the monotony of travel.

Then Jake Sharp procured a franchise to extend the horse-car line to lower Broadway. There went up a cry of bribery, and pressure was used to block it, but the rails were laid nevertheless. The fleet of buses was sold at auction and scattered among cities and towns for hundreds of miles.

In 1884, the elevated reduced its Sunday fare from ten cents to five because travel was so light on that day—a reduction which greatly worried its competitors. James W. Foshay, president of the Broadway Line, feared this would lure passengers from the ten-cent horse-cars, which already were operating at a loss on the Sabbath.

"Sunday travel on Broadway is almost a blank; we might as well keep our horses in the stable," said Foshay. "In the winter I don't believe it pays to run the elevated on Sundays, but it has to be done for the convenience of the public."

Broadway was sparsely built-up north of Thirty-fourth Street, except for two handsome hotels at Forty-second, the Rossmore and the St. Cloud. Virtually the only night life was between Twenty-third and Thirty-fourth, where the crowds thronged the sidewalks, while the lights of omnibuses and carriages darted here and there like fireflies. Electric bulbs illuminated the street from Union Square to Thirty-fourth—a section which today is rather lonely and deserted after dark—while the hotels, playhouses, restaurants, stores, and saloons sent out their blaze of gas lamps.

The playhouses [theaters] were dingy affairs. At first, their only lighting equipment were the gas jet and the calcium for spotlight effects, but in 1881, D'Oyley Cart introduced the electric bulb in his newly constructed Savoy Theatre, making it probably the first building entirely lit by electricity. (The Savoy, by the way, was the birthplace of most of the Gilbert and Sullivan operettas.) In 1882, another theatre, the New York Casino at Broadway and Thirty-fourth, managed by Rudolph Aronson, adopted electric illumination; it was a place I often frequented.

Lower Broadway had the squatty appearance of the average city street. There were as yet no skyscrapers. Four stories was about the limit, and these had to be reached by climbing stairs. I remember Riverside Drive before it was a parkway; Central Park when it was entirely surrounded by a high iron fence, the gates of which were locked at eleven o'clock every night (except when there was skating on the lakes); Sixth Avenue when it had jim crow trolleys; and Harlem when goats roamed all over it, nibbling at waste paper and tomato cans.

Bathtubs in private homes were rare, although there were plenty of tin wash basins, and a few public pumps were still in active use throughout the city. Many barber shops had bathing facilities; it was common on a Saturday night to step in for a

"The Preacher"

bath—twenty-five cents being the average price for a dip—and only spendthrifts would indulge in such luxuries more often. Too much bathing was deemed unhealthy.

Vendors swarmed the streets and hawked their wares without restriction, so did beggars. The gold-brick shark was in his element when the unsophisticated merchant from up-state struck town. And policemen wore heavy moustaches which gave them a brutal appearance. It was said that as soon as an Irishman landed, he joined Tammany Hall and was put on the police force.

Flashily dressed street-walkers wove their way in and out among the night crowds, glancing boldly at the men who passed. They could never be mistaken for decent women, because of their painted faces and low-cut gowns. Eluding the eyes of the police, one of these girls would attract the attention of a victim and then wait for him to join her on a side street. Frequently, the man would be decoyed into a low dive in a cellar, where, besotted with drugged liquor, he was robbed or worse, thus ending the "romantic" adventure.

I was never a "rounder," one who found a thrill in the night life of the dives, yet on several occasions I made the rounds to see if the fabulous stories were true, and I found the places even worse than they had been pictured. I visited all the joints of shady reputation such as Tom Gould's, Oney Ghegan's, the Hay Market, and most infamous of all—Billy McGlory's Armory Hall, where the high-hatted audience proved to my mind that McGlory's was under police protection. It was common belief that the patrons of that joint included more than a few city officials showing their friends a den of wickedness.

At that period I was rooming in Brooklyn with two former Elmira friends, Ruggles and Kingsbury. The three of us stayed close together in the event that should anything out of the ordinary happen we could protect one another or make a safe get-away.

While "doing" the Bowery—"the Street of a Thousand Sins"—we used to meet the "fresh hot corn" man, who still may be seen in Coney Island and parts of Greenwich Village. We never got such

"When the Auto-Hobo Begs"

KIND LADY—"I suppose when I give you this dime
you will go direct to a saloon and invest it in liquor."
POLITE PETE—"You misjudge me, kind lady. I want
it for gasoline for my automobile."

corn at our boarding-house—long, luscious ears oozing with butter, sold on the open street. Drinking was neither a sin nor a crime in those days, so it was only natural for us to take our beer with the rest of the world. Occasionally, we spent Saturday evening at the Atlantic Garden, a very respectable establishment to which men took their families to enjoy good beer and music.

New York so many years ago was a city of 2,340 licensed saloons and a great many "blind tigers," as contrasted with scarcely 500 churches. Arrests for drunkenness totaled about 35,000 a year, one-third of the cases being females. Saloon-keepers agreed that the worst nuisance in town was the free-lunch friend. [In many saloons, the owners put out free sandwiches and other "finger food," counting on the clientele to buy a lot of beer; some "customers"—the "free-lunch friend"—came only for the food.]

Several attempts were made in Manhattan to introduce the barmaid, a popular English character. Eight of them were employed at a "gin-mill" on New Street near the Stock Exchange, but customers "razzed" the girls so much that they were obliged to return to London. Then, a saloon in the basement of Wallack's Theatre, at Thirtieth Street, hired barmaids. Patrons liked the innovation very much, but the police didn't; the presence of a stairway leading from the bar-room to the theatre lobby constituted a violation of law, so that venture also failed.

Hod Brese, a middle-aged farmer I know in Horseheads, who subscribed to Horace Greeley's *Weekly Tribune,* never tired of recalling the time when "Boss" Tweed and his gang were plundering the New York City treasure and Thomas Nast was after their scalps. That lantern-jawed rustic used to make occasional trips to the metropolis and never failed to call at the *Puck* office while I was working there, and we would go to a show together. First he took me to Bible's Garden to see "The Black Crook," which was regarded as extremely immoral because the ballet dancers dressed in tights! That, of course, was long before [Producer] Earl Carroll flaunted beautiful feminine nakedness on the stage in the name of art. Although the naughty 'eighties and 'nineties kept Anthony Comstock in a furor of activity, his mild-mannered and more cultured successor, John Summer, was obliged to overlook a degree of sophistication which would have shocked old Comstock out of a year's growth.

"Satyr and Nymphs," which hung in the cafe of the Hoffman House, was familiar to the early patrons of the Bowery. When I had attained the stage of thorough appreciation of classic art, I was enticed into the presence of the exquisite painting and allowed to feast my eyes upon the lovely voluptuousness of Adolphe William Bouguereau's imagination, while my companions tucked away a few cocktails.

I gazed upon that masterpiece with dire misgivings, however, lest [Anthony] Comstock arrive and pinch the bunch and drag us off as trophies of his raid. Thanks to the stars and planets, nothing of that sort happened and we were allowed to remain intact. I have often thought Mr. Comstock missed a lot by being born too soon.

"Satyr and Nymphs" was the biggest single advertisement which any hotel had during the twenty-odd years it hung in the Hoffman House. One of the proprietors, Edward S. Stokes, paid exactly $1,010 for that canvas and refused to sell it for $30,000 a few years later. Men and women from all over the country visited that cafe to admire—or gloat over—"Satyr and Nymphs" together with other large nude canvases such as "The Vision of Faust" and "Narcissus."

The Hoffman House of the early 'eighties employed seventeen bartenders and had the most palatial drinking-room in the world, decorated with a sumptuous art gallery. In those days most of the great paintings in America belonged to private collections; the Metropolitan Museum of Art had only just opened its present building and was still closed on Sundays. So the exhibition at this café was not without justification. Just as each of the smaller saloons had its "Ladies' Entrance," so did the Hoffman House cafe have its "Ladies' Day" once a week, when a uniformed attendant met each female patron with a printed catalogue of the art gallery.

Prices at this magnificent café were reputed to have been the highest ever known in America, with the exception of the bars in Western gold-mining camps. Plain brandy sold for fifty cents a tiny glass; a better quality could be had for one dollar a glass, while fine Rhenish wine cost up to eighteen dollars a quart—rather high for pre-prohibition days.

Little did St. Anthony dream that the Twentieth Century would usher in the nymph of real life, to be rubbered at with utter impunity in the theatre, on the beach and elsewhere. In this modern age of dress—or undress—reform, we of today do not need shock absorbers to ease our conscience. We no longer gape open-mouthed at the charms of Bouguereau's shameless maidens, for some of our own girls have his painted nymphs "skinned to death."

When the Flatiron Building was erected, there were many predictions that sooner or later it would blow over into the street and no doubt kill somebody. Before it was built, a one-story railroad ticket office stood on the site—the intersection of Twenty-third Street, Fifth Avenue and Broadway—and the dead wall of a structure behind it was a valuable asset to advertisers.

A sad sight in modern progress was the passing into history of lower Fifth Avenue as a residential section—the demolition of stately brownstone mansions of wealthy and noted citizens who were shifting higher uptown. The Judge Company was about the first to move from Park Row to its new building, corner of Sixteenth Street and Fifth Avenue, opposite which lived Vice President Levi P. Morton and other celebrities. One of the early show palaces of Fifth Avenue was the all-marble dwelling of the millionaire merchant A. T. Stewart. The place was not particularly striking in itself, but the white marble rendered it more conspicuous than its surroundings. After Stewart's death this building was torn down to make room for another structure. New York cares little for sentiment when it stands in the way of dollars.

The Arion and Liederkranz sponsored two of the great social events in the New York season. These were rival German singing societies which counted all the local "Dutchmen" of note on either one roster or the other. Tickets to their annual functions, handsomely lithographed in colors, cost ten dollars apiece. Mr. Keppler belonged to the Liederkranz and was a member of its reception committee, so it was easy for him to get me a complimentary ticket. I went as far as the door of the old Metropolitan Opera House, where the ball was about to take place, but when I beheld the array of diamond-bedecked females, big-bellied brewers, wine merchants, poets, actors, editors and artists, I turned tail and went back to my humble lodging-house in Brooklyn. My nerve deserted me at sight of such vulgar display of wealth, and I with barely a five-spot in my clothes. However, I was told it was a gorgeous sight when the grand march, with floats, passed around the throne of King Carnival.

It might seem uncouth to admit that grand opera never appealed to me further than the music. Perhaps my disgust for the bombastic sort of acting was sharpened by seeing those conceited stars offstage at their hotels and noting their self-important carriage in befigured overcoats and high hats, with a sprinkling of diamonds on their shirt fronts.

"The Slide Waltz"

"Dey's no use talkin', Mistah Rafbone; I sartinly does laik t' waltz wif yo'. Mah feet nevah touches de groun'."

Chapter 14

[DURING HIS SEVEN-DECADE LIFE, Eugene Zimmerman became friendly with many persons who were famous when he met them or would soon become famous. In his notes, he writes about some of these people.]

Whenever the subject of caricature is touched upon, the name Matt Morgan is seldom mentioned. Yet in the 1870s, Morgan was a prominent figure in the world of caricature and one of Thomas Nast's principal contemporaries. Morgan was an Englishman with a pleasing black-and-white technique; besides, he was an excellent scenic painter, having painted the scenery for many of the early stage productions.

Morgan's career as a caricaturist may not have been as spectacular as Nast's. He had, however, a reputation quite as enviable. In those days of good shows, any man as capable of painting stage scenery, as was Morgan, would have been considered ace high. I remember attending a Broadway play on an opening night, for which Morgan had painted the scenery—and I might add here that his charming work received as much applause as the actors themselves. His dash in manipulating distemper colors was admirable.

In 1888, Morgan became art editor of *Collier's* "Once A Week," and it was at that period that he and I entered into business relations. It is pleasant to look into the past and contemplate the generous souls that a kindly providence placed in your path. I found Morgan one of that kind, exceedingly thoughtful of the interests of the younger artist. I had been engaged by him to illustrate Bill Nye's weekly letter for *Collier's* "Once A Week," and on the presentation of my first bill for the Nye drawings, I was surprised to find it rejected with this notation across the bottom—"Your bill is not correct. Take this remark for what it is worth. Make it out right. If you will add a few figures to it so that it will look bigger, I am sure it will please Mr. Collier better, as well as Yours Truly." Of course, I acquiesced and continued henceforth to render my statements so perfectly satisfactory that no further coaching was deemed necessary.

Walt McDougall, in his book *This is the Life,* says that Morgan made an unsuccessful attempt at publishing a paper called "The Tomahawk" and returned to England. That might have been long before he assumed charge of the art department of "Once A Week." It was no cinch to start a paper on its way to success in those days because of the undeveloped conditions and high cost of photo engraving (a new discovery) and other meager resources which have since been overcome. (Morgan's son became a cartoonist for the *Philadelphia Inquirer.*)

Bert Levy, the Australian cartoonist, found a warm welcome at the *Judge* office. Later he went into theatricals and invented a clever vaudeville stunt of projecting his drawings upon a screen by means of powerful lights and reflectors, which he was seated at a table, whistling or smoking as a man would do in his studio. It was a huge success financially.

In 1888, I illustrated a humorous *Railway Guide* written by Bill Nye and James Whitcomb Riley. When Nye sat down to discuss terms he reminded me of a two-foot jointed ruler. His bald head was part of his stock in trade and his letter of July 11 gave me explicit directions for putting it on the front cover of the *Railway Guide:*

Dear Mr. Zim:

I think the pictures are great and shall keep them all. I have sent you the cover design, however, and ask you, as you kindly invited me to make suggestions, to try my face again on the Roman coin. Perhaps the photograph will help you, but the principal points I see that need doctoring are the head as to width from forehead to back, just above the ear. When in profile my head is very wide at that point, even more so than the three-quarter photo shows.

At the nose and mouth I think you can get a better "scale" on. My nose is the only thing I am really proud of, except my wife, and most artists make it look too long with a "tit" on the end—if "tit" is a term used in art. The mount is apt to be made too full, whereas it is straight and clean-cut, with a lingering suspicion of comic delivery.

If you could strike such an inspiration on my face as you did on Riley's I would be happy. I don't mind the artist taking liberties with my physiognomy in the text but I want to look as much as possible like George Washington or Julius Ceasar on the medallion outside, so that

people will not be down on me too much. Riley never had a better or stronger picture in his life than the one you made of him.

Yours truly,

E. W. NYE

After that, I illustrated Nye's periodical letters in *Collier's* "Once A Week."

A daily newspaper, be it known, usually has three different cartoons on hand on the eve of a closely contested election—one for victory, another for defeat, a third for doubtful results. In a mayoralty campaign in Philadelphia about twenty years ago, the first returns gave a big lead to the Republican nominee, George H. Earle, Jr., so the "bulldog" edition of the *Inquirer*—a Republican paper in a G.O.P. stronghold—came out with an exultant cartoon by Fred Morgan entitled "The Early Bird Catches the Worm." Later returns, however, elected the grizzled old reform candidate, Rudolph Blankenburg, so the *Inquirer* hastily substituted a cartoon of lamentation for its final edition.

Many classic bulls have been perpetrated in journalism. I recall reading a "greatly exaggerated" obituary of my friend Jay N. Darling—the cartoonist "Ding"—who is doing effective work for the New York Herald Tribune Syndicate.* Ding's masterpiece is "The Long, Long Trail," published in the *Tribune* at the time of Roosevelt's death, showing Teddy's cowboy spirit riding into the Big Dark. It was widely reprinted and has been reproduced in bronze in the lobby of the Hotel Roosevelt, New York. The original is in the Roosevelt Memorial House Museum.

A man need make one such hit in a lifetime and his fame is eternal. Ding has produced many great cartoons. One similar to the Roosevelt tribute appeared just after the death of another famous colonel, "Buffalo Bill." It depicts the wrath of the "Boyhood's Great Idol" bidding goodbye to lads playing Indian, and trailing after a ghostlike procession of redskins and cowboys, stagecoach, buffaloes and covered wagons. "Gone to Join the Mysterious Caravan" is the title.

Ding is the only cartoonist I know of who is a

---

*Darling (1876–1962), employed by the *Des Moines Register,* won two Pulitzer prizes (1923, 1942) for his cartoons.

Doctor of Laws, but, says he, "I hope that somewhere there is another cartoonist with an LL.D.; I hope I don't have to live that down all by myself."

When Charles A. Dana owned the New York *Sun,* Walt McDougall wanted to do cartoons for it, but Dana indignantly refused to "splash the *Sun* with penny valentines"; so did his right-hand man, William T. Dewart, the present publisher.

An ocean voyage often brings one in contact with very companionable people. My third trip to Florida, my wife and I found such acquaintances aboard the Clyde steamer "Apache." Being past the rush reason, there were not many tourists headed south so that the few passengers aboard had practically the ship to themselves. Among these were the popular actress, Edna May Spooner, and her mother, enroute to fill a Summer's engagement at a Jacksonville theatre. In the ship's salon was a very much abused piano with several silent keys to add to the merriment of the party and, to the accompaniment of my daugher, Laura, Miss Spooner sang *The Harvest Moon* and other popular songs of the day. On the Spooners' opening night, many of the ship's party were present and the bank of flowers which passed over the footlights to that splendid actress was sufficient evidence of the deep regard in which Miss Spooner was held by her newly made friends. Strange things happen even on the deep sea to show us how very small a world we live in.

While I was sending a wireless to Grant Hamilton at the *Judge* office, the ship's purser recognized my name and introduced himself as Mr. Ringold, saying, "I've often heard Mr. Bernhard Gillam speak of you, sir." And I recalled having heard Bernhard's family speak of their friend Ringold. Well, that was enough. We were treated like nabobs on that voyage, and, returning later on the same vessel, were given a cabin on deck next to the captain's.

On that trip I made the acquaintance also of Dr. Munyon, whose slogan, "There is hope!" appears to have been worth several million dollars. Munyon and his young wife joined our party at a hotel in Jacksonville. The doctor professed vast faith in his products, for, said he, "There's a pill for every ill."

Munyon impressed me as a rather unique person. A shock of iron-grey hair stood upon his head

like a drum-major's bearskin, with a strong-charactered face beneath. It seemed to me that he was continually having himself paged, for seldom did I enter the dining room that a bellhop was not yelling "Doctor Mun-yon!"—which was the cue for that master of publicity to arise and elevate his index finger in imitation of his well-known pill advertisements.

Transportation for two of my Florida trips was supplied by Joe McCann, formerly an Iron Mountain Railroad passenger agent, who now conducted McCann's tours at the Flatiron Building. While I was exhibiting my work at a Chemung County fair, McCann strolled by, looking for space to exploit his railroad's advantages; being a good friend of mine, I told Joe he need look no further. So he sat in my booth and gave out railroad literature, incidentally passing himself off as the maker of my numerous pictures which adorned the stall. I used to stand with the crowd of "rubes" and listen to Joe lie about how he had drawn those pictures for *Judge,* and give advice to youthful aspirants for artistic fame.

Another passenger agent, Tom Lee, dropped in on me once, suggesting that he would like to do something for me in the way of transportation, and would I accept a thousand-mile book on the Delaware, Lackawanna & Western? I presume it was a subtle form of bribery in recognition of the power of the cartoon in influencing public opinion, but I accepted graciously, and for years thereafter I traveled between Elmira and New York City on Lackawanna passes supplied through the *Judge* advertising department.

In 1888, I had moved back to Horseheads, just outside of Elmira, and was living there with my family, nearly three hundred miles from the metropolis. For a quarter of a century I conducted metropolitan affairs from my village home, traveling back and forth at short intervals to keep in touch with my associates at the *Judge* office. (This long-distance commutation was a result of the nervous breakdown which preceded my first trip to Florida; a doctor had ordered me to return to the calmness and purer air of Chemung Valley. Besides, my wife's family lived there, which was another good reason.)

All the free rides I ever had at the Lackawanna's

expense were paid for by one warning of danger when I had found a wooden culvert afire in an isolated spot where the road had been built on piles over a march—a nasty spot for a wreck. The ties were partly consumed and ready to drop in. Running to a signal tower half a mile away, I gave the alarm. Three minutes later a bucket brigade was headed for the scene.

On a different occasion, I was walking the ties of the Pennsy when I noticed a broken rail, split for about two feet by a heavy freight. I happened to know that a passenger train was due to pass that point within a few minutes, so I hurried the news to a section gang and the oncoming train was flagged in time to avert derailment.

Under John Sleicher's management, the *Judge* office was a rendezvous for celebrities. Sleicher invited the "big shots" to look at his plant and took pride in introducing us to men like Andrew Carnegie, Vice Presidents Fairbanks and Sherman, Senator Beveridge of Indiana, Jerome K. Jerome, and Homer Grey, author of best sellers, whose stories I used to illustrate, and Charles W. Post, of Postum [cereal] fame, whose friendship I cultivated. [On September 4, 1912, Mr. and Mrs. Post hosted the American Press Humorists at their home in Battle Creek. ZIM was president of the organization.] I still have the letters Mr. Post wrote me. One of them was dated at Santa Barbara, Calif., Jan. 20, 1913, and said:

Wife and I work every morning until 12:30 or 1 pruning apricot, pear, orange, lemon, locust and grapefruit trees, rose bushes, etc., and raise merry h——, but we feel fine with the physical work God intended for so-called millionaires.

Despite his wealth, his outdoor activities and his exploitation of health foods, Mr. Post died shortly afterward in a spell of illness and despondency.

I never had direct contact with any of our presidents, although, as I said, I attended Grant's funeral and the dedication of Grant's Tomb, besides working for a farmer's wife who bragged that President Grant in his early days had once made her an offer of marriage. And I once drew a caricature of President Coolidge for a Horseheads neighbor, George L. Mulford, editor of the *Chemung Valley Reporter,* who surprised me by taking it to the Coolidge camp at Paul Smith, New York. It was in the summer of 1926—four months after Grant Hamilton's death, by the way—and "Cal" was very much in the limelight as a trout fisherman, so I pictured him as such. A few days afterward, George received this acknowledgement:

Paul Smith, August 27

My dear Mr. Mulford:
    I greatly appreciate your kindness in bringing to the Executive offices the original cartoon, and I want to thank both you and "ZIM" for it. I very much appreciate also the personal message of friendship and support.
                    Very truly yours,
                    CALVIN COOLIDGE

Nearly two years later I received the following from Northampton, Mass.:

June 24, 1929

My dear Mr. Zimmerman:
    Understanding that you are writing an autobiography, I am pleased to send you a word of encouragement and commiseration since I have lately been employed in an effort of that nature for myself.
    I am sure that the public who have enjoyed the pictures you have been making for more than a quarter of a century will be pleased to read something of the motives which inspired them and the results which you have attempted to secure. We have all been so much amused and inspired by your work that we shall look forward with pleasure to having the more intimate acquaintance with your own self which your autobiography will reveal.
    Hoping that you may have the same success as a writer that you have had as an artist, I am,
                    Very truly yours,
                    CALVIN COOLIDGE

Beneath Cal's New England conscience is a dry sense of humor. Callers at the White House one day found him chuckling over a cartoon by Thomas Nast, published in the *Harper's Weekly* of July 18, 1885. The cartoon was captioned "What Position of President of United States Really Is." Nast depicted the White House as a combined intelligence office and employment bureau, with President Cleveland trying to take care of job-hunters who thronged his quarters with food and baggage. Mr. Coolidge commented that the Presidential office had not changed materially since 1885, although the Civil Service law had cut down the demand for positions. As he read Nast's translation of *E Pluribus Unum*—"Many for One Place"—Coolidge smiled and said Cleveland evidently was able to cope with the situation.

Death very quickly blunted the lance of the cartoonist.

On June 27, 1881, Joseph Keppler produced his famous "Good and Bad Boys" cartoon, wherein President Garfield as a schoolmaster was disciplining certain members of his Cabinet class, while the bad boys outside were indulging in mischief. It was between that date and the following issue of *Puck* that Garfield was struck down by the assassin Guiteau, and as Keppler already had a humorous Fourth of July cartoon in course of printing—a double page, in which Garfield was pictured as one of the merrymakers at a picnic—it became necessary to add some manifestation of sorrow to the issue. Accordingly, the colored cover which had been prepared was laid aside, and Keppler rushed through a black-and-white cover representing the President slain at the post of duty. The assassination of President McKinley occurred at a time when he was being unmercifully abused by opposition papers. A feature of that campaign was Mark Hanna, as "Willie's Pa," depicted by Opper. The cartoons were republished in book form and were on display in a Sixth Avenue department store window when the President was laid low. The book was withdrawn immediately from public view and its sales fell as a result. Two decades later, *Judge* was publishing a cartoon lampooning former presidential candidate William Jennings Bryan for his beliefs at the Scopes evolution trial in Tennessee, when the news came of Bryan's death. The "Evolution Number" of July 18, 1925, had portrayed Bryan on the front cover with a slogan "Pin the Tail on the Monkey." His death eight days later left *Judge* out on a limb, so to speak. The presses were stopped, a new cartoon was submitted, and the copies already printed with the Bryan cartoon were destroyed—a rather costly process, but in accordance with the inflexible code of journalism which says: "Thou shalt not ridicule the dead." However, the issues of July 25 and August 1 contained satirical attacks on him, and it was not until August 8 that *Judge* was able to come out with an editorial apology:

Judge disagreed with William Jennings Bryan on what we believe are fundamental issues. But our disagreement was never so deep that we couldn't sincerely regret what has taken place. Unfortunately, a humorous weekly must go to press several days before its date of publication, so not only will this expression of sorrow seem late but in the meantime there will have appeared in *Judge* reference to Mr. Bryan that in view of his death are untimely. We would have recalled these if that had been possible.

In October, 1897, I received the following letter from A. G. Racey, a young art student at Montreal:

Pardon the liberty I take in asking a very great favour. I am making a collection of American illustrative artists' work before I leave for Paris to study, and write to ask if you have any little sketch laying around your studio that you do not want, and if so, will you make a most ardent admirer of yours happy by letting me have it?

Racey today [about 1929] is staff cartoonist for the Montreal *Daily Star*. He is easily the foremost pen artist in all of Canada. Recently he told me that in '97 he had asked a number of artists for specimens of their work and I alone had responded.

"Your sketch was framed," he said, "and still reposes in a place of honor on my study walls."

One never knows when, by granting the plea of an obscure student, he is warming the heart of a future celebrity. In most cases, however, I am inclined to think it is a curse to possess talent which places one at the mercy of collectors. When the slightest sketch is requested it means a personal reply, if not a half hour's labor on a drawing and mailing the same.

In May, 1896, I met Thomas Edison at his Orange, N.J., laboratory, and accepted his invitation to sketch before one of the first movie cameras ever invented. Hy Mayor accompanied me and also posed. The film was flashed on a screen in Kester & Bials' Music Hall.

Edison told me of an amusing mistake which had just occurred. His operator had accidentally reversed the film in projecting a barnyard scene. Instead of a farmer feeding his chickens, they were coughing up corn, which the farmer caught in his hand and returned to the pan under his arm. Thus originated a feature which has since become very popular.

Another electrical wizard I met was Nicola

"A Thompson-Street Stampede"

SIMPSON (entering)—"Say, fellers, maik yo' selbes scarce! De perlise am comin' up-stairs on a dead run."

SIMPSON (to himself)—"Lord saiks! If dis ain't de best luck I eber had at pokah den mah name ain't Pete Simpson."

Eugene Zimmerman, early 1890s (?)

Tesla, who roomed at the Gerlach Hotel, where I lived several years by courtesy of the *Judge* advertising department.

In those days, Lee DeForest, inventor of the vacuum tube, had his workshop in the Parker Building, Fourth Avenue and 17th Street, on the top floor, directly above the *Judge* office. Members of the *Judge* staff secretly pitied him as a bug who was attempting the impossible—namely to talk through the air without wires.

About twenty-five years ago, the building burned out, consuming DeForest's efforts of years. Now we find the whole world doing exactly what our "bug" had predicted and helped to bring about—while we humorists were busily ridiculing ideas that a quarter-century hence would be hailed as miracles of modern science.

I often saw John N. Willys during the bicycle days at his little repair shop in Elmira, without dreaming that he would become a millionaire through the invention of a horseless carriage.

Billy Arkell's younger brother, Bart Arkell, is a magnate in the food industry, head of the Beech Nut Packing Company, of Canajoharie, N.Y., producers of bacon, ham, peanut butter, mints and many other widely advertised edibles. This concern began as the Imperial Packing Company, and Billy was connected with it, but for the first few years it had an uphill fight, due to the lack of a catchy business title. In this connection, my employer related the following story:

On the day of President Garfield's funeral, my father, brother and I went to Saratoga Springs from Canajoharie and were guests of Albert Spender, who conducted the Saratoga Club House. We supplied him with hams, and while at dinner that day Spender asked me:
"Why do you call your concern the Imperial Packing Company?"
I replied that I thought it was a good name.
"It isn't worth a damn," he said. "Why don't you call it the Beech Nut Packing Company? Everybody will then think you use the hogs that are raised in Virginia, and I'll bet you a red apple you will do a larger business."
"That's a good suggestion," Bart told my father, "and when we get back home we'll change the name."

And we did. For fifteen years we had never made a dollar as the Imperial Packing Company. By changing the name, we were paying dividends in six months. That's what there is to a name.

Enrico Caruso, who was as clever a caricaturist as he was charming in voice, made a sketch of me from *This and That about Caricature* which was published in *La Follia de New York*. The original was sent to me by Mr. Sisca, the editor, and now hangs in my den.

Only twice in my life have I consulted the legal profession. Walter Lindner, whose son was on *Leslie's* editorial staff, once advised me. I made a drawing for him in lieu of a fee. The other occasion was precipitated by a double-page cartoon of mine in *Judge* lampooning the New York police because several of them had been clubbing innocent citizens. It was intitled "Protect Me from My Protectors."

The *Brooklyn Standard Union* took exception to the picture and excoriated me editorially as an ex-sign painter and an anarchist from the country. The facts that I had once been a sign painter and had been brought up rurally were matters of public record, but I declined to be classed as an anarchist and threatened to sue the paper for libel. I said, "I'll have some fun with that editor. I'll make him either give out the name of the fellow who wrote that or else stand suit." The paper was forced to publish a retraction and make settlement for twenty-five dollars—the exact amount of my attorney's fee!

As I grew older I learned to pay less heed to insulting comment. Critics may call me anything they please now, and I would merely grin over it. I have seen too many feet of clay to worry over the fire-breathing gods of brass.

Now and then I ran into Lew Dockstader, the minstrel king. Once I happened into the cafe of the old Marlborough Hotel and found Lew, with Lawrence D'Orsay, the English actor, imbibing certain beverages; and to relieve them of the burden of disposing of all the bar contained, I graciously consented to aid in that task. On a similar occasion I left the New York theatre between acts and wet my lips at a saloon across the way, and there I found James Swinnerton, the comic strip artist. Jimmy seemed unable to remember my name.

"Captain Dusenbury," I whispered impressively, so Swinnerton introduced me to his cronies by that monicker.

During one of the campaigns of my family physician, Dr. Robert P. Bush, speaker of the New York State Assembly, I painted a caricature of him wielding a sabre. Erroneously I placed it in his left hand, which the grand old man, being a former army officer, noticed at once. So, to square myself, I said it was intended to show his extra-ordinary strength in being able to lick his foes with his left hand.

Bursting my head all day for ideas, I need diversion of a less flamboyant nature. I preferred the Weber and Fields sort of "foolishment," and once took a friend to see Weber and Fields; the seats cost me $1.60 each. The fellow went right to sleep and slumbered throughout the whole performance. I assured him that when I invited him again I'd engage a hotel bed instead of a theatre seat, so he would find it more comfortable. How a man could doze in such an uproar of mirth was beyond me. I learned afterward that the fellow was as dull to humor as a clam.

I like musical comedy and legitimate drama. Melodrama is too sad for me. I weep too easily. Although I was never a fight fan, having been born in a neutral country, Switzerland, there was one time when I regretted John L. Sullivan's retirement from the prize ring—and that was when he played the leading role in that melodramatic masterpiece entitled "Honest Hearts and Willing Hands." Even Jack Dempsey did better than that in the movies many years later.

I made a special trip to John L.'s saloon on Sixth Avenue to obtain an autographed portrait. The "Boston Strong Boy" happened to be out, whereupon his valet said, "I'll get you a photo."

"But," I protested, "I'd like Mr. Sullivan's autograph also."

"Aw, that's alright," the valet assured me, "I'll write his autograph on it. I often do."

Far from appreciating this courtesy, I edged away and promised to call again. I later obtained an unforged signature of the world's most spectacular prize fighter. Sullivan, when I finally met him, was in good humor, but since he was on the water wagon, I had to do the drinking for both of us,

while he chatted about some of the notable battles in his career. There was no one else in the saloon, so I had the ex-champion practically to myself. When I left, it was with a very friendly regard for His Pugilistic Highness. He did not impress me as being the hard-boiled bruiser that we had pictured him in cartoons.

Frequently, I dropped in at Jim Corbett's "rum shop," which was on the site of the present Saks' Department Store. I drifted in because I was thirsty and, incidentally, to study the sort of characters that frequented such a joint. I used to see Tom Sharkey, the big-chested sailor-boxer, strutting along Fourteenth Street near his place of business across from the Old Tammany Hall. In Atlantic City, I had also met another champion, Bob Fitzsimmons.

I have always been partial to circus clowns. My friend, Homer Davenport, was successful as a circus clown long before he became a cartoonist and later created the famous "$-sign suit" for vaudevillian Mark Hanna. I am sure that clowns had something to do with shaping me into a slapstick humorist.

As a youth, while employed at the bakery, I was allowed to eat up the scorched cookies. Some of these I used in bribing the janitor at the Broadway Wigwam, a cheap show-house in Paterson, to sneak me into the gallery where I would hide beneath the benches until the doors opened.

At least once a year, the circus pitched its tents in the outskirts of Paterson, on land now owned by millionaires, mansions, and stately business blocks; father always took me to these shows. P. T. Barnum would sit at the entrance where patrons could get a good look at him as they went into the Big Top. When Barnum was first pointed out to me, I thought he was the greatest man the Lord ever made. He had brought Jumbo to this country the year before I had begun to work on *Puck*. I had seen the huge elephant so often, I felt almost personally acquainted with it.

(In July, 1865, Barnum's American Museum, at the corner of Broadway and Chambers, had burned down. My father-in-law had told me that His Army regiment, returning from the Civil War, had marched past the museum the day following, while it was burning fiercely.)

George L. Fox was the original Humpty

Dumpty who, I believe, set the pace for all his future ilk; many clowns owe their origins to him. Later, Charles Seeley acquired his acrobatic training on the tan-bark of his home town. I recall seeing him at the height of his fame, in a clown outfit, driving a funny pony rig through Elmira, with half the boys of the Chemung Valley calling after him. To the street urchins who called out, "Hello, Charlie!", Charles Seeley was three stories higher than a king. I saw Mr. Seeley again as an old man, shortly before he passed on to the Big Top, and I loved him for all the joy he had given me as a youth; I hope he is now happy.

A little more than two decades ago, a baby leopard was named after me. It was born in Bellefonte, Pennsylvania, in the John Robinson Circus. Two others born in the same litter were named "Hig," for Frank W. Higgins, governor of the state of New York; and "Sloat," after Congressman Sloat Fassett, a native of Elmira where the circus was to make its next stop. Fassett and I were guests of honor when the outfit hit the town.

Press Agent "Doc" Watson was responsible for the naming of those leopards. The following stop happened to be at Watkins Glen, New York, where Waddell announced the birth of a sacred calf, which he called "Telegram," in honor of the Elmira newspaper which circulated there. He named a Royal Bengal tiger, "Leffingwell," for the mayor of Watkins Glen. I shrewdly suspect that all those beasts were reborn and renamed by the "doc" in every state the circus toured that season. That fellow had a wonderful imagination.

Chapter 15

[I]N 1890, ZIM AND HIS FATHER-IN-LAW had finished building ZIM's house in Horseheads. It was a house admired throughout the Chemung Valley and featured a two-story office with natural lighting; ZIM, however, found the room distracting and preferred to work in a corner of the living room.

With a wife and two children, ZIM was not settled into Horseheads and the lifestyle typical of the town. He stayed busy, creative, and reasonably happy, but there was tragedy. The death of his close friend Bernhard Gillam in 1896 had left him devastated. In 1908, his adopted son, Adolph, Jr., died of tuberculosis at the age of twenty-five; that was an even more tragic blow, one he never wrote about. ZIM spent less time in New York, and for a while almost shut himself off from the national publication scene.]

In 1905 I had put out a book entitled *This and That about Caricature,* the object of which was to answer a question which fond mothers ask with exasperating frequency: "What shall I do with my son to make him a cartoonist?"

My stock reply is, "If the youth has an artistic nature, love of fun, perserverance, and can withstand disappointments, then (perhaps) you can make a cartoonist of him."

The first edition of 2,000 copies [at $1.50 each] was soon exhausted, and in 1910 a second edition was published by the Correspondence Institute of America, revised and retitled *Cartoons and Caricatures, or, Making the World Laugh* with an introduction by John Maxwell, editor of *The Home Educator.*

The C. I. of A., located at Scranton, Pennsylvania, was a get-rich-quick correspondence art school. Its president was Louis Conrad. Instead of employing an artist to criticize the work of pupils, the Institute entrusted that job to a few female stenographers. [However, the institute had the endorsements of both Scranton's mayor and its superintendent of schools.]

Maxwell had a run-in with his employers, quit the organization, and set about exposing its unscrupulous methods—methods which he himself had aided in putting across. In his zeal for revenge, Maxwell stole a list of names and addresses of students, whereupon he was arrested and imprisoned for a year. After that, the Government prosecuted the concern for fraudulent use of mail. Maxwell was taken to Harrisburg, Pennsylvania, by deputy sheriffs, to give evidence, and I was subpoenaed by the Federal Grand Jury to appear as a witness.

I knew nothing about the Institute's affairs at the time I authorized them to reprint my book, nor

Eugene Zimmerman, late 1890s

had I seen their complete art course. A statement in the C. I. of A. textbooks to the effect that I had personally revised the lessons was untrue and misleading. One of the defendants offered me $1,500 if I would okay that course before the trial. This I refused. But since the fellow seemed in a mood to spend money, I reminded him that I had sold the

right to publish only 5,000 copies of my book, the copyright to remain with me, whereas the Institute had put out 15,000 copies. Modestly I pressed claim for an additional $500 royalty, which the defendant paid.

Finally, the case was settled out of court. The three partners were each fined $1,000 and costs, and ordered to quit the correspondence school business. This scandal attracted so much attention and I received so many inquiries from art students who had been fleeced that I was obliged to send out a printed form explaining the situation. After the Institute had been disbanded, the printers were left with a large number of the books unpaid for and undelivered. Leslie-Judge Company bid for the lot, sold them for a dollar a copy, and made a nice profit.

When *This and That about Caricature* first appeared, H. T. Webster, the syndicate cartoonist, who was then on the Chicago *Inter-Ocean,* drew a cartoon showing me so overwhelmed with orders that, unable to stand the shock, I was about to leap into a river labeled "This Water Reserved for Despondent Comic Artist." In a letter, Webster wrote:

> If you believe that old saying that "Imitation is the sincerest flattery," you would surely be flattered if you could see the number of alleged comic artists in this city mangling up your work day by day and selling it. There is more graft in this business than in insurance.

In 1913, the idea occurred to me that there might be a gold mine in doing honestly what the C. I. of A. had been carrying on crookedly, so I launched a

Eugene Zimmerman about 1925–30

ZIM correspondence school of cartooning and caricature.*

My correspondence school has had its ups and downs, while rival organizations have pilfered material from *This and That about Caricature*.

[For a fee, ZIM would criticize the work of potential students; they could then determine whether to sign up for the course or not. Because of ZIM's encouragement—very few students were discouraged—most who had paid their fees signed up. In 1913, at the age of fifty-one, with numerous free-lance opportunities, and his school bringing in a good income, ZIM retired from the *Judge* staff. Although he indicated that one of the reasons for resigning was a lack of confidence in the Sleicher management, a stronger reason might have been his ability to earn a respectable, even generous, income in Horseheads, without the necessity or pressure of going into New York City at regular intervals. His world was not limited to free-lance work and the school. It's doubtful that any of ZIM's

---

*In 1905, Grant Hamilton had developed a multi-lesson correspondence course that could have been the basis for both the C.I. of A. and the ZIM courses.

students became professional full-time cartoonists, but his techniques did influence numerous professional cartoonists. The cartoon school suffered a drop in enrollment during 1917–18 when, as ZIM says, "the World War took most of my pupils into military service." The school closed in the early 1920s.]

Not being on the staff of any publication [during World War], I lacked the advantage some artists had of working on salary to "make the world safe for democracy." I drew about sixty war propaganda cartoons, receiving commendation from Secretary of the Navy Daniels, Postmaster General Hayes, and Charles Dana Gibson, who was director of the Division of Pictorial Publicity of George Creel's committee which "put over" the war with the reading public.

My first plunge into humorous writing had been an assignment from Mr. Sleicher to do a page for *Judge* on the subject of "Astrology and Its Relationship to Art." Later, the success of Bill Nye's *Comic History of the United States* inspired me to write and illustrate three foolish histories of Horseheads and one of Elmira, each limited to 1,000 copies selling at a dollar each. [The first history of Horseheads was published in 1911, the second in 1927; the third history was published in 1929. The *Foolish History of Elmira* was published in 1912. Each of these books was not only well received but also received that attention of many of ZIM's professional colleagues throughout the country.] My purpose was to propagate local interests and induce the outside world to shove its shekels under our door. Included were caricatures of leading citizens, and advertisements, such as:

Take a tip—Flat collar buttons don't roll under the bed nor stick out like a wart on the back of your neck—Thomas & Messing, 10¢.

And pseudo want-ads of the following type:

The scarcity of money to meet the demands of perpetual subscription lists, compels us to open a counterfeiting plant. Any one having such an outfit to dispose of or rent for a given period on a percentage basis, will kindly communicate with us by personal letter.

A Special Offer: The proprietors of our local restaurants have kindly agreed to give to each purchaser of this book a fine chicken dinner (at the customary price) this unusual offer to stand good for the entire year.

One of my foolish histories fell into the hands of Paul T. Gilbert, editor of *Cartoons Magazine,* of Chicago; as a result, I wrote and illustrated a department in that monthly entitled "Homespun Phoolosophy" for several years [1914–16] until the magazine suspended publication about the time of the World War. Later, when *Cartoons* was revived in New York I carried on a similar department, "ZIM's Phoolosophy."*

The New york publishers of *Cartoons* sponsored an American Association of Cartoonists and Caricaturists, of which I was choosen president in 1926; Bud Fisher and Rube Goldberg were vice presidents, and Freeman H. Hubbard became secretary. The A. A. C. C. started ambitously, maintained an information bureau, supplied publicity matter to the press, assembled a number of well known cartoonists at a banquet, and took part in an international art exhibition at the Palazzo Rucilsi in Florence, Italy, but when *Cartoons Magazine* gave up the ghost in 1927, the A. A. C. C. passed into the limbo of *Puck* and *Leslie's Weekly,* the Populist Party and the three-toed horse. So far as I am aware, that was the only attempt ever made to weld the cartoonists of this or any other country into a permanent organization.

Chapter 16

THE SPREAD OF CARTOONISTS DURing the past three decades may be likened to the multiplication of rabbits in Australia; they have increased so rapidly that it may become necessary to devise humane methods of extinction. *Judge* is partly responsible for this. During my three years

---

*Many of these essays were collected and published in book form in 1916.

connection with *Puck* I never once saw an outsider enjoy the freedom of *Puck's* art department, which maintained a sort of haughty dignity. *Judge,* on the other hand, kept open house for visiting talent, got the pick of their work, and started some of America's foremost cartoonists and magazine illustrators on the road to fame. In the days when James Montgomery Flagg was known as Jim Flagg and his comic character "Nervy Nat" was occupying *Judge's* back page, Harrison Fisher, Howard Chandler Christy, and Penrhyn Stanlaws were serving a tough apprenticeship as occasional contributors. Even George Luks, the distinguished modernistic painter who has won more medals than a general, used to draw comics for *Judge.* I marveled at Luks' pastel sketches. He would carry a pad with a handful of pastel stumps in a coat pocket, and jot down little scenes in his travels about the city. What George couldn't produce from that handful of pink chalks wasn't worth mentioning. A tiny spot of color here, a dab there, and he had an organ grinder surrounded by dancing street urchins. Then he would sell his stuff to any paper that would publish it. When asked if he had a success formula, George replied: "Sure, I have a success formula. *I know what I want and go get it.*"

In the cartoon field the old *Judge* fostered such celebrities as Hy Mayor, Walt McDougall, Art Young, W. A. Rogers, Gus Dirks, Richard Fenton Outcault, Charles W. Kahles, Mike Woolf, and "Chip" Bellow, whose father was a rival of Nast in Nast's palmiest days.

Outcault, who was born when I was eight months old and died before this book was being written, was employed successively by Joseph Pulitzer, W. R. Hearst and James Gordon Bennett, all in New York City. He contributed the first comic series to the first colored supplement ever printed by a daily paper—the one gotten out by Pulitzer's *World* on November 18, 1894. His first big hit, "The Yellow Kid," was created for Hearst's *Journal* two years later, and his even more famous "Buster Brown" decorated Bennett's *Herald* in 1902.

In 1902, while Outcault's "Yellow Kid" was amusing children and philosophy professors alike, and Rudolph Dirks was drawing "The Katzenjammer Kids," Kahles originated "Clarence the Cop" for the *World,* Clarence being an unfortunate policeman who was always trying to do someone a

Eugene Zimmerman, 1926

good turn. Tiring of this, Kahles turned to a new character, "Hairbreadth Harry," who was forever rescuing the fair Belinda from the villainous clutches of Relentless Rudolph.

The comic strip is now a popular feature of every big American daily except the business journals and a few highbrow papers like *The New York Times, The Boston Transcript,* and *The Christian Science Monitor.* Its popularity is due to (1) the development of photo-engraving, (2) decline of hot political partisanship, and (3) rise of the newspaper syndicate.

Before the invention of photo-engraving, the wood-cut had held sway for centuries, and then lithography came to the fore. All colored cartoons for *Puck, Judge, The Ram's Horn* and other weeklies were drawn on stone.

There was a certain charm about the lithographic cartoon while in course of construction which one does not experience on black-and-white. Working with crayon upon the soft, gray, stone surface required unusual patience. The weight of a double-page stone was about fifty pounds, according to its thickness. Therefore, a lithographic cartoon was usually finished in the same position in which it was begun. The handling of such burdens required

considerable effort and extreme care. Besides, their preparation for the press consumed much time, whereas the photo-engraving process permitted a drawing to be done in colors on cardboard and reduced to any desired size upon zinc plates.

At first, Puck's artists were obliged to draw upon one large stone, all at the same time; that is, the center double spread and the back and front pages were executed upon one large slab, the three artists sitting around a table, each laboring upon his assignment. That, of course, was before the circulation reached an extent to require transfers and when the edition was printed directly from the original stone.

In *Puck's* later years, duplicate stones were made by means of transfers, and still later a cheaper method was adopted by which the entire edition was printed from zinc plates made by transfers, the original stone being preserved for making duplicate transfers. A transfer is made by means of a print or impression from the original stone upon coated paper. This coated-paper print is then transferred to another stone or metal plate and etched with acid in the same manner and by the same process as the original drawing upon the virgin stone.

Leslie-Judge's twenty-fifth anniversary which fell on President Roosevelt's birthday, October 27, 1906, found New York in the throes of a lithographers' strike, and we were up against it for emergency methods of reproducing colored pictures. We tried drawing them on rose board and reproducing with zinc plates, tints being added by the Benday process—a very unsatisfactory arrangement. I was actually ashamed of the sickly appearance of our cartoons during this period; and yet, good or bad, the magazine had to be published. What was to have been a glorious anniversary number of *Judge* appeared as one of the weakest issues ever put on the news stands.

Months of experimenting evolved the three-color process of photo-engraving. Thus, the strike proved a boomerang to the Lithographers' Union, for it diverted their part of cartoon production into other channels, the work of the lithographers being done by zinc etchers. However, it took only a few hours—now it's about half an hour—for a daily paper to reproduce a black-and-white cartoon by photo-engraving, while the colored lithograph for a weekly periodical required one week to finish. Often, an idea became stale before it could be printed. When at last the success of photo-engraving was assured, *Puck* and *Judge* abandoned the field of political cartoons, becoming comic weeklies.

This planet of ours may not be improving morally, but at least our election campaigns are no longer slugging matches.

When you and I were young, the type of cartooning that paid real money was editorial caricature, and the artist's chief job was to vilify his employer's political foes. Nowadays, people refuse to take their politics seriously, and the cartoonist who pays the heaviest income tax is the fellow who grinds out six comic strips a week and a whole page in colors for Sunday—or hires an understudy to do it for him.

In the period of the nineties, according to the Chicago *Journal,* cartoonists earned "from $2,000 to $25,000 a year, according to their industry and ability." Bernhard Gillam was getting $25,000 annually at the time of his death in 1896, which was the highest income of any cartoonist in the world up to that time. Today, the juiciest plum on the cartoon tree is reputed to be plucked by Bud Fisher

Eugene Zimmerman, about 1905

(Harry Conway Fisher) whose yearly income was broadcast in the press at $250,000 a year. Whether or not that sum is correct, I am not prepared to say. Maybe it is even higher.

In commercializing a daily feature nowadays, good drawing is relatively important. The idea counts most and speed follows a close second. The producer of a daily strip works on schedule, eats and sleeps on schedule, plays golf on schedule. No doubt, when his time comes, he will pass into the Hereafter on schedule.

Better than the finest studio, to my mind, is the cartoonist's ability to observe on which side of a cow the farmer sits when he milks her, the physiognomy of a fireplug or mailbox, the difference between a Ford and an Austin. One well known cartoonist of my acquaintance pictured corn growing like wheat atop of the stalk.

On most publications the cartoonist supplies his own ideas. As Herbert Johnson puts it:

> Cartoon ideas come to me as the result of deliberate cerebrations and constructions. When I am absolutely up against it, the editor sometimes gives me an article to illustrate, an editorial to read, or suggests something which helps. This is rare, however. A cartoonist is expected to hit 'em out. The editor may tell him when to bunt, but doesn't bat for him.

A few of the newspaper syndicates issue editorial cartoons which are popular and widely circulated, but in general that form of art is not easily syndicable, because it lacks the timeliness that an editorial cartoon requires, as it must be drawn a week or two before release date in order to permit national distribution. Moreover, it cannot conform to local conditions or to the distinctive politics of the paper. The latter problem was cleverly solved in a political cartoon by Dorman H. Smith syndicated for Hallowe'en, 1927, showing a bogie-man hovering over the White House, with a choice of two opposing captions—one poking fun at President Coolidge, the other ridiculing his foes.

Kahles' "Clarence the Cop" was, I believe, the first serial comic strip published in a daily paper, although "Mutt and Jeff" was the earliest one which is still running. "Mutt and Jeff" appeared originally in Hearst's *San Francisco Chronicle,* in November, 1907. At first it was confined to A. Mutt's race-track selections; Jeff was added later and has kept Mutt company ever since. The feature proved so popular that Hearst tried it out singly in other newspapers of his national chain, then decided to use it in all of them simultaneously in order to give the readers a circulation-boosting treat at minimum cost to himself. Thus was formed what I believe to be the first daily newspaper art syndicate. Eventually, the Hearst Syndicate began selling to non-competing, non-Hearst papers throughout the country, rival syndicates were organized, and the age of the daily strip was ushered in.

King Features, which puts out a majority of the Hearst comics and serves about 2,000 newspapers here and abroad, is said to be the world's largest syndicate in number of strips handled, in distribution and in earnings.

George McManus's "Bringing up Father" is reputed to have the widest distribution of all comic strips, for it is published daily on all five continents and translated into Japanese, Spanish, Italian, Swedish, and German.

"There are few cities in North or South America where territory is open that 'Bringing up Father' is not sold," I was told by J. V. Connolly, editor and general manager of King Features. "It is so valuable an element for building up circulation that newspapers buy from us the exclusive rights to this feature in territories seventy-five to one hundred miles adjacent to their cities."

McManus made a fortune out of "The Newlyweds and Their Baby." He was born in 1883, the year I joined the *Puck* staff.

Our American language is indebted to comic-strip artists for the coining of popular phrases such as, "It's a lot of boloney" (one of Al Smith's favorites, originated by Rube Goldberg)—"Ain't it a grand and glorious feeling!"—"flivver"—"banana oil"—"foolish question number 9187"—"the Toonerville trolley"—"when a feller needs a friend"—"He's the cat's whiskers"—"He's so dumb, he thinks Sandy Hook is a Scotchman"— "You tell 'em, lumber; you've been through the mill"—"You tell 'em, goldfish; you've been around the globe"—and hundreds of other gems, which have become imbedded in every-day speech. A wisecrack is like sap; the more you boil it down the richer will be your syrup.

The comic strip of fifteen years ago usually ended with an explosive climax of the brickbat or rolling-pin type, such as Charles Chaplin was giving to movie fans. I recall a masterpiece by Goldberg—who had been fired from a $6-a-week engineering job and is now getting well over $1,000 in his Saturday night pay envelope—showing undertakers at a banquet celebrating the opening of the football season. "I couldn't get away with anything as raw as that today," he confided recently.

"Mutt and Jeff," however, is still of the slapstick variety and probably will remain so. At the first wave of Bud Fisher's popularity, I received an offer to draw a strip imitating "Mutt and Jeff," which I refused to do. In Decmeber, 1918, years after I had left *Judge,* Grant Hamilton conceived the idea of cashing in on Chaplin's popularity by publishing in *Judge* each week a full-page comic strip take-off on Charlie's exploits, using a dog to personify the film

*"How the Blackvilles Lost the Game
with the Darkeytowns"*

JEFFERSON (at the bat)—*"Dis am de las' innin', de
score am even, dere's free men on bases, two out, I've had
two strikes and free balls; now watch me swat a home
run!"*

UMPIRE (hoarsely)—*"Striker out!"*

comedian, and other canine characters. Hamilton wrote enthusiastically:

Chaplin is the biggest man in the movies, and all know him. *Film Fun* can increase its circulation by thousands by putting Chaplin's portrait on the cover. We have proved that.

John A. Sleicher was quickly sold on the idea, and wrote me:

You don't want to hook on behind the Fisher wagon. My idea was the same as yours, that you might get up something entirely original and not a mere imitation of "Mutt and Jeff." We are trying out the Chaplin dog and I hope it will meet all your expectations.

The dog ran in *Judge* for about two years before it died a natural death. Another page in colors I did was "Louie and Lena," for the McClure people, who asked for a page similar to "The Katzenjammer Kids"; it continued for about a year.

The modern strip tends toward "human-interest appeal"—every-day life in homes, offices, factories. Its puppets remind us of ourselves and our friends.

"The funniest people are all around you," he continued, "in the street cars, on the sidewalks, everywhere. Almost anywhere you look you'll see a funny-looking man, woman or child. I know lots of fellows who, if they were to appear on the stage, would make an audience laugh their heads off merely to see them, but on the street we don't notice them."

In the movement away from slapstick, many of the newer strips have given up humor altogether, and we are treated to a tabloid education, carefully censored and pre-digested, in strip form—history of the world, synopses of literary classics or best sellers, autobiographies, fairy tales for children, Parisian styles and even problems in etiquette. This recalls the story of the tourist who boasted he had

MERRY X-MAS.

SAY! SEEN ME PRESENT?

The Alfred E. Neuman character, who became the symbol of MAD *magazine, had been around since at least the late 1880s.* ZIM *had apparently drawn a few such characters in the late nineteenth and early twentieth centuries. This one was drawn in 1922.*

gone through the entire Louvre in twelve minutes. "I could have made it in nine flat," he said, "if I had worn spiked shoes."

Other comparatively recent developments in the comic-strip are simpler technique—the use of fewer lines to express ideas—and the advent of the continuity or serial strip, which has plot in addition to the "gag a day" which non-serialized strips have.

The continuity strip is profitable because, as one syndicate manager told me, "it tends to sell the next day's paper to the readers, whereas the 'gag a day' strip is complete and does not have the same hold-over interest. Moreover, after a syndicate has sold a newspaper on a continuity strip, that paper is less apt to cancel the strip in the middle of the story." There is some divergence of opinion as to who started this form of serialization.

George Matthew Adams, president of the syndicate bearing his name, wrote to me:

I believe the Adams Syndicate was the first one to introduce successfully the idea of continuity in the daily comic strip. It did this with Ed Wheelan's "Minute Movies," and the idea has been adopted—or attempts have been made to adopt it—by practically all the leading syndicates.

Bud Fisher, writing his autobiographic "Confessions of a Cartoonist" for *The Saturday Evening Post,* gives the credit to Sol Hess, a witty Chicago jeweler. "I believe the continuity strip originated in his anecdotes and ideas," Fisher declares, relating how newspaper artists and reporters used to gather daily at luncheon in Stillson's restaurant, Chicago, where "the boys" welcomed Hess "for the fun the jeweler got out of grabbing the check." Eventually Hess gave up the jewelry business and is now making a handsome income on a strip of his own, "The Nebbs," drawn by W. A. Carlson, of the Bell Syndicate, the same outfit which distributes "Mutt and Jeff."

In his "Confessions," Mr. Fisher made a challenging statement: "I expect to see the number of comic strips now being published in newpapers greatly reduced in the next few years." Managers of most of the leading syndicates agreed with this when I put the question up to them, the consensus being that "There is a very large overabundance of comic strips in the field today and many of the weaker ones are bound to drop by the wayside. No strip can coast on its past popularity. The consolidation of newspapers also tends to reduce the number of comics which can be absorbed by the market."

Mr. Adams was even more explicit, adding that:

Because of the rapid jump in big salaries for many of the old-time strips, the condition of an overloaded market resulted, placing a very low type of comic strip on the market, which, naturally, must have to pass. . . . Creators of some of the better-known strips have largely lost their interest—in many instances actually turning over to understudies the drawing and preparation of their strips, in the same manner as many of the big names are now being used through the medium of "ghost" writers.

Mr. Connolly, of King Features, was almost the only dissenting voice in the ranks of syndicate managers I canvassed, and he said:

> The actual trend is for *more* comics. Newspapers that published four comics on Sunday are now publishing eight pages of sixteen comics, two on a page. Whereas, before, a few comics were scattered throughout the paper, now papers carry a full page of comics daily, and many papers publish *two pages* of comic strips daily.

Since Mr. Connolly is editor and general manager of the world's largest syndicate, he speaks with a not-to-be-ignored voice of authority. Nevertheless, it seems to me, as Clare Briggs once remarked, that "most of the published comic strips are mere space wasters," and this form of art evidently has reached the saturation point.

Chapter 17

IT'S NEARLY TIME FOR OUR HORSE-heads deer hunters to pack their deck of cards and chips for the season's chase. My preference is for smaller game. When brain fog approaches, I cast aside brush and pen, shoulder a gun and whistle for a dog. The village of Horseheads is well stocked with mongrels, so I never lack a canine escort to that charmed spot where cottontail and partridge abide. Usually half a dozen volunteers are at my heels. Animals of sensitive nature have no business aspiring to such a position, because in the course of a day's hunting, a dog must be willing to accept with good grace the responsibility for misses made by his temporary master's gun.

Through gift, purchase, or theft I have come into possession of valuable rabbit hounds—at prices ranging from $3.75 to as low as two bits—

and once I owned only half a dog. Partnership, however, is not satisfactory, for dogs require punishment and one cannot kick his own half without giving pain to the other fellow's property. Most of my holdings met untimely and violent deaths through their own carelessness, which usually happened outside of their professional capacity. Among them was Patsy, the only dog famous enough to fill me with pride. He gained renown overnight at a Masonic fair.

As a committee member I was consulted on special features for separating the public from its coin. We hit upon the idea of a wheel of fortune, upon which I painted many figures, including a likeness of Patsy. Patsy was a winner from the start. All during the week of the fair a bunch of tinhorn gamblers could be found in that locality rooting for him. At the conclusion, receipts showed a clear $4,000 profit, most of which was traced to the influence of that uncouth rabbit fur. Patsy could not stand success, however, and lost his life in a moment of exultation. When I wrote my first *Foolish History of Horseheads* I inscribed on the opening page a touching eulogy:

> This book is most respectfully dedicated to the moving memory of my late dog Patsy, who met his doom while attempting to wreck a trolley car. Tried and true was he, and homely as a hedge fence, also honorary member of many dog societies of the neighborhood.

His soul climbed the rugged pathway to Eternity, and if there be a canine Heaven located on the Dog Star I am sure Patsy is there with the rest, lapping up his share of the Milky Way.

One winter day a mail carrier from R.F.D. No. 4 returned from his journey through the hills of Chemung County, announcing that rabbit tracks were visible in the show. Cottontails were scarce, gunners eager and plentiful. The moment that joyous news was broadcast by our efficient public servant, every musket in the vicinity was taken from its corner and pressed into service. Excitement was contagious. I hastened along with gun and dog—not to hunt, of course, but just to see what was going on. In due time we reached bunny's footprints. Hounds were unleashed and the music of their calliope rent the air. Half a mile away one innocent little rabbit had vanished into its hole where a single gun could be trained on it. Presently a constable appeared on the scene, and began a roundup of violators of the game law. Twenty were arrested for hunting without having their licenses on them. Six had ferrets, three possessed clubs, and four carried revolvers without permits. All told, there were about sixty of us. Later developments showed that our mail carrier had been in league with the constable and had spread the news to perk up business.

One of the many delightful old fellows who crossed my path was Enos Cook. Enos' occupation since the Civil War was hunting and fishing for the community. While still suffering from a nervous breakdown upon my return from Florida, I chose this genial companion as a lifelong friend, for Enos understood exactly how to treat a nervous condition. He knew every inch of woodland and every stream in Chemung County, because he hunted, fished and trapped there and gathered its herbs and roots for medicinal purposes. Thus he saved my life by keeping me outdoors when I had been due for an early demise.

In those palmy days we would hike to a creek, set our poles for spring suckers, then I would bring forth my drawing kit to fill my *Judge* assignments. There at my disposal I had all the material for comedy that Nature offered—the study of birds, fishes, shrubbery, foliage and the like. Thus I became a student of woodcraft. I learned to imitate the piping of quail, the lowing of cattle, the *ba-a-a* of sheep, the neighing of horses. By mimicry I could call squirrels or a bevy of quail to within a reasonable distance.

On one occasion, while angling alone beside a brook, I talked so convincingly to a bull that he decided to accept the challenge. Now, there are two things in this lovely world that I deeply respect when headed in my direction: one is a railroad train, the other a playful old bull. While I was disputing this fellow's right-of-way, he demonstrated beyond question the soundness of his argument by wading through the brook. Our debate up to that point had been conducted from shore to shore—a distance which I found exceedingly desirable—but when the discussion waxed warm and the bull decided to press his argument at closer range, I saw very clearly that I was in the wrong. And, like a true gentleman, I conceded to him all the land in question, together with some neighbor-

Eugene Zimmerman, 1922

ing farms, a new bamboo pole, linen line, hooks, sinkers, and a handsome string of suckers—and hastily withdrew from the scene.

Whenever I have occasion to draw such a picture, I go into a sort of trance and re-enact that adventure in my mind, whereupon my wife asks, "Heavens! Why are you making such faces?"

And I reply, "Don't disturb me, please. I'm being chased by a bull."

One other fishing trip, this time with a friend, I found a cow mired in the much bottom of the stream. Only her back and head were visible. I saw at once that the cow's efforts to free herself had only sunk her deeper. My companion hurried to the farmhouse for help, while I procured rails from the nearby fence to build a solid flooring beneath the helpless animal.

No engineering project was ever conducted with

more deliberation than the salvaging of that cow. The farmer brought a horse, ropes, tackle blocks, chains and crowbars—enough paraphernalia, in fact, to open the Suez Canal. We got a chain around her chest, constructed a skidway of fence rails and, with the horse's aid, extricated the cow. But the poor creature wasn't herself for many weeks afterward because of exhaustion and exposure in cold spring-water. The matter was never reported to the Carnegie Medal Committee [for heroism].

During my thirty years of acquaintance with Enos Cook I traversed virtually every square yard of the game country in Horseheads and adjoining townships. But early one evening I became bewildered in my geographical reckoning and, having no compass in a dense forest, I was at my wits' end. The elderly guide was nowhere to be seen, which made my predicament decidedly alarming.

Twilight was not far off. The possibility of camping over night alone in so spooky a place was not pleasant to contemplate, so I set up a terrible shouting.

"Hallo-o-o, E-e-nos!"

I yelled until blue in the face, yet my voice only re-echoed to mock my loneliness. Then I mustered all my remaining courage and the entire force of my lungs, letting out a final yell before I lay down to die.

Unexpectedly, from behind a tree stump not five rods away, an answer came in the purest vernacular: "Well, what in blank-it-te-blank do you want? Are you tryin' t' scare all the game out o' the woods?"

Enos went on to explain that he had been watching a grey squirrel atop a tall tree in the hope of drawing a bead on it, to round out the day.

"If ever you git lost agin," he added, "don't go yellin' like a loon fer help. Jes' notice what side o' the tree the moss is on, an' if you got the sense of a woodchuck you'll know that's north."

When weary of tramping, we would sit down and spin yarns. Unintentionally, the ancient woodsman supplied me with many comics for *Judge.* Enos was a philosopher. He liked his toddy, but his golden rule was, "Never drink licker when carryin' a gun, an' always extract yer shells when you set it down in a public place, 'cuz fools what picks it up an' examines it ain't all dead yet."

Playing tricks on good old Enos was ever the delight of his cronies, nor was he displeased, for Enos himself was a practical joker. It was an epoch when baseburners and sawdust boxes were in vogue at our grocery, and chairs were filled with idlers from sun-up till the wooden shutters were fitted into place at night. That was the environment I encountered upon my entry to Horseheads. Now, our village contributed not a little to the annals of the Revolutionary War, but those incidents are read and forgotten, while such important events as the shooting of the cast-iron frog have been handed down by word of mouth for two generations. It occurred this way:

Before navigation was suspended on the Chemung Canal and that waterway was abandoned, its shores bred a multitude of frogs which were much sought after by epicures of the locality and brought a good price in market. One day, an unusually big croaker was sighted on a rock. The news was carried to Enos, who approached cautiously with a loaded gun and a true marksman's eye, and blazed away.

The amphibian barely stirred. Apparently it had a tough hide, so another barrel was discharged. Then investigation revealed that the frog weighed three or four pounds and had been propagated in the molding-room of the local iron foundry. The community had assembled to watch the fun and offer advice, but all they got out of Enos was, "All right, Bubbie, that's on me."

Secretly he laid his plans for reciprocating. To one of the perpetrators he sold a mess of dressed toads in the guise of frogs' legs, and to another he palmed off a two-pound sucker bespattered with vermillion spots to resemble a speckled trout. In each instance Enos was paid a fancy price. And, of course, he told the story to the town gossips, so the laugh was on the other fellows.

Some of the small town fun practiced in Horseheads years ago would land a man in prison if perpetrated in a big city. For instance, several young fellows took a jackass out of a pasture field and held up the aged chief of police, depriving him of badge and jail keys, then locked up the jack in one of the two cells and the chief in the other. After that they went to a banker and informed him that two of his relatives were in jail and wished to consult him about bail. By this time half the village was on to the fun and had gathered to give the

"Four Views of Uncle Pothwaite's Educated Ears"

| Normal. | Listening for the dinner-horn. | Angry with Aunt Mandy. | During the new minister's call. |

banker a laugh. Local authorities were inclined to take a serious view of the matter, but the cost of a trial and conviction would add to the taxes, so the matter was dropped. This was before the introduction of autos and good roads, when time hung heavy on our hands, and one had to make his own fun.

I remember reading in the *Chemung Valley Reporter* that a local firm had just installed a two-ton safe. The *Reporter* merely mentioned the incident to let the rest of the world know that Horseheads was still in the forefront of industrial progress, but neglected to give the following details:

The firm's office is situated on the top floor of a two-story brick structure. Hoisting a safe to such tremendous altitude as the top of the only flight of stairs is not without risks to life and limb. Great precautions were exercised in this civil engineering feat. All nearby ropes, hawsers, single and double pulley blocks, planks and joists were rounded up, every married family shelling out its quota of cotton clothes line to bring this vast job to a successful climax. Meanwhile, all the wheels of commerce and local traffic ceased to pulsate and every man

"Take the Most Valuable"
SECOND BURGLAR: *Don't be crazy, Petey. Let de safe go an' tackle dese slot machines."*

able to leave his sick bed or his chosen seat at the nearby hostelry was there to offer suggestions and stand in the way. Since then, in a big city, I have seen safes drawn up to the 48th story of a skyscraper on a slender cable, with a political rally in operation directly beneath it, and not one of the thousands of eyeballs turned from the speaker to offer suggestions or guard against calamity.

Some years later the Chemung County Rod and Gun Club purchased a plot of ground in my vicinity for the raising of pheasants. Twelve hundred of the little birds were hatched under my supervision, with the assistance of "Ted" MacDonald, a railroad telegraph operator. My chief worry was to protect them against rats, cats, weasels, mink, hawks, owls, and other foes. Experience in the sign shop with an awning maker had taught me to use the sailmaker's needle. With this knowledge, I produced a burlap mattress, which I filled with new hay, and for many nights we slept out-of-doors to guard the young chicks which were housed in a hundred and twenty-five small coops. Despite our vigilance, we lost two-thirds of the flock. That next-to-nature life was ideal, however, and how we did sleep! Any disturbance in the coops was detected by means of the old hens' SOS, which gave us the location of the trouble. Besides, we had a keen dog who did police duty. In this case, my services were donated to the cause of stocking the surrounding country with the newly introduced game bird.

Once, a rumor was current that a wildcat had been seen prowling at large after nightfall—not a very pleasant thing to contemplate in a peaceful community. Most of the residents retired early, while others crouched behind closed blinds, listening for the cat's yowls. I was naturally wakeful, so one very dark night I boldly set forth, shotgun in hand, to round up the vile disturber. In scant attire and slippered feet I sneaked from tree to tree, when suddenly a neighbor's hound pounced off his porch with a tremendous howl, which sent me scurrying home to bed. I regret that no timekeeper witnessed the performance, for I feel sure I broke the local record for the hundred-yard dash on that occasion. Thereafter, I was no longer troubled with sleeplessness or a desire to hunt wildcats.

The region in which I live is rich in historical lore. Some of the important battles of General Sullivan's campaign against the Indians were fought here; in fact, Horseheads derived its name from the skulls of the many worn out horses slaughtered by Sullivan's army. Every household hereabouts has its quota of flint arrowheads. When it was learned that I had a mania for collecting relics, farmers began bringing me all sort of Colonial antiques—warming pans, spinning wheels, grandfather's clocks, old weapons and the like—so that my home is now a museum. One day while at the *Judge* office, the porter informed me that a wooden bicycle had come by express. It proved to be a big flax spinning-wheel, the like of which he had never seen before. The best place to collect such curios as sabres, pistols, and other military trappings is in the department stores, where they can be acquired so much cheaper than on the battlefield during an engagement, and you can invent your own legends about them. Indian relics have always had a fascination for me, but all I have left now, after many forays of moths, are the flints, which they found indigestible. Among other things those pesky critters devoured were two elegant war bonnets I prized most highly.

Our theatre was an ordinary village hall with a medium-sized stage and long rickety-backed benches. Before the adoption of electricity, a few kerosene lamps supplied weird illumination. The hall contained a huge wood stove which rendered one corner uncomfortably hot while the rest of the house was sufficiently bleak to demand overcoats. One day I was approached by a gentleman with "SOS" written on his features. He wanted me to manage a cakewalk which had been advertised for that night but could not go on until at least the rent of the hall had been placed in the landlord's palm. So I became ticket seller as well as manager, and to save the expense of a collector I contrived to sell the tickets with one hand and take them up with the other. I had sent word for "the gang" to patronize the show, and thus succeeded in selling out the house, with a resultant profit of sixty dollars.

On another occasion I stood sponsor for an "Uncle Tom's Cabin" troupe, stranded at Horseheads without cash or credentials. There were seven Thespians, including a 200-pound Eva, all with hungry stomachs. Since no one else seemed willing to grubstake them, I acted the part of financial Samaritan, receiving in turn an attachment on six flaxen and mohair wigs and a death grip on whatever gate receipts there might be. There was no artificial ice for the famous scene in which Eliza crosses the ice-filled river, so I made some out of six soap boxes by mixing a little skill and ten cents worth of kalsomine in the same pail. One bloodhound of doubtful pedigree was included in the assets, and two more just as good were borrowed from the keeper of the local dog pound to assist in hastening Eliza's footsteps. But since the dogs hadn't time to become acquainted and rehearse their part in advance, they got into a scrap at the wrong time and the asbestos curtain had to be rung down hastily over the scene.

Chapter 18

As I WRITE THIS, THE VILLAGE FIRE bell is calling for volunteers. It is 10 P.M.; I am in bed and here I shall remain. Twenty-five years ago a straight-jacket would not have kept me from responding to that dismal knell, but twenty-five years ago there was no Volstead Act, and smoke-eaters knocked out in performance of duty were given ample means of resuscitation. Today, the best you can expect is sympathy and a glass of water.

I have already told how the burning of a wine shop was indirectly responsible for starting me on an art career. In my eighteenth year, I had joined a newly organized group of fire-fighters, Acme Hose No. 2, at Horseheads, and served as secretary of the outfit until I began work on *Puck* in 1883, and even then I did not resign from the company itself.

At the time I joined Acme Hose, I anticipated performing marvelous deeds of heroism, but the opportunity never arose. I was in no sense a spectacular fireman. I never rushed pellmell into a flaming structure to save a twenty-five cent mirror nor bellowed orders through a brass trumpet. Usually I stood outside the danger zone listening to critics and awaiting the call for relief—which I sometimes

carried in a black bottle with a Canadian Club label on it.

The first fire in which I participated occurred July 4, 1881, when I nearly burned down a barn while shooting firecrackers. There was also another ignominious Fourth at Horseheads. I was master of ceremonies, and the day began with a grand fusileer "pee-rade" headed by the village cornet band of eight pieces. At evening, nearly the entire population—about 800 souls—assembled in the public square where a suitable platform had been erected for the discharge of $18 worth of fireworks bought by popular subscription. A basket containing the precious set pieces, skyrockets and roman candles, which had been carefully guarded for a week beneath the bar of a local hotel, was brought forward and placed upon the platform.

No sooner had I announced the gorgeousness of the closing event that was about to take place than an unauthorized spark fell into that basket, possibly from a cigar, and in less than no time at all those $18 worth of fireworks were "pyrotechning" through the sultry atmosphere. Everybody concentrated on getting out of harm's reach. The cornet band, rendering one of its favorite quick-steps, was already under way and in considerable disorder. Even men so rheumatic that they had not walked for years were able to leave the scene with perfect agility, discarding canes or crutches as evidence of physical recovery. Within three minutes by the town clock, the public square of Horseheads, N.Y., was an exceedingly lonesome place. Those who witnessed the ceremony from a safe distance said afterward it was the grandest display they had ever seen.

When the smoke cleared, and spectators began searching for friends and relatives, they found no casualties but many hats, umbrellas, galoshes, and lunch baskets strewn over the battlefield. The story of the famous night is now told to our grandchildren by those who were in the thick of it and is remembered today as the greatest Fourth of July celebration in the town's history.

The fiercest blaze we ever fought was at the Standard Oil Company's transit station at West Junction, a suburb in 1882, when one of the oil tanks was ignited by lightning. It was necessary for us to force steam into the tanks, thus completely ruining our hose. I happened to be boarding at a local hotel at that time and the excitement there at 6:30 A.M., with nightshirted women and men rushing hysterically through the halls, tickled my funny bone and later supplied grist for my cartoon mill.

One method of cashing in on my fire-fighting associations came thirty-five years later when the American La France & Foamite Corporation asked me to draw a monthly page of fire-equipment cartoons for its house organ, which it mails to every fire headquarters in the land. I originated "The Dingville Fire Brigade" cartoon in 1919 and this has been running continuously ever since.

R. A. Mollman, chief engineer of the Millstadt, Ill., Fire Department, once wrote that "we small-town firemen expect to be kidded and probably would be highly disappointed if we were not," which is exactly what I am doing with the Din-

gville Brigade of bewhiskered derelicts and their old-fashion pumper. These fossils devise ludicrous schemes for battling flame and saving lives in their home town, at Mt. Vesuvius, within the Arctic Rim, on the Sahara, and other assorted places. One cartoon showed the fire laddies at a Chinese laundry, during a drought, taking water from a large tub where clothes were soaking. The nozzle was emitting such garments as the ancient pumper could push through the hose, while the proprietor, who had robbed the village water supply for his business, was expostulating. A sixty-page booklet of these cartoons, reprinted from the house organ, was sent to all fire chiefs.

A fire at St. John's Military Academy [Manlius, New York], where my nephew [Adolph, Jr.] was

The Dingville Fire Brigade testing out their new Aerial equipment at the first stupendous opportunity, when a careless tinker's firepot ignited a quantity of old sermons stored in the belfry of the church and left the victim beyond the reach of human aid—besides endangering valuable surrounding real estate.

Because that spindleshanks of a Smith kid was seen with a pack of cannon fire crackers in his possession on the night of July three, the Dingville Fire Brigade was ordered to sleep in harness, prepared for an emergency call, with full equipment of chewing tobacco and hard cider, as were the Minute Men of the Revolutionary Period.—By order of His Honor, the Mayor of Dingville.

studying in 1906, prompted me to invent an automatic fire extinguisher, which I labored over for months and finally patented. Satisfied that it was ready for a test, I took an embryo model to the *Judge* office, much to the joy of a bunch of professional wags. After describing the working features of my great discovery I asked my colleagues to follow me to the roof, so I could favor them with a thorough demonstration. Yes, they followed, but it was to my dismay, for I had not given due concern to the power generated by merging sulphuric acid with a soda solution. The device sprang a leak, ruined my best Sunday suit and, worst of all, ceased to loom as a formidable weapon against fire.

Although I had spent upwards of $300 in perfecting several models, I did not derive a cent of income from this invention except the $50 for all rights which I sold ten years later to an interested party in Syracuse. I never heard the end of it from the *Judge* staff. Frequently they greeted me with, "Well, how's the fire extinguisher coming along?"

Twenty years ago [1908] there was a fire in the *Judge* office; an aftermath of it came to me a few weeks ago in the form of a letter from Israel Zadikow, a young Brooklyn cartoonist:

Dear ZIM:
   While passing a book shop on 13th Street and Fourth Avenue, I saw some original drawings twenty to thirty years old by F. Opper, Dalrymple, T. E. Powers, Albert Levering, Rollin Kirby, Carr, C. R. McAuley, S. S. Pughe, L. M. Glacken, John McCutchion, Gordan Grant, Fan, and many others. All these were for sale at a quarter apiece. Failing to see any drawn by you, I inquired inside. The proprietor took my breath away by saying he had some small originals by ZIM from the eighties at ten dollars apiece.

To which I replied:

Dear Zadikow:
   Your letter amused me very much. The fact that you did not run on to more of my originals of early days is because most of them were consumed in the *Judge* fire January 10, 1908. Hence, you will observe that it is the scarcity, not the quality, that governs the market value of a man's work. Thousands of my pen-and-inks which went up in smoke might now be commanding as high as ten cents apiece instead of ten dollars per. Evidently the dealer wanted to keep them in his family, for such a price as he placed on them would certainly render them heirlooms.

I remember visiting the cottage of a relative at Auburn, New York, for a ten-day vacation. On the ninth day that cottage and four others caught fire which we were cruising on Lake Owaske. Hastening back, we found that flames had consumed everything except an empty trunk belonging to me, which I advised my relative to throw into the bargain, as I had no use for an empty trunk. There were sheep in the pasture nearby and a small dog added to the excitement by driving them into the lake, whereupon we turned our attention to rescuing mutton. It would have been funny if it had been less serious. My losses were about $800 with no insurance. All I had to wear home was a pair of

with an American La France pumper and modern water works are doing the work which once required three companies of about twenty-five men each and a firehouse full of apparatus.

My chief value to the Horseheads department has been as superintendent of fairs for making money to be used in purchasing apparatus; also, I have created many novelty features for the firemen's annual parades. The festivals became so popular that they drew patronage from the surrounding countryside; for this service, the department has given me several gold medals which I have never worn. I am not a medal hero, by the way, and some day a junk dealer may carry them off at his own price.

In 1906, I had staged a fair for the Horseheads volunteer firemen. It lasted a week. I had made water-color caricatures of about twenty of the Elmira exempts—a group of red-shirted old-timers—all in one immense frame occupying about twenty square feet. I planned this feature as a drawing card for the fair and compliment to the old fellows. We set apart one evening as "Exempt Firemen's Night." Our village band met the guests and escorted them to the hall. It seemed that half of the city of Elmira had also accompanied them. The ancients came primed with money which they spent like the proverbial drunken sailors. The hall

trousers and an outing shirt.

Eventually the old department became a new one and the antiquated apparatus was sent to the junk heap. Nowadays, from four to six able men

was jammed, and the late Will Y. Ellett, at that time assistant fire chief of Elmira, was there to give our boys a glad hand. After performing that function, Bill sniffed the air in the fashion of a setter dog scenting a quail, led me aside and said hastily: "Keep quiet, but show me where the coat room is." When we got there, he began a survey of overcoat pockets; from one he took a smoldering briar pipe which had partly eaten its way into adjoining textile. Lifting the coat from the hook, he placed his number 12 fireman's hoof upon it and made a general inspection of all the clothing before we resumed our place among the merrymakers. Bill told me afterwards that but for this precaution, a panic undoubtedly would have resulted, for the hall had only one exit and a long flight of stairs, well designed for a holocaust.

The fair was a huge success. At its conclusion, the caricatures were presented to the Elmira "exempts" who had them framed and hung in their parlors, where they remain today. The Exempt Association has since dwindled to a pitifully few veterans waiting for the final gong.

In a rash moment I once consented to run for alderman at Horseheads. No sooner had I been elected [1891–93] and sworn to do my duty than I was commanded, under threat of prosecution, to repair a sidewalk for a shiftless taxpayer. Presently, a bridge required attention. Carpenters were not available—because they did not take kindly to slow-moving payment by town orders—so I planked the bridge myself. Whenever trouble arose, the word was passed, "Let ZIM do it; he's the street committee."

I have been honored periodically with the decorating committee chairmanship of local fairs of firemen, Masons and Odd Fellows, each of which exacted two weeks of time and energy. (Add "Mark" to my initials, E. Z.) There is a lot of glory attached to such activity, but it fades when the function ends.

[In Teal Park, Horseheads, is a wooden band stand, designed by ZIM and built in 1910 by him and his father-in-law. The funds for the construction of the bandstand were partially raised by the residents of Horseheads. ZIM not only donated the bandstand, but also the band. Although he never played a musical instrument, he enjoyed music. In the late 1880s, he donated instruments to

The ZIM Band about 1912

"Paralyzing Pertinence"

MRS. HANDOUT—"And who is responsible for your impoverishment?"

TATTERS—"Easy people like you, mum, whose continuous generosity makes gettin' a job unnecessary an' de idea irksome."

Mabel and Eugene Zimmerman, early 1930s

many of the children of Horseheads and created the first ZIM band. The band was active until about 1900; from 1909 until 1916, the ZIM band again made regular appearances in the bandstand. There were about thirty musicians ranging in age from about twelve up to adulthood. ZIM donated most of the uniforms. A small photograph of ZIM was always kept on the bandstand during concerts although he refused, perhaps out of modesty, to be photographed with the group. The ZIM bandstand was decorated with ZIM's caricatures of a bullfrog and two grasshopper musicians.

[ZIM was forever donating his time to the community, and gave freely of his money and his artistic ability. He sent flowers to the ill, usually along with a whimsical drawing.

[In 1928, at ZIM's suggeston, Horseheads put a plaque on a boulder to honor General John Sullivan and his packhorses, which were killed in 1779 after being broken by a harsh march in campaign against the Indians; in 1789 settlers found the horses' skulls and so named the village.]

When I look back into the past and think how satisfied and comfortable we were in our miserable condition, I suspect that the world is going backward instead of forward and that modern improvements are more of a menace than a benefit to the human race. The fellow who learned a trade is out of luck today, for this is a period of experts and specialists. All a man is required to do five and a half days a week is to screw a nut on a bolt in an auto factory and get a dollar an hour for his speed and ingenuity.

As I write, the frosts of three-score and eight winters are creeping into the hair of my once noble blond head, and lines of care have deepened beyond the power of beauty specialists to eradicate. Friends may rest assured, therefore, that this masterpiece bristles with truth, even though it be lightened here and there with a flourish of cap and bells. I have witnessed the passing of many pioneers of my profession and am one of the few survivors left of that once famous group. I have no regrets. If I were starting my career over again, under similar conditions, I would follow substantially the same course.

And now I have come to the end of this book. I have nothing to add except that I feel like Joe Cannon felt in an incident quoted by my friend, the late W. A. Rogers, in his autobiography, *A World Worth While;*

We were all seated in a room in his house in Washington, which had several large windows opening, I think, to the south, "Uncle Joe" looked up at one of the large windows, kept his gaze there as though he saw some presence outside, and said:

"I am getting on in years and I have seen many of my friends leave this fine world. My mind doesn't dwell on the uncertainty of life; I enjoy living. I am interested in all that makes it worth while; but if I saw an old, muffled figure out through that window and it pointed its long bony finger at me and said, 'Come!' I should be ready to obey."

Editor's Epilogue

ON THURSDAY, MARCH 21, 1935, EUgene Zimmerman became ill and was treated for indigestion. For the next five days he continued to work, although at a much reduced level. He awoke on Tuesday, March 26, saying that he felt better. About 7:45 A.M. he fell to the floor. His wife and daughter, who were in the kitchen at the time, went to his room. At the age of seventy-three, Eugene Zimmerman, who had written his last newspaper column the previous evening, was dead of a heart attack.

ZIM is buried in the Maple Grove Cemetery in Horseheads. In 1939, the people of Horseheads built a seven-foot granite memorial in Teal Park.

In a seventy-three-year life, Eugene Zimmerman gave the world more than forty thousand sketches, pen-and-ink drawings, lithographs, and wash-colors, a large number of which appeared in the nation's major magazines. He produced hundreds of newspaper columns, four different comic histories, and a twenty-volume cartoon correspondence course. To the people of Horseheads he gave his spirit of community. To all Americans, he gave an insight into human nature, making them laugh at themselves, and he tried to do it with kindness. But, most of all, the man who was known as ZIM gave the people of America himself, asking only for love.

Eugene Zimmerman about 1920

Bibliography

Eugene Zimmerman contributed to more than one hundred magazines. His primary work was for *Puck* from 1883 through 1885, and for *Judge* from 1885 to about 1910. Other major contributions to magazines included "Homespun Phoolosophy" in *Cartoons Magazine,* 1916–18; "ZIM's Page" in *Art and Life,* 1924–25; and the Dingville Fire Department series in *The Modern Fire Chief,* 1928–30. For newspapers, ZIM drew a "how-to" column for *The New York Press* in 1911, a syndicated comic strip, "Louie and Lena," in 1911; and a continuing series of articles for the *Elmira Star-Gazette* during the last decade of his life. During his lifetime, almost every major American newspaper and magazine published at least a paragraph—most published full stories—about him. In addition, his death on March 26, 1935, led to obituaries in almost every American newspaper. The Horseheads Historical Society has the largest collection of articles about ZIM.

Arkell, W. J. *Old Friends and Some Acquaintances.* Los Angeles, 1927.

Barber, Charles. "Zim's Centennial." *Chemung Historical Journal* 8 (September 1962).

Brasch, Walter M. *Black English and the Mass Media.* Amherst, Mass.: University of Massachusetts Press, 1981; paperback rev. ed., Lanham, Md.: University Press of America, 1984.

Byrne, Thomas E. *Chemung County, 1890–1975.* Elmira, N.Y.: County Historical Society, 1976.

Campbell, Mary, and Campbell, Gordon. *The Pen, Not the Sword: A Collection of Great Political Cartoons From 1879 to 1898.* Nashville, Tenn.: Aurora Publishers, 1970

Caricature: Wit and Humor of a Nation in Picture, Song and Story. New York: The Judge Co., 1905.

"Cartoons and Their Makers." *Munsey's Magazine* 21 (August 1904): 737.

"Court Jesters to Father Knickerbocker." *The New Broadway Magazine,* February 1908, p. 598.

Flantz, John. *Life: The Gentle Satirist.* Bowling Green, Ohio: The Popular Press, 1972.

Hill, L. Draper. *'What Fools These Mortals Be': A Study of Joseph Keppler, Founder of* Puck. Senior history thesis, Harvard College, 1957.

History of the Genesee Country. Chicago: S. J. Clarke, 1925.

Hoskings, Arthur Nicholas. *The Artist's Year Book.* Chicago: The Art League Publishing Association, 1905.

Jerome, Robert, and Wisbey, Herbert. *Mark Twain in Elmira.* Elmira, N.Y.: The Mark Twain Society, 1977.

Kather, Jan Strasser. ZIM: *The Life Story of Eugene Zimmerman.* Student paper, Elmira College, 1977; published 1978, Horseheads Historical Society.

Lardner, Ring. *Regular Fellows I Have Met* (illustrated by Eugene Zimmerman). Chicago: Bruccoli-Layman, 1919.

Marden, Orison Sweet. *Little Visits With Great Americans.* New York: The Success Co., 1904.

Marschall, Rick. "Penman of the Past." *Nemo, A Magazine of Classic Comics,* June 1984, pp. 59–65.

Mathews, E. C. *How to Draw Funny Pictures* (illustrated by Eugene Zimmerman). Chicago: Drake, 1928; rev. eds. 1935, 1936.

McDougall, Walt. *This is the Life!* New York: Knopf, 1926.

"Men Who Make You Laugh." *The New York Times,* November 3, 1907.

"Modern Cartoonists and Their Works." *The Quaker,* September 1899, p. 257.

Mott, Frank Luther. *A History of American Magazines.* Cambridge, Mass.: Harvard University Press, 1957.

"New Readers in American Illustration." *The Bookman* 11 (June 1900): 334–41.

Nye, Bill. *Bill Nye: His Own Life Story.* New York: Century, 1926.

———. *Wit and Humor, Poems and Yarns* (illustrated by Eugene Zimmerman). Chicago: Thompson and Thomas, 1900.

Nye, Bill, and Riley, James Whitcomb. *Railway Guide* (illustrated by Eugene Zimmerman). Chicago: Dearborn Publishers, 1888.

Press, Charles. *The Political Cartoon.* East Rutherford, N.J.: Fairleigh Dickinson University Press, 1981.

"ZIM." *Romance* 20 (June 1896): 105–7.

Zimmerman, Eugene. *A Jug Full of Wisdom; Homespun Phoolosophy.* Horseheads, N.Y.: Eugene Zimmerman, 1916.

———. *Cartoons and Caricatures.* Scranton, Pa.: Correspondence Institute of America, 1910.

———. *Fire; Heroic Deeds for the Dingville Fire Department.* Buffalo, N.Y.: Holling Press, 1922; published for the American LaFrance Fire Engine Co., for distribution.

———. *Foolish History of Horseheads.* Horseheads, N.Y.: Chemung Valley Reporter, 1927.

———. *Foolish History of Horseheads.* N.Y.: Eugene Zimmerman, 1929.

———. *In Dairyland.* Horseheads, N.Y.: Eugene Zimmerman, 1914.

———. *Language and Etticket of Poker.* Horseheads, N.Y.: Eugene Zimmerman, 1916.

———. *This and That About Caricature.* New York: Syndicate Press, 1905.

———. *ZIM's Correspondence Course in Cartoons and Caricatures.* Horseheads, N.Y.: Eugene Zimmerman, 1913. 20 volumes.

———. *ZIM's Foolish History of Elmira and Its Tributaries.* Horseheads, N.Y.: Chemung Valley Reporter, 1911.

———. *ZIM's Foolish History of Horseheads.* Horseheads, N.Y.: Eugene Zimmerman, 1911.

Index

Pughe, S. S., 79
Punch, 57

Quimby, Harriet, 91

Racey, A. G., 107
Ram's Horn, The, 77
Reid, Whitelaw, 67–68
Riley, James Whitcomb, 9, 24, 104
Rochester Democrat & Chronicle, 80
Roebling, Washington A., 75
Rogers, W. A., 60, 64, 65, 93, 114, 131
Roosevelt, Franklin D., 26
Roosevelt, Theodore, 88–89, 116
Rosenfeld, Sydney, 57

St. John's Military Academy, 126–27
"Satyr and Nymphs," 102
Schwartzman, Adolph, 57, 62, 63, 76, 78, 79
Sims, Robert, 55–56
Sleicher, John A., 18, 86, 89, 91–92, 93, 106, 113, 118
Spangenmacher, George, 50–51
Spendler, Albert, 109
Standard Oil of New Jersey, 18, 92
Statue of Liberty, 75
Stokes, Edward S., 102
Stucker, Paul, 94
Sullivan, Gen. John L., 110, 131
Swinnerton, James, 109–10

Talmage, Rev. Dr. Thomas DeWitt, 64
"Tattooed Man," 67–68, 72, 76
Teal Park, 28, 129–30
Tesla, Nicola, 107, 109
This 'n' That About Caricature, 18, 111
Trudeau, Gary, 23
Twain, Mark, 54

Van Dugan, Jones, 89

Waldron, A. T., 89, 92
Wales, James A., 23, 57, 60, 65, 76, 77, 79–80
Walker, Brian, 25, 30
Watson, "Doc," 111
Webster, H. T., 112
Weiss, Edward M., 49
Wes-Kos, 30
White, William Allen, 19
Willys, John N., 109
Wood, Art, 25
Worden, A. T., 29
Worth, Thomas, 23, 29

Zadikow, Israel, 127
Zim, 10
Zim Band, the, 10, 129–30
Zim House, 12, 15, 30, 32, 111
Zimmerman, Adolph (brother), 17, 18, 37, 49
Zimmerman, Adolph (nephew), 32, 84, 111, 126–27
Zimmerman, Amelie Klotz, 17, 37
Zimmerman, Eugene (cousin), 38
Zimmerman, Eugene (ZIM), 9–13, 23, 86; adopts nephew, 18, 32; builds house, 18; correspondence course, 19, 111–13; death, 19, 132; early years, 9; early years in Europe, 17, 28, 35, 37–38; early years in Horseheads, 17, 27–29, 32; early years in Paterson, N.J., 17, 28, 39–53; elected alderman, 18, 129; first sign-painting job, 52; foolish histories, 113–14; goes to *Judge,* 79–80; goes to *Puck,* 58; Grotesque school, 9, 24; latter years in Horseheads, 53–57, 120–31; marriage, 18; nervous collapse, 18, 33, 83; profiled, 24–27; racism discussion, 12–13, 28–30, 61, 96; recipes from *Judge,* 19, 92
Zimmerman, Joseph, 17, 37, 39, 42, 43, 48, 83
Zimmerman, Laura, 17, 32, 85